D0099558

Protecting Children in the Age of Outrage

Protecting Children in the Age of Outrage

A New Perspective on Child Protective Services Reform

Radha Jagannathan

Michael J. Camasso

Rutgers University

OXFORD

UNIVERSITY PRESS

OXFORD
UNIVERSITY PRESS

Oxford University Press is a department of the University of Oxford.
It furthers the University's objective of excellence in research, scholarship,
and education by publishing worldwide.

Oxford   New York
Auckland   Cape Town   Dar es Salaam   Hong Kong   Karachi
Kuala Lumpur   Madrid   Melbourne   Mexico City   Nairobi
New Delhi   Shanghai   Taipei   Toronto

With offices in
Argentina   Austria   Brazil   Chile   Czech Republic   France   Greece
Guatemala   Hungary   Italy   Japan   Poland   Portugal   Singapore
South Korea   Switzerland   Thailand   Turkey   Ukraine   Vietnam

Oxford is a registered trademark of Oxford University Press
in the UK and certain other countries.

Published in the United States of America by
Oxford University Press
198 Madison Avenue, New York, NY 10016

© Oxford University Press 2013

All rights reserved. No part of this publication may be reproduced, stored in a
retrieval system, or transmitted, in any form or by any means, without the prior
permission in writing of Oxford University Press, or as expressly permitted by law,
by license, or under terms agreed with the appropriate reproduction rights organization.
Inquiries concerning reproduction outside the scope of the above should be sent to the
Rights Department, Oxford University Press, at the address above.

You must not circulate this work in any other form
and you must impose this same condition on any acquirer.

Library of Congress Cataloging-in-Publication Data
Jagannathan, Radha.
Protecting children in the age of outrage: a new perspective on child protective services
reform / Radha Jagannathan, Michael J. Camasso.
p. cm.
Includes bibliographical references and index.
ISBN 978–0–19–517696–4 (hardback : alk. paper)—ISBN 978–0–19–972101–6 (e-book)
1. Child welfare—United States.   2. Child abuse—United States.   3. Social work with children—
United States.   4. Social case work with children.   I. Camasso, Michael.   I. Title.
HV741.J244 2013
362.7′2560973—dc23
2012029874

ISBN 978–0–19–517696–4 (hardback : alk. paper)
ISBN 978–0–19–972101–6 (e-book)

1 3 5 7 9 8 6 4 2
Printed in the United States of America
on acid-free paper

To my parents, who remain my guiding force.
Radha

To Dr. Al Roberts, who knew that the real enemy of the scholar is the hourglass—taking our measure even as it takes away our time.
Radha and Michael

CONTENTS

PREFACE

Against the backdrop of what must sound like an interminable drumroll of sensational media stories cataloguing child rape, abductions, starvation, beatings, and deaths, substantiated child maltreatment cases have been decreasing dramatically in the United States. Whether the source is the National Incidence Studies of Child Abuse and Neglect reported to Congress or trend data published by the National Child Abuse and Neglect Data System (NCANDS), cases of sexual abuse and physical abuse have declined both in absolute numbers and as a rate per 1000 children at risk. Child maltreatment in these reports refers to a parent's or caretaker's recent act or failure to act that results in death, serious physical or emotional harm, sexual abuse or exploitation, or imminent risk of serious harm (CAPTA, 42 U.S.C.A. §5106g). This is the definition we use in this book.

The apparent progress our public child protective services (CPS) agencies have made in combating child abuse, however, does not fit well into a public and professional narrative that features skyrocketing reports of alleged maltreatment, a workforce constantly ridiculed as uncaring and incompetent, service budgets viewed as stressed by extreme state cutbacks, and an ever-expanding chorus pleading for real child welfare reform. Although many remain unconvinced of the "progress" of CPS, some have speculated as to how a seemingly grossly dysfunctional organization could experience any success.

One explanation for less substantiated child maltreatment traces the impact of public welfare reform on the child welfare system, finding causes in the renewed calls for personal responsibility and economic self-sufficiency. Another finds the cause in our "war on drugs," which has helped child welfare agencies to come to grips with the impact of illegal drugs on children and their families. Poverty reduction has been cited as a reason, but recent increases in the numbers of poor families and children make this a complicated argument at best.

In the pages that follow we propose what to many professionals in the child welfare field will appear to be a radically different explanation for our society's decisions to protect children from harm and for the significant drop in the numbers of substantiated cases of child abuse. At the center of this conceptual and analytic approach is our contention that social outrage emanating from horrific and often sensationalized cases of child maltreatment plays a major role in CPS decision making and in child outcomes. The ebb and flow of outrage invoke three levels of response that are consistent with patterns of the number of child maltreatment reports made to public child welfare agencies, the number of cases screened-in by these agencies, the proportions of alleged cases substantiated as instances of real child abuse or neglect, and the numbers of children placed outside their homes. First, at the community level, outrage produces amplified surveillance and a posture of "zero tolerance"; second, public child protection workers, in turn, carry out their duties under a fog of "infinite jeopardy" that impacts the number of investigated cases while yielding lower numbers of real maltreatment cases. Third, with outrage as a driving force, CPS organizations are forced into changes that are disjointed and highly episodic and that follow a course identified in the natural sciences as "punctuated equilibrium." Through manifestations such as child safety legislation, institutional reform litigation of state CPS agencies, massive retooling of the CPS workforce, the rise of community surveillance groups and moral entrepreneurs, and the exploitation of fatality statistics by media and politicians we find evidence of outrage at work and its power to change social attitudes, worker decisions, and organizational culture. Hence, although the origins of our explanation can be traced to the collective emotional anger of a concerned and animated general public, we attempt to show that the consequences of social outrage do not manifest themselves as free-floating hostility or moral panic but instead show up as deliberative processes that ensure ongoing organizational turmoil and adjustment.

We have structured the book in a fashion, we hope, that will allow the reader to critically judge the validity of our model both conceptually and empirically. In Chapter 1 we provide an introduction to the critical role played by outrage in CPS decision making. We introduce the reader to the notion that these decisions have measurable rational *and* emotional components, both of which need to be considered in any effort to reform public child welfare. Chapter 2 examines the role that social outrage played in New Jersey, in which a crisis of confidence engulfed the CPS system and forced a court-mandated takeover of the system. We also examine the impact of legal accountability through court orders and consent decrees nationally. New Jersey, we believe, provides a representative case study of community, worker, and CPS agency responses to outrage. The focus in Chapter 3 is a discussion of the normative and technological bases of risk assessment strategies that have motivated "decisions to protect" in child welfare agencies. These strategies have by and large neglected any contribution of outrage. This chapter details the poor performance record of traditional "risk as hazard" approaches and what the child welfare literature has to say about how to improve traditional risk assessment in the detection of child maltreatment. Chapter 4 examines the resources that have long been used to explain levels and rates of child abuse and neglect. We take a look at workforce issues, particularly worker caseloads, unionization, pay, professionalism, and quality, and then examine the issues of case management, quality control, technology, and worker training strategies. The success of "inputs" explanations has proven to be stubbornly limited, here again we believe, because of failure by policymakers and government officials to take into consideration the punctuated, abrupt changes in workforce dynamics produced by social outrage. Chapter 5 provides the reader with a discussion of societal and extraagency accounts for inappropriate CPS decision making and current maltreatment levels. Here we focus primarily on poverty, racism, and welfare reform—three of the most popular macroexplanations for child maltreatment numbers and rates. In Chapter 6 we put our model to an empirical test using a national data set that allows us to examine the relative impacts of outrage,

CPS agency inputs, and social risk factors such as race and poverty. The implications of our analyses for state CPS agency design and child welfare reform in general are addressed in Chapter 7. It is in this Chapter that we attempt to link our findings to a management model and general quality control effort that can be utilized to better understand, predict, and prevent child abuse and neglect in the United States. This model points up the critical importance of confronting the emotional as well as factual bases of child maltreatment risk at both the direct practice and administrative levels of agency operations.

Although the conceptual framework we employ, analyses we conduct, and remedies we promulgate will no doubt interest the wide range of professionals, administrators, academics, and researchers who have made child welfare their life's work, we believe this book will stimulate a much broader discussion as well. Anyone interested in the limits of rational decision making in public bureaucracies—political scientists, economists, and professional managers included—is sure to find parallels in medical settings, law enforcement, public welfare, and any number of other public settings. Community activists, media relations specialists, opponents and proponents of the privatization of public agencies, and others concerned about impression/image management are certain to see the opportunities and dangers that accompany any use of highly emotional focusing events to set public policy or organizational agendas. The book's most natural audiences, however, are the purveyors, victims, and spectators of America's ever-growing "angry culture"—some content and exegesis here are sure to be quite maddening.

ACKNOWLEDGMENTS

As noted in our dedication, we owe a great deal to the late Al Roberts, Professor of Criminal Justice at Rutgers University. Al, with a caring, hectoring style all his own, demanded that we write a child welfare book that really explained why public child protective services agencies "do the things they do." Professor Roberts motivated us to get outside the traditional child welfare box of explanations. We deeply regret that we will not be able to hand him a copy of this book.

We owe much gratitude to the faculty and students who read parts or all of the draft manuscript. We give special thanks to Professors Sara McLanahan and Marta Tienda, both of Princeton University; Stefan Mend, Rutgers University; and Meera Jagannathan, University of North Carolina at Chapel Hill. Stefan's knowledge of punctuated equilibrium theory as it has been applied in political science was singularly helpful. We would also like to thank two anonymous reviewers for their thoughtful comments and constructive criticism. Professor Duncan Lindsey, University of California, Los Angeles, and editor of *Children and Youth Services Review*, published an early paper of ours in which we outlined the conceptual importance of moral outrage of child protective services decision making. His acceptance of this paper stimulated our interest in subjecting outrage mechanisms to a rigorous empirical test.

We are very grateful to Maura Roessner and Emily Perry, Oxford University Press, for their editorial assistance. Maura's patience was once again the perfect antidote for our procrastination. We also acknowledge the editorial help provided by Meera Jagannathan—her work on the book's many charts and tables was invaluable. On issues with the National Child Abuse and Neglect Data System (NCANDS) we were assisted by Dr. John Gaudiosi, Mathematical Statistician at the Children's Bureau.

Finally, our acknowledgements would not be complete without recognition to our spouses. Chet and Anne were once again supportive as we engaged in still another endeavor to slake our Faustian thirst for knowledge.

Protecting Children in the Age of Outrage

1

CHILD WELFARE REFORM AS
ANGER MANAGEMENT

Children begin by loving their parents; after a time they judge them; rarely,
if ever, do they forgive them.

Oscar Wilde (1893)

In a March 2007 newspaper column, the well-known conservative pundit George Will writes that America has become an angry nation with "fury as a fashion accessory, indignation as evidence of good character" (Will, 2007). Peter Wood (2006), an anthropologist at Boston University, documents what he sees as the new ubiquity of rage in American life and its crystallization into an "angri-culture." Although reasonable individuals might debate the pervasiveness of such an angri-culture across broad sectors of our society, it would be difficult to find people who are not maddened to some degree about the way our children are protected, especially when that protection involves public child welfare organizations. Horrifying cases of child abduction, rape, starvation, or murder in Florida, New York, or Washington, DC appear to fade from media coverage, if not from memory, only to be replaced by seemingly even more gruesome cases of child maltreatment from New Jersey, Illinois, Utah, or Maryland. No state or city looks to be immune; no child or family can be certain they will not in some way be touched by the awful specter of child abuse.

There is no doubt that there is some validity in the claims of a number of social scientists and critics of the media that a portion of this broad-based anger with our child welfare institutions is due to sensationalized reportage that engenders hysteria and hostility by obfuscating both the exceptionality and the disproportionality of especially horrific child maltreatment events (Welch et al., 2002; Zgoba, 2004). We believe it is mistaken, however, to view the anger generated by media accounts, no matter how distorted or sensationalized, as simply the incipient form of moral panic or a pretext for irrational social action. The decisions to protect—or, to be more precise, the decisions that have failed to protect—play a crucial role in the dynamic that has driven a great deal of efforts we call child welfare system reform. As Thomas Price (2005) remarks: "So it goes in the American child welfare system, scandal triggers public outrage which spurs reform, leaving children's advocates and child welfare workers constantly ricocheting between hope and despair" (p. 348).

Thomas Price and the purveyors of social panic theory have been able to pinpoint the special type of anger that imbues communications about child maltreatment. This broad-based anger or outrage, if you will, articulates failures to protect as violations of accepted social mores and values. Violations of what the public perceives to be "acceptable risks" are at the core of the outrage response to cases of child maltreatment. Because outrage, unlike other angry expressions such as moral indignation, loathing, or mere exasperation, demands redress, it cannot be dismissed easily like some sort of hysteria. As we show in this book, failures in decisions to protect children are inextricably bound up with failures to redress social outrage inasmuch as both types of negligence contribute to perceptions of overall risk magnitudes (Covello et al., 1988; Sandman et al., 1998).

MEASURING UP TO EUROPE

If sensational news accounts of child abuse and neglect cases serve as the precipitating factors of much public outrage, it is the professional social science and child welfare professionals who have provided contexts, color commentary if you will, on how these seemingly inexplicable events can be better understood. One commonly used frame of reference is Northern and Western Europe, where we are told public expenditures are more likely to be invested in the improvement of "child well-being" and not simply child protection. Whereas the latter places emphasis on the incidence of child physical abuse, child abuse fatalities, child sexual abuse, physical/medical neglect, emotional abuse and neglect, or psychological maltreatment (Brittain & Hunt, 2004, p. 307; Lindsey, 2004), the former has a much broader focus and includes a child's material well-being (poverty), health and safety (infant mortality, immunizations), educational well-being (literacy), family relationships (two-parent families), risk-taking behaviors (obesity, smoking, drugs, unprotected sex, fighting), and subjective well-being (self-reports of life satisfaction) (UNICEF Innocenti Research Center, 2007; Bradshaw et al., 2006). In most head-to-head comparisons with the Western European democracies, the United States cuts a sorry figure on measures of child well-being, more often than not coming in dead last (Bradshaw et al., 2006; Gabel & Kamerman, 2006). The country usually employed as the standard against which the United States fails to measure up is Sweden. This narrative, taken from Freymond and Cameron (2006), is quite typical:

> Sweden, along with the Nordic countries of Denmark, Finland, Norway and Iceland, follow a social democratic model of social protection where the core concept is equality. Social rights are associated primarily with citizenship and benefits provided by the public sector are delivered in the form of free services or all-inclusive benefits...No separation is made between protecting children and supporting families in Sweden....(p. 292)

According to Freymond and Cameron, England, Canada, Australia, Ireland, New Zealand, and the United States have a liberal tradition (in the classical sense) of social protection, in which greater emphasis is given to the market than to the state in allocating resources. The state must above all maintain a residual role: welfare benefits must be very low and minimum incomes and income support must constitute the main form of state intervention. Liberal social protection laws and policies have incorporated the values of self-reliance, individualism, and family privacy (Freymond & Cameron, 2006, p. 293). Even among this libertarian group of countries the United States fares poorly, which is the conclusion of Waldfogel's (2010) recent examination of child well-being in Great Britain and the United States.

The working hypothesis in these international comparisons of child well-being appears to be that if more investment is made by the United States to reduce poverty and fashion a family/child safety net of policies and services, child maltreatment levels will decline as a consequence. Simply increasing money expenditures, however, might not be enough to move the country higher on international rankings. The United States boasts among the very highest levels of single-parent families with parents who have never married (Camasso, 2007). Such single-parent families are less likely than single-parent families resulting from divorce—the more typical European dynamic—to provide the prospects for both parents' engagement in a child's socialization process. Americans, moreover, tend to be more inclined than Europeans to engage in risk-taking or risky behavior, a cultural trait that arises from Americans' more libertarian worldview (Kupchan, 2008; Rifkin, 2005; Sjoberg, 2000).

It is also worthy of note that the United States, among all the Western industrialized countries, "provides the most extensive, regularly reported and systematic data on the condition of children and indicators of child wellbeing," this according to the Organization for Economic Cooperation and Development (OECD) (Kamerman et al., 2003, p. 8). Not intending to be apologists for the performance of the United States, we wonder how more complete data from better performing European countries would affect America's child well-being stature in the world. Perhaps a reporting system less capable of hoisting America on its own petard would make comparisons with Europe a bit less dramatic.

CALLS FOR REFORM

That the United States may have the worst system for ensuring child well-being among wealthy democracies only serves to fuel the domestic anger around failures to take better care of our children. Blame has been hurled in all directions: e.g., unfit parents, unregistered sex offenders, lenient judges, family breakup, and unraveling social values; however, it is the public child protective services (CPS) agency and its workers that are usually singled out for special excoriation by the media, the public, child welfare professionals, and academics—especially academics. Take, for example, this montage of pejoratives used by David Stoesz to portray U.S. child protective services. Stoesz (2005) sees the child welfare system as a "network of negligence" (p. 157) built upon "professional ineptitude" (p. 161), yielding a "culture infused with mediocrity" (p. 164) with workers of poor education "performing tasks that have little empirical or ethical bases" (p. 168). William Epstein (1999) denounces the child welfare profession for not understanding its operations and how they are related to outcomes and for the lack of self-discipline or character to find out. This is a bit over-the-top, perhaps, but a view shared by many in the media, on expert panels, elected officials, and legal watchdog organizations (Geen & Tumlin, 1999; Golden, 2009; DeParle, 1997). In a study conducted by the Annie E. Casey Foundation (2003) on the condition of the frontline human services workforce, the Foundation concluded that child protective services and other government agencies treating the problems of children and families are reaching a state of crisis.

> Frontline jobs are becoming more and more complex while the responsibility placed on workers remains severely out of line with their preparation and baseline abilities. Many are leaving the field while a new generation of college graduates shows little interest in entering the human services sector. Millions of taxpayer dollars are being poured into a compromised system that not only achieves little in the way of real results but its interventions often do more harm than good. It is clear that frontline human services jobs are not attracting and keeping the kinds of workers we need, and that regulations, unreasonable expectations and poor management practices mire workers and their clients in a dangerous status quo. (p. 2)

Alvin Schorr's (2000) seminal article, "The Bleak Prospect for Public Child Welfare," continues to be rewritten each year—only the names and the publishers change in these compositions designed to draw attention to our failures to protect the innocent.

Almost from its very inception at the U.S. Children's Bureau in 1912 and as the Child Welfare Services Program, under Title IV of the Social Security Act in 1935, public child welfare has been an enduring target for reform at the federal level. An extensive discussion can be found in Schene (1998) and Lindsey (2004) or on the Child Welfare Information Gateway (2011).

Schorr (2000) has classified these many efforts to reform public welfare into three principal categories: viz. administrative, practice, or systems, although many pieces of legislation are, without doubt, mixtures of each. Schorr finds examples of administrative reform in legislation, especially in the 1980s, that attempted to merge services into "superagencies" and increase integration into community-based agencies. Practice reform turns on issues of optimal service delivery models and has run through phases such as permanency planning, family preservation, case management, and "best practices" case practice. System reform, according to Schorr, is exemplified by legislation in the 1990s that separated protective services from family services and that isolated CPS from initiatives designed to address broad social problems such as poverty, discrimination, or social justice. The persistent themes that run through child welfare reforms are organizational effectiveness and efficiency, financial resources, necessary services, minimization of decision errors, worker quality and training, computerized management, and quality control data systems.

Notwithstanding decades of attempts to reform child welfare, the clamor for more reform continues unabated. A 2006 report from the U.S. Government Accountability Office (GAO), for example, in a survey of state child welfare agencies, identified three challenges that needed to be resolved to improve child protective outcomes: providing an adequate level of services, recruiting and retaining caseworkers, and finding appropriate homes for children. A 2010 Report to Congress issued by the Department of Health and Human Services (DHHS), Administration for Children and Families (ACF), and the Office of Planning, Research, and Evaluation (OPRE) (Sedlak et al., 2010) concludes that the majority of maltreated children do not receive CPS investigation and recommends that better working relationships need to be established between CPS and potential sentinel sources, especially schools (p. 9.4). A 2003 study of state CPS policies conducted by Walter R. McDonald & Associates for OPRE and ACF found substantial variation across states in policies/procedures regarding mandated reporters, investigation objectives, standards of evidence, types of maltreatment, required timelines, and due process requirements, noting that such variations "may have meaningful impacts on achieving" the goal that children are safe from abuse and neglect (p. 6.1).

Most experts in the child welfare field appear to believe that current legislative reforms have not gone far enough. In 2009 issues of the Princeton University–Brookings Institution publication "The Future of Children," over a dozen leading academics and practitioners conclude that more needs to be done to ensure adequate funding for child abuse prevention (Paxson & Haskins, 2009). Another compilation of expert research and opinion sponsored by the Annie E. Casey Foundation identifies a pressing need for CPS programs and policies undergirded by a reliable data reporting, collection, and analysis system. According to the editors, Haskins, Wulczyn, and Webb (2007):

> If this [CPS] system looks somewhat reasonable on paper, it has flaws that are widely recognized. These include inadequate training of the professionals running the system, a shortage of high-quality foster homes, a shortage of effective intervention programs to provide needed services, a dearth of preventive services, an abundance of paperwork and a somewhat ineffective though improving system of accountability. (p. 2)

A collection of essays edited by Lindsey and Shlonsky (2008) calls for a system that embraces both CPS and child well-being, integrated in much the same manner as the public health service diagnoses and treats both infection and lifestyle sources of pathology.

The substantial number of federal reforms and the ongoing discussion around still more reforms have all but obscured our attention away from the manner in which child welfare policies are conceived and put into practice. A few scholars, outside the social work and child welfare professions, notably Baumgartner and Jones (1991, 2009) and Nelson (1984), have observed that these policies follow change trajectories that are disjointed and episodic. Often the impetus for a policy initiative is an "alarmed discovery," demanding immediate corrective action(s). Subsequent discoveries or crises necessitate new responses that can just as well lead to the destruction of previous policies and institutions as to their reinvigoration. This sort of "punctuated change" has also been seen operating at the state level by Gainsborough (2010), but here the alarm is more likely to be tinged by scandal.

STIMULATING REFORM WITH APPEALS TO THE SHADOW

If CPS policy changes are not gradual and incremented, but instead are driven by alarming discoveries and the outrage they spawn, it is critical that we understand why horrific cases of child maltreatment serve as such catalysts. One compelling argument is offered by some psychiatrists who maintain that cases of inhumanity bring out energies, desires, and drives in all humanity that cause us great emotional pain (Stein, 1995). For Jung (1959) confrontations with bad or evil persons, objects, or events bring the shadow to our consciousness—that portion of self that the ego calls evil for reasons of shame, social pressure, or family. Exposure of the shadow also summons up energies for redress—this is especially true in cases in which we face the shadow archetype, i.e., manifestations of pure evil. In Jung's (1964) own words:

> The sight of evil kindles evil in the soul. There is no getting away from this fact. The victim is not the only sufferer, everybody in the vicinity of the crime, including the murderer, suffers with him ... Evil calls for expiation, otherwise the wicked will destroy the world utterly, or the good suffocate in their rage which they cannot vent and in either case no good will come of it. (p. 410)

If Jung's assessment is correct, our encounters with cases of shocking child maltreatment not only open avenues for emotional catharsis, they also provide windows of opportunity for social action. Indeed, a number of political scientists (Baumgartner & Jones, 2009; Nelson, 1984; Gainsborough, 2010) have identified archetypical cases of child abuse as the focal events responsible for lurches in public attention, political agenda setting, and policy instability.

The archetypical case of child maltreatment buttressing the Adam Walsh Child Protection and Safety Act is well known to many Americans. In 1981, Adam, a 6-year-old Florida child, was kidnapped from a mall while shopping with his mother, brutalized, murdered, and decapitated. The graphic account of parental anguish and public outrage can be found in the book *Tears of Rage* (Walsh, 2008) written by Adam's father.

The nexus between the horrific incident and legislative action is unambiguous in the Walsh case; however, its analogue can be found to some degree, more or less, motivating all sorts of legislation and community actions seeking to protect children from child maltreatment. For example, embedded in the pages of testimony providing statistical and financial evidence for the necessity of the Child and Family Services Improvement Act (2006) we find this heartrending account.

> Starting from her brick apartment tower, Rose walks a block to Gun Hill Road, takes the 28 bus to the subway station, catches the 5 train to Harlem, makes her way down 125th Street, boards the Metro-North train to Dobbs Ferry and rides a shuttle—at each stop, she places two metal crutches ahead of her and swings forward on two prosthetic legs. The journey would have been worth it had there been something worthwhile at the end of the line. But there wasn't. Issa (her son)

was warehoused at a residential treatment center. This is a form of care so utterly ineffective that even the head of the trade association for child welfare agencies, the Child Welfare League of America, had to admit they lack "good research" showing its effectiveness and "we find it hard to demonstrate success...." Issa is not paranoid, he's not schizophrenic, he's not delusional. The only label pinned on him is Attention Deficit Hyperactivity Disorder. But his handicapped, impoverished single mother couldn't do what middle-class and wealthy families do: find a good psychiatrist and hire some home health aides. She couldn't do that because the federal government does almost nothing to help pay for alternatives. (Committee on Ways and Means, U.S. House of Representatives, 2006, p. 80)

This case and several others like it proved to be compelling for legislators who supported expanding the flexibility of Title IV-B to fund nonresidential treatment modalities.

Indeed, it is a widely held opinion among child welfare historians that it was a singularly incomprehensible act of cruelty to a little girl named Mary Ellen Wilson that started the modern child protection movement (Bremner, 1971; Nelson, 1984; Myers, 2006; Wiehe, 1992). When Mary Ellen, a severely malnourished 11-year-old child, appeared in court shortly after being rescued by officials from the Society for the Prevention of Cruelty to Animals from 8 years of maltreatment, she gave this testimony:

My father and mother are both dead. I don't know how old I am. I have no recollection of a time when I did not live with the Connollys. I call Mrs. Connolly mamma. I have never had but one pair of shoes, but I cannot recollect when that was. I have had no shoes or stockings on this Winter. I have never been allowed to go out of the room where the Connollys were, except in the night time, and then only in the yard. I have never had on a particle of flannel. My bed at night has been only a piece of carpet stretched on the floor underneath a window, and I sleep in my little undergarments, with a quilt over me. I am never allowed to play with any children, or have any company whatever. Mamma (Mrs. Connolly) has been in the habit of whipping and beating me almost every day. She used to whip me with a twisted whip—a raw hide. The whip always left a black and blue mark on my body. I have now the black and blue marks on my head which were made by mamma, and also a cut on the left side of my forehead which was made by a pair of scissors. (Scissors produced in court.) She struck me with the scissors and cut me; I have no recollection of ever having been kissed by any one—have never been kissed by mamma. I have never been taken on my mamma's lap and caressed or petted. I never dared to speak to anybody, because if I did I would get whipped. I have never had, to my recollection, any more clothing than I have at present—a calico dress and skirt. I have seen stockings and other clothes in our room, but was not allowed to put them on. Whenever mamma went out I was locked up in the bedroom. I do not know for what I was whipped—mamma never said anything to me when she whipped me. I do not want to go back to live with mamma, because she beats me so. I have no recollection of ever being on the street in my life. (Bremner, 1972, p. 186)

The *New York Times* recorded on April 22, 1874, that particulars of the Mary Ellen Wilson case "caused such excitement and indignation in the community" of New York City and a large outcry emerged calling for the punishment of Mary and Francis Connolly, the child's adoptive parents. Mrs. Connolly was found guilty and was sentenced to 1 year of imprisonment at hard labor.

Outrage has also provoked child welfare reform through a judicial vehicle known variously as the court order, injunction, or consent decree. This route to reform typically begins with a civil rights organization or national advocacy group filing a lawsuit against a governor or state human services commissioner for failure to protect children under the United States Constitution, a state's constitution, or federal child welfare legislation. One organization that has been particularly active in filing lawsuits against state CPS agencies is Children's Rights, Inc. The executive director of Children's Rights, Marcia Robinson Lowry, in fact, maintains that lawsuits are critical to reform because they provide a source of sustained pressure for constructive change (Lowry, 1998).

Although lawsuits filed by advocacy groups are typically guided by class-action legal theory, they are almost always motivated by an archetypical case of egregious maltreatment. In the legal action that Children's Rights brought against the City of New York (*Marisol A. v. Giuliani*, 1995) for the city's alleged noncompliance with federal child welfare statutes, the plaintiff was 3-year-old Marisol. According to the complaint:

> Reports that Marisol was being abused by her mother went uninvestigated and those concerned were given bland assurances that the child was thriving. But child welfare officials had no idea how she was doing. Fifteen months later, a housing inspector happened upon Marisol, locked in a closet in her mother's apartment, near death. She had been repeatedly abused over an extended period of time, eating plastic garbage bags and her own feces to survive. (Lowry, 1998, p. 124)

Then there is the Children's Rights intervention in New Jersey, *Charlie and Nadine H. v. Corzine* (1999, 2003), a class-action lawsuit filed on behalf of 11,000 children receiving care from the state's Division of Youth and Family Services (DYFS). Movement on this litigation appeared to have reached a stalemate until the mummified body of 7-year-old Faheem Williams was found by investigators in the basement of a Newark, New Jersey home.

> Faheem's cousin, Wesley Murphy...admitted that while the family was living in Irvington (NJ) he had killed the child with a wrestling move in which he had forced his knee into the child's abdomen...Sherry Murphy, another cousin, admitted that she left the boy's body on the floor, then put it in a plastic hamper, which she took with her when she moved to Newark. A day before the body was found, police found Faheem's two young brothers, Raheem and Tyrone, emaciated and starving in an adjacent room. (Associated Press, 2006)

The state Human Services Commissioner revealed that DYFS workers had closed Faheem's case 11 months earlier without investigating a claim that the brothers had been beaten and scalded.

Litigation against child welfare organizations continues to take place in dozens of states with many CPS agencies operating under court order (Geen & Tumlin, 1999; Kosanovich & Joseph, 2005). Many court cases have proven to be an effective vehicle for channeling public outrage into a forum that promises the redress of personal damages and institutional breakdown. Just how effective this reform litigation has been in improving child welfare agency function, however, remains the subject of considerable debate (Sandler & Schoenbrod, 2003; Behn, 2001).

Arousing our disgust and anger through the invocation of an especially horrific case of child maltreatment is not limited to judicial or legislative reform efforts. It remains a common literary device, employed in scores of child welfare textbooks and professional journal articles, and is motivated by an exceedingly clear objective—grab the reader's attention. Here are two examples from books used in graduate and undergraduate schools of social work.

Winton and Mara (2001) began their book with young Laura:

> Laura had shot her stepfather in the back, killing him. She was being charged with murder in the first degree and was to be prosecuted as an adult. The state attorney's office subsequently called and requested a full psychological evaluation of Laura. The standard psychological evaluation was completed and revealed the clinical characteristics of a sexually abused adolescent.
>
> The case eventually was set for trial, and, despite the circumstances, the state attorney's office sought to prosecute the fourteen-year-old girl as an adult. That prompted a tremendous backlash in the community, with many women's support groups and children's rights groups springing to Laura's defense. The day of the trial was emotionally charged for everyone involved, as both sides subpoenaed and called on all kinds of witnesses and experts. The defense argued the scenario of self-defense of a battered child who was sexually abused, while the prosecution presented Laura as a fourteen-year-old who took the law into her own hands and should be punished for this act of murder.
>
> Laura testified in open court about the abuses that began when she was seven. She vividly described scenes in which her stepfather emotionally abused her by calling her *ugly* and *stupid* and telling her that no boy would ever want to look at her. She described how her stepfather began coming into her room periodically in the middle of the night, telling her that he loved her and caressing her. Over the years this led to fondling, digital penetration, and then full intercourse. She recounted numerous occasions when he took her out in his truck and they had intercourse. Afterward he would buy her a new dress, tell her not to tell anyone, and threaten her with a shotgun.
>
> As a teenager, Laura started to recognize that she needed to end the abuse. She described pleading with her stepfather to stop the abuse, which he did for a short time, only to begin again, threatening her life as well as her mother's. As she

testified in court, Laura exhibited the terror she had felt during these horrific scenes. (p. 2)

In her book *Reforming Child Welfare* (2009), Olivia Golden provides the reader with a brief glimpse into the life of Lora.

"Lora," age 13, is the oldest child in a sibling group of four....In April 2003, [community agency staff] reported physical abuse of Lora by her stepfather....Lora was removed by CFSA....In June of 2003, Lora reported sexual abuse by the stepfather during the time he still resided in the family home. [Her mother] currently is receiving treatment for a blood clot on her brain which resulted from a brutal incident of domestic violence by the stepfather....(p. 2)

We could cite many more of these vignettes, but believe the point has been made that accounts like these engender attention even as they come up short on explanation.

In her book *The Future of Child Protection* (1998), Jane Waldfogel declares that child protective services in America has an image that is "often drawn from the case of one particular child who has been in the headlines or the television news" (p. 1). In effect, CPS is viewed by the public as the Facebook pages of Laura, Lora, and Mary Ellen,. Waldfogel goes on in the next few pages to list five cases of child maltreatment that received enormous publicity and engendered immense public outrage: viz. Lisa Steinberg, Elisa Izquierdo, Lance Helms, Michelle Gray, and Nadine Lockwood. However, instead of following up the shock with an argument—which is quite commonplace in child welfare essays—"we need to take these cases to heart and reform CPS protection to insure they don't happen again," Waldfogel offers this observation:

The cases that arouse public outrage are not a random, representative sample of child abuse and neglect cases. Rather, they are special in some way, usually in that they involve either the death of a child or the maltreatment of several children and, more often than not, the failure of the child protective services system. These special cases may be useful for examining how well the system protects children under the most extreme circumstances, but they provide no insight into the overall population of children in need of protection and the general operations of the child protective services system. (p. 5)

Waldfogel's statement reveals a perspective on the relationship between the archetypical case and general CPS agency operations that is widely, if tacitly, held in the child welfare profession. (See, for example, Gainsborough, 2010; Nelson, 1984.) The extraordinary evil that men and women sometimes do to their children is viewed as so exceptional that such occurrences have little to offer in understanding our decisions to protect children. This, of course, is much the same argument offered in the public hysteria and moral panic literature in which both the corrosive and beneficial impacts of outrage on child protection institutions are very often minimized or trivialized.

OUTRAGE AND CHILD WELFARE OPERATIONS

Rather than serve as some sort of distraction in the real work of protecting children, it is our contention that public outrage, driven by the archetypical case of child maltreatment, plays a pivotal role in structuring the daily operations of CPS organizations. We believe this impact emerges in a fashion that closely parallels the organizational impact that the economist Max Weber identified as the "routinization of charisma" (Weber, 1947, pp. 324–334). Charisma or "personal magic" confronts organizations with a dilemma that requires some kind of rapprochement between business as usual and the visionaries (and their followers) who are contemptuous of anything associated with the routine. If an organization is to survive a charismatic challenge, it must find ways to integrate these nonroutine elements into its operational fabric—it must transform the extraordinary into ordinary operations.

In much the same way, CPS agencies seek to confront the horrific case(s) of child maltreatment without losing the organization in a morass of improvisation and potential chaos. The principal solution to this problem, we believe, is through "the institutionalization of child risk as moral outrage." We believe this routinization manifests itself in three ways that exert profound influences on CPS management and operations. The first is the inculcation by state and local agencies of the community standard for "zero tolerance" (Price, 2005; Wilson, 2010). In the parlance of public health meeting this standard requires maximum surveillance, screening in of false positive as well as true positive cases, and the guarantee of no false negatives. Adoption of the zero tolerance standard introduces a second form of routinization best described as "infinite jeopardy." The term has been used by Robert Behn (2001), narrowly, to describe the anxiety among civil servants over how ethics rules could be interpreted in public bureaucracies. We define the term more broadly as a component of CPS agency culture in which culture, simply put, "is the way we do things around here" (Deal & Kennedy, 1982, p. 4). The principle of infinite jeopardy helps motivate the thoughts, speech, actions, and technologies that are transmitted laterally and longitudinally in CPS. The ethos of infinite jeopardy places high values on "keeping your head down" and other risk-averse behaviors.

Attempts to routinize outrage produces yet a third dynamic into CPS operations, one that all but ensures adaptation will be frenetic, episodic, and partial. Punctuated change or "punctuated equilibrium" is a conceptual and empirical model that has its origins in the natural sciences (Eldredge & Gould, 1997; Raup, 1991), predicting system shifts rapidly from one stable point to another. This model has been employed by social scientists to describe the S-shaped transition curves that characterize many policy processes, budgetary changes, and group dynamics (Gersick, 1988; Baumgartner & Jones, 2009). We believe that concentrated bursts of change, punctuating periods of relative stability, have applications to CPS operations and decision making, and provide a formal test of its efficacy in Chapter 6. As we will show, outrage-driven legislation, lawsuits, government task forces, and special panel reports can and have exerted impacts on both the structure and process of CPS organizations. In reform legislation and consent decrees we can find interventions targeted at executive leadership, mid-level managers and supervisors, the technostructure, as well as the operating core of CPS that comprises the front line workers. Even the support staff, such as legal counsel, public relations, and research/quality assurance staff, have been targeted for improvement in the aftermath of especially horrendous maltreatment cases.

The pressure to routinize and restructure, in turn, changes what Mintzberg (1983, 1979) characterizes as the essential flows of an organization: viz. formal authority regulated activity, informal communication, and decision making. It is Mintzberg's insight that flows are often hierarchical with the dominant flow providing an organization with its essential character and culture. It is also possible for flows to hybridize if context and environmental conditions in the market, polity, or citizenry warrant such modification. Thus a CPS agency, which in Mintzberg's framework would be classified as an amalgam of (1) machine bureaucracy, dominated by standardization of work processes and the flow of formal authority, and (2) professional bureaucracy, based on standardization of skills and regulated activity, can rather easily transform into an organization dominated by ad hoc decision processes, if equilibrium is upset (see Mintzberg, 1983, pp. 58–64). Of course, CPS bureaucracy struggles to reach new stability, guided by modified SOPs and new rules.

OUTRAGED DECISION PROCESSES

The principal argument in this book posits that archetypical instances of child maltreatment release an ad hoc decision flow that profoundly destabilizes the manner in which child risk is conceptualized and operationalized by CPS workers, mid-level managers, and even agency leaders. Most notably, critical decisions around acceptable risk are respecified, moving them away from a public health conception of risk, i.e.,

Risk = f(Hazard)   (Eq. 1)

[where risk is the likelihood of harm or loss and hazard is a scientifically validated source(s) of potential danger (Blake, 1995) that is a function of the magnitude of threat (toxicity and dosage) multiplied by the probability of exposure (Sandman, 1999), i.e.,

Hazard = f(Magnitude of Threat • p(Exposure)]   (Eq. 2)

to a more socially sensitive definition, i.e.,

Risk = f(Hazard,Outrage)   (Eq. 3)

[where hazard is defined as above and outrage articulates feelings of righteous anger].

The notion that risk perception and assessment are not simply a result of technical hazard is not new; risk has been long conceptualized in the fields of environmental science, food safety, chemical engineering, and others as the function of technical (hazard) and emotional (outrage) components (Covello, Sandman, & Slovic, 1988; Kasperson, 1986; Sandman, 1999). As we show in Chapter 3, however, such specification is uncommon in child welfare and CPS. Notwithstanding the recognition in the environmental science and engineering field of the importance of outrage to risk measurement, the tendency in these disciplines has been to portray outrage as something residing in the general public that can be "managed" by an organization through strategies such as health education, public relations, or careful risk communication (Sandman, Weinstein, & Hallman, 1998; Sandman, 2003). The citizenry and media are "handled" in much the same way as Erving Goffman's crime victim is during the process of "cooling out the mark" (Goffman, 1952). If successful, risk communication strategies can limit the impact of the extraordinary violations of social norms such as coal mine disasters, oil spills, adverse drug reactions, consumer product malfunctions resulting in injury or fatality, etc., on an organization's operating core. Exceptional decision making need not suffuse the exercise of routine operating decisions and risk as hazard can once again be employed.

It becomes more difficult (we would say impossible) to protect an organization's operations from the effects of public outrage when children become a focal point, and this is openly recognized in the risk communication field (Covello, Sandman, & Slovic, 1988; Sandman et al., 1987). When the business of the organization is the protection of children, this capacity is reduced even more. When CPS organizations are confronted by public outrage, the exceptional mixes rather easily with routine decision processes, creating a risk assessment strategy that we believe can be modeled as follows:

$$\text{Risk to Child} = f(\text{Hazard, Risk to CPS Worker}) \qquad (\text{Eq. 4})$$

where

$$\text{Risk to CPS Worker} = f(\text{Outrage, Worker Competence/Insulation}) \qquad (\text{Eq. 5})$$

with Eq. 4 and Eq. 5 leading to

$$\text{Risk to Child} = f(\text{Hazard, Outrage, Worker Competence/Insulation}) \qquad (\text{Eq. 6})$$

Collecting the terms from Eq. 6 and augmenting this risk model with CPS organizational level inputs (e.g., workforce size, experience, agency budgets, etc.) together with child-relevant social policies and economic conditions, we obtain this CPS decision outcome specification:

$$\begin{aligned}
\text{CPS Decision Outcomes} = f(&\text{Risk to Child through Hazard and Outrage,} \\
&\text{Risk to Child/Worker from Outrage, Worker} \\
&\text{competence/insulaton, CPS organizational Inputs/} \\
&\text{resources, Social Policies, Economic Conditions)} \quad (\text{Eq. 7})
\end{aligned}$$

The model explicitly locates the impact of community outrage as an exogenous component that influences CPS worker decision processes along with worker expertise and organizational protections from jeopardy. Subsequent outrage shocks would be hypothesized to produce trajectories of S-shaped change–stability curves with consequences for the relative weights given by CPS decision makers to risks from hazard and outrage.

In the chapters that follow, we explore our model's relevancy for understanding not only the processes of risk assessment and decision making in CPS but the outcomes of these risk assessments and decisions as well. In Chapter 3 we describe how model components 1, 2, and 3 (Eqs. 1, 2, and 3) provide us with a better understanding of how judgments of risk in CPS are informed by social outrage. Model components 4, 5, and 6 (Eqs. 4, 5, and 6) provide focus for our discussion in Chapter 4, where we describe how CPS agency resource inputs, most especially the frontline workforce, are shaped by bursts of social outrage. Chapter 5 introduces the reader to the extraagency forces that thoughtful social scientists have used to explain poor CPS agency performance. These factors are incorporated under economic conditions and social policies on the right-hand side of model component 7 (Eq. 7). Chapter 6 provides an econometric, empirical test of model component 7 (Eq. 7), employing 17 years of national data from the National Child Abuse and Neglect Data System (NCANDS).

Before we launch into the formal test of the model's efficacy in explaining CPS decision-making process and outcomes, we introduce the reader, in Chapter 2, to child protective services in New Jersey. We trust the case study material presented will help convince the reader, as it did us, of the pivotal role played by outrage in state CPS reform and of the importance of conducting a deeper and broader analysis of the outrage dynamic.

2

A STATE OF PERPETUAL OUTRAGE
NEW JERSEY

"Innocence always calls mutely for protection."
–Graham Greene (1955)

In New Jersey, the Division of Youth and Family Services (DYFS) was, until 2006, the state agency charged with the protection of children from maltreatment. When the authors arrived in New Jersey in 1984 to accept positions at the Rutgers University School of Social Work, DYFS had firmly secured a reputation of scorn from a broad array of politicians, family court judges, academics, and media within New Jersey and from bordering states as well. The derision stemmed from the widely held perception that DYFS was not doing enough to protect children from maltreatment—maltreatment in their own homes, maltreatment in foster care, and maltreatment in the state's institutions. In December 1985, for example, an employee at a day-care center in Maplewood, New Jersey was indicted for 229 instances of sexual assault on 33 children aged 3 through 6 years. Allegations that the abuse had occurred over a 6-month period put the agency in the national spotlight and generated a public outcry for staff resignations and organizational restructuring (*New York Times*, 1985). Others had also documented DYFS' painful history of problems and efforts to reform in the 1970s and 1980s (see, for example, Advocates for Children of New Jersey, 2003; Nelson, 1984).

Especially alarming to the many agency critics were the child fatalities from abuse and neglect that appeared to be occurring even when cases were under long periods of DYFS supervision. In 1990, for example, the New Jersey Department of Human Services reported that 39 children died from abuse or neglect in the state, and of the 39, 22 children were or had recently been under DYFS supervision (Waldman & Balasco-Barr, 1995). From 1998 to the end of 2002, 123 children died from abuse or neglect in the state with over two-thirds of these children receiving DYFS investigation and services. The average prison time for individuals found guilty of child homicide in these cases was 11 years (Alaya, 2003). Many in the state complained that the incarceration time was not enough and, indeed, the punishment given to New Jersey's perpetrators was less than in many other states. What was not mentioned very frequently in media accounts or politicians' displays of anger was how New Jersey compared with other states on the frequency with which child deaths occurred. In 2002, New Jersey reported a child death rate due to child maltreatment of 1.41 deaths per 100,000 at-risk population: the rates in the District of Columbia, Missouri, and Texas that year were 11.59, 3.79, and 3.38 per 100,000 (U.S. Department of Health and Human Services, Children's Bureau, Administration for Children and Families, 2004). Interstate comparisons or comparisons with the national average (which hovered around 2.00 per 100,000), however, were never winning arguments with the public or their elected officials as DYFS sought to defend itself from a seemingly continuous barrage of criticism.

In 1999, the chorus of DYFS detractors got even larger when the advocacy group Children's Rights, Inc. filed a class action lawsuit in state court claiming that the agency had failed to adequately protect the civil rights of thousands of children in the child welfare system (Association for Children of New Jersey, 2007; Children's Rights, Inc., 2010). Yet despite the continuing deaths, the lawsuit, several oversight panels, several critical reports, and scathing media coverage, the DYFS child protective services staff pressed on from the mid-1990s through 2002, even making some modest progress in reducing the number of children abused in foster care and decreasing individual worker caseload sizes (Association for Children of New Jersey, 2003, 2007). Annual child fatalities, too, had appeared to moderate moving from the consistent mid-thirties to the mid-twenties (New Jersey Department of Children and Families, 2010). To a public exhausted by bad news and the legion of critics it must have appeared DYFS, like a serviceable Timex watch, would "keep taking a licking but still keep on ticking." The new year, however, held a horrific surprise for the organization—one that was to utterly destroy public confidence in DYFS and shake the agency to its very operating core. That surprise was the mummified body of 7-year-old Faheem Williams.

LET THERE BE BLAME

On Saturday, January 4, 2003, Newark, New Jersey police received a telephone call from the boyfriend of Sherry Murphy, a 41-year-old go-go dancer, that he had found two children, ages 7 and 5, locked in a room that was "in a terrible state" (CNN, 2003). On January 5, in a house filled with garbage, urine, feces, and vomit, police discovered the two boys, Raheem Williams and Tyrone Hill, dehydrated and starving, their heads covered with lice (Livio & Patterson, 2003). Murphy, who had agreed to look after the youngsters while the boys' mother, 30-year-old Melinda Williams, served jail time on an assault charge, was now the subject of an intense missing persons search.

On the sixth of January, police recovered the body of Faheem Williams, the twin brother of Raheem, locked in a basement room in the same house, stuffed in a plastic container hidden in a closet (Livio & Patterson, 2003). An autopsy showed that the child had died from starvation and blunt force trauma to the stomach (Kleinknecht & Sterling, 2003). DYFS had been involved with Melinda Williams and her children since 1992, and had received 11 complaints of physical abuse or neglect over a 10-year period, but closed the Williams case in February of 2002 (Livio, 2003; Association for Children of New Jersey, 2003).

In terms of absolute horror, the Williams case was reminiscent of the death in 1989 of Dyneekah Johnson, the 5-year-old girl whose body was found clad in her Sunday school dress on a garbage pile in an empty Newark lot. Notwithstanding the intense media coverage and threats of lawmakers to make basic changes to DYFS, the words of the then agency director William Waldman resonated what was to become the customary agency retort to criticism for nearly a decade. When asked if the DYFS system had broken down in the Johnson case, Waldman asserted that "failures in this case were not due to problems or weaknesses of the system but were the failures of specific agency personnel to carry out established policies and procedures" (DePalma, 1989, p. B4). A 2003 policy brief written by the Association for Children of New Jersey (ACNJ) lamented that no real reform had taken place in DYFS during the 1990s and that the agency appeared on track to suffer more tragedies, more crises, and more lawsuits (Association for Children of New Jersey, 2003).

In 2003, the social and political climate in New Jersey did not offer DYFS the option of explaining away an archetypical case of child maltreatment as the handiwork of a "few bad apples" (Patterson, 2003), crushing caseload sizes, or too few cell phones and/or cars for workers. Above the din of the usual chorus of politicians, lawyers, and academics offering to create and/or staff expert panels, fashion new statutes, or lobby for larger child welfare budgets (see, for example, Kleinman, 2003; Moran, Witlow, & Jerome-Cohen, 2003) stood a governor, James McGreevey, and a commissioner of human services, Gwendolyn Harris, who believed that radical, structural reform was the only real remedy for child protective services in the state. The Governor's immediate response to the Williams death was to call for the extraction of DYFS from the Department of Human Services and the creation of a Cabinet-level unit to oversee investigations into abused and abandoned children (Livio & Donohue, 2003). Both as a candidate for governor and as a state legislator, McGreevey had advocated for the passage of a law compelling DYFS to disclose all details of its involvement in a case in which a child had died. Harris called for an overall structural reform (Livio & Donohue, 2003) and in February issued a report entitled Transforming Child Protective Services in New Jersey: DYFS Transformation Plan (Harris, 2003). The 13-page report placed DYFS in a "state of emergency," forbade caseworkers from closing a case in which a child had not been seen on a family visit, and called for the formation of a new child protection division, the Division of Child Protection and Permanency, reporting directly to the Commissioner's Office. The report also called for the use of Quality Service Reviews (QSR), a case auditing program that was in use in Alabama and Utah, and for the expedited, full implementation of the federally supported Statewide Automated Child Welfare Information System (SACWIS). Harris also promised openness to broad community and professional input, reinforcing the Governor's commitment to a child protective services (CPS) accountability based on operational transparency and broad access to fatality and extreme abuse records. McGreevey reprised many of the February report's recommendations in his "Bold New Initiatives" press release in May 2003. He also called for the creation of an independent Child Advocate Office and Cabinet for Children with statewide planning for child welfare and child protective services (State of New Jersey Governor's Office, 2003).

It appeared that the Governor and Commissioner were on the verge of leading child protective services in New Jersey on a pathway to real reform. At a graduation awards ceremony held by the Rutgers University School of Social Work, Harris was awarded the School's 2003 Public Policy Leadership Award by Dean Mary Davidson for her work on transforming DYFS (New Jersey Department of Human Services, 2003). May, however, did not lead to the flowering of the state's reform efforts, nor did June or July. But October and December proved to be the cruelest months of all.

In early May 2003, Richard Lezin Jones and Leslie Kaufman (2003) published a piece in the *New York Times* titled "Foster care secrecy magnifies suffering of New Jersey cases." Using information made available through an open records policy that McGreevey had championed, the authors presented a portrait of incompetence and cover-up that dismayed even the most sympathetic of DYFS supporters. These journalists cited data that showed that one in five of the children in the agency's foster care system had been physically abused. They also stated that DYFS makes great efforts to conceal its failures from the birth parents, lawyers acting on behalf of the child(ren), and legislators seeking reform.

Faced with withering criticism from the Williams death, another dozen child fatalities since February (Livio, 2003), and this new revelation about foster care abuse, Governor McGreevey made the decision on June 24, 2003 to abandon his own efforts to guide child welfare reform by agreeing to settle the 1999 lawsuit brought by Children's Rights, Inc. Among the terms of the settlement was the requirement that any state plans designed to address child protective services issues be approved or disapproved by a "Child Welfare Panel of Independent Experts" comprised of individuals from the University of Medicine and Dentistry of New Jersey, the Annie E. Casey Foundation, and the Center for the Study of Social Policy, located in Washington, DC (Livio, 2003). The panel was empowered by the court to (1) identify legally enforceable deadlines and goals that had to be achieved, and (2) determine if the state was making sufficient progress in achieving these goals. The Governor also promised to immediately allocate more money for new case managers, additional caseworkers, and equipment, and to determine whether any of the 11,600 children in foster care were in danger.

Pressure continued to mount on DYFS staff even as morale sunk to all-time lows. The Williams case opened the floodgates of reports of new abuse and neglect cases from throughout the state. The total number of children under DYFS supervision rose from 46,985 in January of 2003 to 58,302 in July, a 24% increase. Worker case loads rose to an average of 41 per caseworker, the highest level experienced since 1996 (Association for Children of New Jersey, 2003; Livio, 2003). Hetty Rosenstein, president of the union representing the nearly 1,500 DYFS caseworkers, lamented that "the caseloads are amazing…it's at crisis proportions" (Livio, 2003). An August report issued by the U.S. Administration for Children and Families informed DYFS that the agency was performing badly in several critical areas of its foster care system and would be expected to return millions of dollars in aid to the federal government (Livio, 2003). All the time, the body count of deceased children continued to mount, reaching 37 by December 2003, the highest annual total since 1990 (Livio, 2003).

Now, not only were case managers and caseworkers being dismissed, top level management was being purged as well. In June 2003, Ed Cotton, former director of Nevada's Division of Child and Family Services, replaced James White as the director of DYFS (Lezin Jones & Kaufman, 2003). When announcing Cotton's appointment, New Jersey

Department of Human Services (NJDHS) Commissioner Gwendolyn Harris boasted that nearly a third of DYFS's district office managers and a host of top officials, including its head of investigations and one of its top legal advisors, had decided to take early retirement. In September, McGreevey signed a law creating the Office of Child Advocate to investigate complaints about DYFS and appointed Kevin Ryan, a close friend, to head the office (Lipka, 2004).

But once again, just when it appeared that DYFS was on the verge of making a dramatic turnaround, a case was reported to police in Southern New Jersey on the night of October 10, 2003, that would evaporate away any credibility that the agency had mustered. A resident of Collingswood, New Jersey, stated that "a little kid was eating out of the neighborhood trash cans" and that he did not believe this was the first time (Livio & Patterson, 2004). The "little kid" turned out to be 19-year-old Bruce Jackson, the adopted son of Vanessa and Raymond Jackson, the parents of 11 children of whom three others were also adopted. When Bruce was brought by law enforcement to a physician for a medical evaluation it was determined that the 4-foot, 43-pound adult had suffered from extreme growth stunting because of long-standing neglect and systematic starvation (Livio & Patterson, 2004). After criminal charges were filed against Bruce's parents on October 24, the other adopted children received medical examinations with startling results. Tyrone, a 10-year-old boy, measured 3 feet 2 inches and weighed 28 pounds; Keith, a 14-year-old boy, was 4 feet tall and weighed 40 pounds; and nine-and-a-half-year-old Michael was 3 feet 1 inch tall and weighed 22 pounds—all were diagnosed with the effects of malnutrition and starvation.

What was perhaps more startling than the results released by the police department or medical care professionals, however, was the revelation that the Jackson family had been under DYFS supervision of one sort or other since 1991. From 1999 through 2003, it was disclosed in a report issued by the newly created Office of the Child Advocate, that DYFS caseworkers made 38 visits to the Jackson home without any record notation of inadequate nutrition, insufficient amounts of food in the home, or child development issues around food intake. In a violation of DYFS's own policies, none of the adopted children had seen a physician since 1996 for a required annual physical examination (Lipka, 2004). DYFS, it appeared, had been the unwitting partner in an almost 10 year outrage, even going so far as to praise the Jacksons in case notes for "doing an excellent job" and for being "very consistent on doctor's appointments" (Livio & Patterson, 2004). Nor did it make the general public feel much better when the press reported that caseworkers confided to investigators that they were unfamiliar with the annual medical evaluation rule and had never asked the children themselves about their health.

The fallout from the Williams case was a fusillade of criticism matched in intensity only by its ferocity. Some of the news accounts and editorial opinions published made the invective attributed to David Stoesz (in Chapter 1) appear rather mild. Amid reports of additional cases of foster home abuse (Paterson, 2003) and more child fatalities, Gwendolyn Harris resigned as Commissioner of Human Services in December (Kocieniewski, 2003). The Governor soon after announced her replacement with James Davy, his most trusted aid (Livio, 2004). In the same week in January that

McGreevey appointed Davy, Colleen Maguire, Deputy Human Services Commissioner for Children's Services, resigned. She had been hired 10 months earlier to "lead DYFS out of crisis" (Livio, 2004).

LIFE UNDER COURT ORDER

On February 18, 2004, Department of Human Services Commissioner Davy unveiled the state's plan to "rebuild New Jersey's Children's Services" entitled A New Beginning: The Future of Child Welfare in New Jersey (New Jersey Department of Human Services, 2004). The slightly modified version of the plan approved by a federal judge on June 11, 2004 was 237 pages and addressed such wide-ranging topics as reforming case practice, achieving permanency for children, and creating a research and data analysis unit at DYFS. Steve Cohen of the Annie E. Casey Foundation and chair of the Child Welfare Panel of Independent Experts called the plan "the most comprehensive reform of child welfare in the nation" (New Jersey Department of Human Services, 2004, p. 1).

Like the Transforming Child Protective Services in New Jersey report issued a year earlier, the new plan contained a good deal of lofty rhetoric about essential principles, strategic vision, and core commitment; unlike the preceding plan, A New Beginning promised substantial, tangible resources for the rebuilding:

- $125 million in 2004 and $180 million more in 2005 to be added to the DYFS budget of more than $500 million.
- Hiring 1,000 caseworkers and 435 support staff to augment the 1,800 workers and 2,300 support staff currently on the payroll.
- The recruitment of 1,000 new foster families to add to the current 5,000 families.
- Increasing the monthly rates paid to foster families by 25%.
- Expanding substance abuse services for parents with $5 million in new monies.
- Expanding mental health services to accommodate 4,000 families in 2005.
- Establishing a New Jersey Child Welfare Training Academy to train the entire DYFS staff in "state of the art safety and risk assessment protocol" (Lezin Jones & Mansnerus, 2004; New Jersey Department of Human Services, 2004).

A New Beginning also contained an impressive listing of specific child welfare outcomes to be achieved and the expected dates for their accomplishment. While the litigation agreement with Children's Rights, Inc. identified 11 improved outcomes for children, the state's plan called for 13 improved outcomes. Each of these outcomes, moreover, was linked to one or more measurable, quantitative indicators. The outcome "decrease the length of time in care with a goal of reunification," for example, was linked to four indicators: (1) length of stay for all children by entry cohort, measured at the 25th percentile, median, and 75th percentile, (2) probability of a permanency exit (reunification, adoption, or legal guardianship) within 12, 24, and 36 months of entry to care, (3) probability of nonpermanency exit, and (4) an additional indicator that will measure the system's performance in achieving permanency for children who have already been in care for a long period of time (New Jersey Department of

Human Services, A New Beginning, 2004, p. 207). A total of 22 outcome indicators were specified, with another half dozen to be formulated. The plan also contained 109 benchmarks that were to be used by DYFS and the Child Welfare Panel to determine if the deficiencies outlined in the settlement agreement were being fixed or improved. Each of these benchmarks was operationalized by baseline data, an interim target, a final target, and a methodology (New Jersey Department of Human Services, A New Beginning, 2004, pp. 212–232). A review of the plan by Noonan et al. (2009) identified between 240 and 255 "enforceable elements," a number they believed was daunting in both specificity and scope.

Amidst the praise and enthusiasm for the new DYFS restructuring plan were rivulets of skepticism—at first small and dripping, later torrential and inundating. Many in the media questioned New Jersey's commitment to real reform. In a *Philadelphia Inquirer* editorial, the writers expressed concerns over the Governor's lack of leadership, tepid support by legislators, and a bevy of benchmarks they saw as vague and incomplete (*Philadelphia Inquirer*, 2004). The editorial staff of the *New Jersey Star Ledger* lamented that although the plan contained some text on budgets and timelines that were specific, "those details make long stretches of vague social work-speak stand out in disappointing contrast" (*New Jersey Star Ledger*, 2004, p. 2).

Media opinion appeared to resonate a cautious cynicism expressed by a wide range of child welfare stakeholders. Cecilia Zalkind, ACNJ's Executive Director, saw A New Beginning as "light on accountability." She believed the plan sent a message that there was no consequence for not doing your job (Livio, 2004). Marcia Loury, Executive Director of Children's Rights, stated that civil service reform was not addressed and that notwithstanding the report's efforts to show progress since the June 2003 settlement, feared that very little had changed (Livio, 2004). DYFS caseworkers and their union representatives complained that reform was responsible for caseloads rising to unprecedented levels. Since November 2002, just before the Williams death, the number of caseworkers responsible for at least 100 children had grown from 13 to 69 and the number responsible for more than 75 children had risen from about 90 to 275. The average DYFS caseload had grown from 33 children to 42 (Livio, 2004). Foster care parents, too, were uneasy with some provisions of the plan, especially the goals of keeping foster children in their own communities—even if these communities were not safe—and requiring biological and foster parents to work collaboratively and hold regular meetings (Livio, 2004).

The DYFS plans (and its planners) were also being examined by two especially prominent groups of critics, state legislators and the Child Welfare Panel of Experts— the former who believed DYFS was trying to do too much and the latter, too little. In January, prior to the release of A New Beginning, Children's Rights, Inc. requested that the Panel provide an accounting of what progress had actually been made since June 2003. An initial monitoring report was not due from the Panel until January 2005, but Marcia Loury was expressing concerns about DYFS mismanagement and foot-dragging (Livio, 2004). The Panel obliged with an impromptu document that confirmed many of Loury's suspicions. New Jersey Department of Human Services, it alleged, had actually lost foster homes, had failed to hire much needed staff, and had spent only a fraction of the money it had dedicated to reforming DYFS. Moreover, the Panel questioned the accuracy of DYFS numbers on fundamental criteria such as the number of foster homes in the state and the number of children's safety evaluations completed (Livio, 2004). In March, the state's Joint Budget oversight Committee unanimously voted to approve only half of the monies promised by the Governor to launch DYFS reforms. Legislators balked at the high cost of restructuring and questioned whether any real reform could ever take place on the grand scale that was being proposed (Livio, 2004).

Caught in the straits between this Scylla and Charybdis, New Jersey Department of Human Services did what its harshest critics would have predicted: it crashed into both. On July 19, Commissioner Davy acquiesced to the Panel's 42-page list of "building blocks....which must be addressed in the short run in order to make the [DYFS] plan feasible" (Livio, 2004). This list included the hiring of a deputy commissioner to oversee the new Office of Children's Services, adding 250 caseworkers, creating a DYFS employee training academy, recruiting and licensing 1,000 new foster homes, and setting requirements for hiring and promotions. Several days later, the commissioner asked a federal judge to free the state from sanctions if it failed to deliver on several components of the reform plan, explaining that the state wanted to preserve "its right to defend itself at a later date if the reform plan falls short..." (Livio, 2004). No matter that a federal judge rejected this request several weeks later, DHS and DYFS had managed to portray themselves as irresponsible in the eyes of the Panel and among many in the legislature as well (Livio, 2004).

Setbacks to child welfare reform continued to accumulate through what was left of 2004. Governor McGreevey announced on August 12 that he would resign from office, effective November 15, more than a year before his term would have expired. He cited his affair with a former aide who had threatened to file a lawsuit accusing the governor of sexual harassment (Mansnerus, 2004).

An agency survey conducted by USDHHS, ACF as part of its Child and Family Services Review (CFSR) program found that DYFS was *not* in substantial conformity with 13 out of 14 outcome and system factors, which the federal government deemed critical to high functioning child protective services. The survey found that children were left too often in unsafe situations because caseworkers did not visit enough and that DYFS took too long to investigate complaints of abuse. Serious problems were also detected in getting children into permanent homes, keeping siblings together in foster homes, establishing face-to-face contact with clients, meeting children's education needs, and providing enough medical and mental health services. DYFS case review practices, quality assurance, training, service array, responsiveness to referrals, and foster home licensing were all judged to be seriously substandard (New Jersey Department of Children and Families, 2008; Schwaneberg, 2004).

In early December, the Office of Child Advocate released to the public a historical and forensic analysis of 12 children who died while under DYFS supervision. Kevin Ryan, the Office Director, recounted in great detail how systemic breakdowns in 11 of the 12 cases contributed to the lamentable results. Marcia Loury opined that the stories of the 12 children are illustrations of what happens if reform doesn't take place (Livio & Schuppe, 2004, p. 1).

The year 2004 ended in much the same way it ended for DYFS in 2003, with a mounting child death total and another signature case of unspeakable horror. Jmeer White, a 14-month-old toddler, died of malnutrition 2 months after a caseworker noted his small size but accepted his mother's explanation that "he had always been small" (Spoto & Livio, 2004). At the time of death, the child weighed 10 pounds. The new Acting Governor called the case a terrible and sickening tragedy and blamed DYFS, by name, for mishandling the case (Larini & Stewart, 2004). Acting Governor Richard Codey and key legislative leaders were now openly questioning the wisdom of financial support for the state's $320 million reform plan. Louis Greenwald, Assembly Budget Committee Chairman, summed up the mood of a great many in the state with this rebuke of Commissioner Davy and work thus far:

> We are looking for the hard data, so we can understand the correlation between the effort, the dollars, the training, and the results. The members of this committee have concerns not about your efforts or intentions, but in practical results. (Livio, 2004, p. 35)

TARGET PRACTICE DOESN'T MAKE PERFECT

As poorly as events had transpired for DYFS in 2004, they provided only an intimation of things to come in 2005. In accordance with the settlement of the 1999 lawsuit, *Charlie and Nadine H. v. Whitman,* and now the class action, *Charlie and Nadine H. v. McGreevey,* the New Jersey Child Welfare Panel of Experts was scheduled to issue its first official monitoring report by the end of March. The general focus of the report was on DYFS progress on improving child safety since the settlement date in June 2003 with a specific concentration on how well the agency was implementing the reform plan "A New Beginning" from June 2004 through December 2004. Before NJDHS could release the report it was leaked to the press—a practice that was becoming more and more commonplace as the DYFS crisis deepened. The media painted an unfavorable picture of poor leadership, unavailable worker training, unmanageable caseloads, and insufficient community services (Livio, 2005). Although the coverage was largely accurate, it did not communicate the gulf that was widening between the Panel and NJDHS. The Panel had concluded that the state "had failed to meet the commitment for this monitoring period" and that "significant course correction rather than minor adjustments were necessary" if real reform was to take place (New Jersey Child Welfare Panel, 2005a, p. 12).

The monitoring report offered some significant insights on the management dynamics at NJDHS and DYFS that appeared to be driven by the sheer number of enforceable components in the consent decree. Panel members commented on the rush to meet deadlines before sufficient resources were put in place to ensure that objectives were actually met. The sense was given that decision making was frenetic, disorganized, and not often prioritized. In fact, the report recommended that DYFS should attempt to do a smaller number of fundamental things and do them well rather than continuing to implement all portions of the reform plan with equal priority (New Jersey Child Welfare Panel, 2005a, pp. 12–13). The NJDHS response was quizzical and contentious: "We are concerned this [report] is a prediction and feel the monitoring should relate to those tasks that have occurred during the monitoring period. There appears to be a recurring theme in their [the Panel's] document that we are not in compliance with things that haven't even been scheduled to occur yet" (Livio, 2005, p. 31).

A Period Two monitoring report was scheduled to be released in September 2005. It would evaluate reform progress from July 2004 through June 2005, emphasizing action in the last 6 months. The Panel made clear in the Period One report and subsequent correspondence that it was expected that Commissioner Davy and DYFS meet 56 specific goals to improve the training and caseload size of caseworkers, recruit additional foster homes, and improve decision making when substantiating abuse and neglect cases. In mid-June, Davy asked the Panel for an extension, citing budgetary constraints and civil service considerations; the Panel refused (Livio, 2005). Two weeks later, a confidential letter from the Panel to Davy was leaked to the press that indicated that DYFS was viewed as making "significantly inadequate progress" toward meeting the terms of the class action lawsuit (Livio, 2005).

The letter was a harbinger of both the tone and content of the Period Two report. In a section entitled "Areas of Seriously Inadequate Progress" the Panel discussed reform areas in which the state "accomplished much less than it could and should have," where this "lack of progress had a negative impact on the lives of children and families," and where even "progress three months after the monitoring period still had not been substantial."

> *Building the skills needed to effectively help children and families.* Training is well behind schedule, as are the critical activities designed to establish a new practice model—developing family team meetings, improving assessment of child and family strengths and needs, and formulating individualized service plans.
>
> *Stabilizing and improving operations critical to safety and permanency.* Adoption operations were seriously disrupted as the existing system was shut down before a new one was ready to take its place. The State cannot yet ensure regular, face-to-face contact between workers and the children for whom they are responsible, nor can it demonstrate that children entering care are routinely getting the medical care they need.
>
> *Finding appropriate placements for children in out-of-home care.* The State has made little progress in reducing the number of very young children placed in congregate settings. There has been minimal attention to reducing the number of children who have temporary placements in shelters because a more stable setting is not available for them. There has also been little improvement in reducing the number of children in out-of-state placement and planning for permanency for those who remain out of state.
>
> *Creating the organizational structure and supports needed to achieve better outcomes for children and families.* The development of an effective Office of Children's Services has been slow and hampered by continued issues of authority within the larger Department of Human Services. The State has not yet fulfilled

its commitments to improve hiring and promotional standards and civil service examinations for child welfare staff or to adequately reimburse non-profit providers so they can hire and retain well-qualified staff. (New Jersey Child Welfare Panel, 2005b, pp. 7–8)

As to the reasons why reform was lagging at DYFS, the Panel placed it on the doorstep of leadership.

"In our view the leadership has not routinely and effectively met some of the fundamental challenges inherent in an effort of this magnitude. In particular, we believe that there have been significant gaps in each of the following areas":

- reinforcing the vision and purpose behind the many changes underway;
- communicating with and consistently engaging staff and community partners, and remaining open and accessible to these critical stakeholders;
- setting and keeping priorities;
- attending to the "big picture" and ensuring that the many different pieces of the reform effort are coordinated with one another;
- building and sustaining the capacity for effective implementation;
- ensuring that the right people are in the right jobs and that they have the support they need to do those jobs;
- delegating responsibility clearly and holding staff accountable for producing results; and
- routinely monitoring and evaluating progress and making prompt mid-course corrections where necessary.

As a result, implementation issues have largely been left to "the field," sometimes without adequate support and often without the honest, thorough communication and feedback and access to executive leadership needed to identify and resolve problems as they arise. Managers and staff in the field, meanwhile, have too often found themselves pulled from one issue to another without ever having the time and sustained attention needed to implement changes well. (New Jersey Child Welfare Panel, 2005b, p. 9)

This monitoring report introduced the citizens of New Jersey to an agency in chaos (Livio, 2005; *New Jersey Star Ledger,* 2005). Much the same image was projected by a state legislative panel in their report entitled "Annual Report for Period July 1, 2004–June 30, 2005" (DYFS/DHS Staffing and Outcome Review Panel (SORP)/Citizen Review Panel (2005). Created by the state assembly to "keep an eye" on DYFS, SORP concluded the reform itself—or, more correctly, the manner in which reform was being carried out—was a major problem. In their words,

After reviewing and discussing the information provided to the panel, the SORP concludes that the fundamental components of reform identified by the SORP have not been adequately addressed and, in some instances, have not been addressed at all. With the requirement of the lawsuit settlement to meet 46 pages of enforceables, it may have been difficult for the State to prioritize those areas which directly impact case practice, child safety and permanency. In addition, the SORP remains gravely concerned that the reform effort was designed from the top down rather than from the bottom up, placing emphasis on restructuring. This misplaced emphasis, combined with the broad-scoped litany of enforceables and their unrealistic timeframes has totally destabilized an already troubled child welfare system. An unintended consequence of the massive reorganization has been the loss of child welfare and community resource expertise as key district office and adoption office personnel either accepted newly created non-direct service positions or were relocated from one county to another. As a result, the reform has not had a significant positive impact on field operations as hoped for, and, in some instances, has made it even more difficult for DYFS staff to protect children and serve families. [DYFS/DHS Staffing and Outcome Review Panel (SORP)/Citizen Review Panel, 2005, p. 4]

The avalanche of criticism soon buried DYFS director Edward Cotton, and he resigned on September 24, 2005 (Lezin Jones, 2005), but it was not enough to mollify Children's Rights, Inc. In early October the organization served Commissioner James Davy with a notice of mediation, giving DYFS 10 days to produce the concrete action steps that would address deficiencies identified in the Period Two Monitoring Report. If the mediation proved unsuccessful, Children's Rights, Inc. threatened to file a motion for contempt and noncompliance in U.S. District Court. The likely outcome of any rejudication of *Charlie and Nadine H.* was a takeover of children's services in New Jersey by the federal government (*New Jersey Star Ledger,* 2005, p. 12). Davy predicted that mediation would actually "detract from the children," and accused Children's Rights, Inc. of grandstanding (Livio, 2005, p. 18) and charging excessive legal fees (Livio, 2005, p. 19).

In this increasingly hostile atmosphere, mediation ended without any agreement between NJDHS and Children's Rights, Inc. on implementation of the Panel's recommendations. Children's Rights held true to its promise and asked U.S. Judge Stanley Chisler to hold NJDHS and DYFS in contempt, but in a change in legal tactics also asked that incoming Governor Jon Corzine be made "accountable for fixing the problems he has inherited and that the judge support him with the broad remedial powers of the federal court to cut through bureaucracy and force changes" (Livio, 2005). Corzine had made correcting the problems plaguing DYFS one of his priorities and had pledged to get involved personally. He was about to get his chance.

Commissioner Davy continued to dispute the findings of the monitoring reports, and in a December 5 opinion piece wrote that "New Jersey is making steady progress and is in substantial compliance with the requirements of the reform plan..." (Davy, 2005, p. 9). Marcia Loury responded to the piece by questioning if Davy was in touch with reality (Livio, 2005, p. 21). Two weeks later Kevin Ryan, director of the Office of Child Advocate, released a new report analyzing the involvement of DYFS with the families of eight children who had died between March and October 2005. Ryan asserted "these children's stories tell us how far we have to go and it seems like a very long way to go" (Livio, 2005, p. 1). Cecilia Zalkind of ACNJ quipped, "this report more than anything demonstrates the continuing disconnect between how reform is being carried out by central office in Trenton and the actual work in the field with the worker out investigating abuse and neglect" (Livio, 2005, p. 1). This would be the last critique of DYFS that James Davy would need to respond to as Commissioner of Human Services. Incoming Governor Corzine announced that Davy would be stepping down and that the new Commissioner would be Kevin Ryan.

COURSE CORRECTION

The New Jersey Child Welfare Panel greeted Governor Corzine and NJDHS Commissioner Ryan in February with a preliminary version of the Period Three Monitoring Report scheduled for release at the end of March 2006. The Panel gave this overview:

> As has been the case in prior periods, we find that the State's performance in these critical areas during the last six months of 2005 was well short of what the public and the Court could reasonably expect. Indeed, in some areas, where prior shortcomings could be explained in part by the amount of time needed to lay the groundwork for future improvements, the record compiled from July through December is particularly disappointing.

> Problems of note include the following:
> - Despite an enormous investment in staff to recruit, train, and support resource families, the number of licensed non-relative families *decreased* by 90 from the end of June to the end of December 2005; for calendar year 2005 as a whole, this figure decreased by 163.
> - The caseloads of workers assigned to child protection units—investigators and assessors—*increased* during this period. Compared to the beginning of the period, by the end of December, a higher percentage of these intake workers had more than twelve open cases, and a higher percentage had more than eight new investigations assigned during the month. Caseloads of permanency workers declined only very slightly, as did the number of permanency workers with extraordinarily high caseloads of 30 or more families.
> - The very limited data available strongly suggest that most children entering out-of-home care in 2005 did not receive a comprehensive medical and mental health examination, nor is there documentation of routine provision of services for children who needed follow-up treatment.
> - The number of cases referred for investigation increased rapidly, apparently because of a breakdown at the centralized hotline rather than a surge in calls. Workers in the field report confusion about why some cases are referred for investigation and being overwhelmed by the number of new investigations. (New Jersey Child Welfare Panel, 2006, pp. 1–2)

Ryan forwarded a copy of this report to a state assembly committee investigating DYFS expenditures and progress. The committee chair, Joseph Cryan, termed the findings shocking and state funds poorly spent. He warned Ryan not to ask for one more penny in the upcoming budget hearings if he could not devise a strategy to realistically improve the agency. Cryan concluded, "Outside of when we lose kids, today is one of the saddest days in the history of child protection" (Livio, 2006, p. 1). Children's Rights, Inc. associate director Susan Lambiase said the public had been duped by previous NJDHS administrations and that both her organization and the state legislature had been misled (Livio, 2006).

In April 2006, Ryan requested $110 million in additional funds to support the reform of DYFS. The Budget Committee Chairman replied to the solicitation with disbelief and an accusation that NJDHS and DYFS had wasted hundreds of millions of dollars on a court mandated overhaul of the child welfare system with no proof that "one child had benefited." Greenwald, referencing the three monitoring reports, noted that the state was behind on employee hiring, training, and technology, and exclaimed, "I don't know how you spend any more money" (Livio, 2006). The Budget Committee vowed to reject any budget request for child welfare until Ryan produced a workable business plan.

In the spring of 2006, it appeared that all the players in the DYFS drama had fought each other to the point of exhaustion. An editorial published in March in the *New Jersey Star Ledger* captured the consensus that had been growing among state politicians and child welfare professionals alike: focus on a few basics and do them in a cost-effective manner. The editors offered this advice:

We believe the state must challenge portions of the court-ordered plan under which DYFS has been operating which has proven counter-productive on several key points.

Each worker is now expected to be expert in all things DYFS does, but most have not been trained for any of those responsibilities.

Adoption is the best illustration of this problem. County adoption resource centers, staffed with experts in adoption laws and needs were dismantled as part of the reform plan. But most field workers still have not been trained to handle adoptions. The number of kids waiting to be adopted has risen to 2,300, one of the longest waiting lists in years. New Jersey social service agencies and advocacy groups urged the McGreevey administration, which was in power when the court settlement was negotiated, to fight elimination of the adoption centers as part of the court's reform plan.

DYFS is not a lab rat, they warned. Some reform measures placed social service dogma ahead of what was practical. Good goals were required in the wrong sequence. (*New Jersey Star Ledger*, 2006, p. 10)

Commissioner Ryan had made some of these same points a few days earlier in a meeting with legislators, albeit absent the instigation to confront the Panel and Children's Rights, Inc. The motion for contempt, however, made confrontation inescapable and in mid-July the plaintiffs and defendants agreed on a compromise that created a new cabinet level Department of Children and Families and a new modified settlement agreement (Livio, 2006, p. 1). It was announced by Governor Corzine that the Department's first commissioner would be Kevin Ryan. Both the McGreevey and Codey administrations had resisted the creation of a new department, arguing that its formation would increase bureaucracy, cost too much, and have no impact on improving the safety of children. It was also announced that the new reform would have a new monitor, Judith Meltzer from the Center for the Study of Social Policy (CSSP) headquartered in Washington, DC (Livio, 2006).

New Jersey's new iteration of child welfare reform was titled Focusing on the Fundamentals and was characterized by the New Jersey Department of Children and Families in this fashion:

- focusing on the fundamentals by prioritizing key first steps, including reductions in caseloads, workforce development, and management by data;
- incorporating the best thinking of New Jersey stakeholders and frontline workers and supervisors, which inspired changes in adoption practice, resource family development, services, and placements;
- supporting a collaborative relationship with a single Monitor of the settlement agreement, allowing the State increased flexibility to make improvements and adjustments when needed; and
- establishing accountability on outcomes for children and families, rather than on a crushing checklist of more than two hundred legally enforceable tasks. (New Jersey Department of Children and Families, 2006, p. 1)

The modified settlement divided reform into two phases; the first, covering the period from July 2006 through December 2008, pledged to concentrate on improving the quality of CPS investigations and reporting capabilities, and the second, beginning in January 2009 and continuing at least until December 2010, turned attention to return on investments and child welfare outcomes. Phase 1 contained 10 specific areas that would be monitored for continuing improvement:

Development of a New Case Practice Model: design a new case practice model that allows the State to synthesize best practices and test different approaches to better serve children and families.

Fundamental Training: prioritize training for new frontline staff, new supervisors, and investigators, while phasing in the development of in-service training for existing staff, beginning with concurrent planning, which supports improved permanency practices, and training in new data and management tools.

Critical Services, including Healthcare: improve delivery of critical services that help keep families together, reunite families that are separated, address the well-being of children in out-of-home care, and help foster families and adoptive families provide for our children.

Placements: change the focus from eliminating out-of-state placements to placing children close to home and where the child's individual needs are best met. In some cases, this means sound placement practice could result in a placement in Pennsylvania or a facility that provides highly specialized services not currently available in New Jersey.

Caseloads: continue new State investments in staff in order to achieve caseloads that are manageable and support good practice. Recent and extensive analysis of staffing records, data and management will allow the state to target future staffing and placement to address staffing shortfalls and caseload issues by the local DYFS office.

Adoption: invest in developing local adoption expertise in every office and create impact teams to address the alarming backlog of children awaiting permanency. This priority will reverse the previous settlement mandate to eliminate specialized adoption practice and, instead, support specialized practice in each local DYFS office.

Recruiting and Licensing Foster and Pre-adoptive Families: link the efforts of resource family recruiters and support staff more closely to licensing in order to transform the welcome recent surge in applications into a wider pool of available families for children.

Management by Data: implement and support Governor Corzine's broader initiative of "government under glass" by collecting and making public critical child welfare indicators. (New Jersey Department of Children and Families, 2006, pp. 2–3)

The Phase 2 monitoring components were designed with an eye on improving compliance with federal CFSRs as well as allaying state legislators' fears that money was merely being wasted. The modified settlement called for the following:

- Outcome indicators: Targets safety, permanency, and stable and appropriate placements for children.
- Performance indicators: Targets achieving reasonable caseload standards; executing timely investigations; supporting a sufficient pool of resource families; ensuring visitation for children with parents, siblings, and caseworkers; and maintaining high quality in healthcare, adoption and overall case practice.
- Advanced practice: Targets development of improved practices in contracting, quality improvement, and needs assessment, while requiring maintenance of high levels of practice in the areas of resource families and workforce development. (*Charlie and Nadine H. v. Corzine and Ryan*, 2006)

PATH TOWARD IMPROVEMENT

In February 2007, the court appointed monitor, Center for the Study of Social Policy, released its Period 1 Monitoring Report, an evaluation of CPS reform from July 2006 through December 2006. The report concluded that "the new Department of Children and Families (DCF) should be pleased with its accomplishments in its first six months of operation" (Center for the Study of Social Policy, 2007, p. 3). The monitor went on to applaud the state for a clear vision, strong leadership, and commitment to building a high quality workforce. In a table inventorying DCF achievements, the monitor observed that the agency had fulfilled all 48 settlement agreement requirements for the 10 Phase 1 monitoring areas. And although acknowledging that a great deal of work remained to be done, CSSP believed that DCF was well-situated to continue on a positive trajectory (Center for the Study of Social Policy, 2007).

In what appeared to be a collective sigh of relief, child welfare professionals, academics, and pundits from throughout the state lauded the new DYFS in DCF for turning the page on years of crisis and failure. The editorial board of the *New Jersey Star Ledger* thanked Governor Corzine and Commissioner Ryan for finally putting New Jersey "on a positive path toward a child welfare system that can protect children, make fragile families whole and stop being a dangerous embarrassment to the state" (*New Jersey Star Ledger*, 2007, p. 16). Columnist Tom Moran singled out Kevin Ryan for turning DYFS around and for fixing a broken system (Moran, 2007). The Association for Children of New Jersey wrote that child welfare reform appeared now to be on the right track—there were some troubling trends such as dramatic drops in children entering foster care and under DYFS supervision, but these too could be indicators of an improving system, it hypothesized (Association for Children of New Jersey, 2007).

The new progress in child welfare reform was not without detractors, especially in the New Jersey legislature. DCF was having great difficulty making the SACWIS operational despite spending over $45 million and anticipating an additional $25 million expenditure. The Chair of the Assembly Human Services Committee called the data system a "boondoggle that was way over budget and years late" (Livio, 2007). The Human Services and Budget Committee, additionally, called the goals achieved in Monitoring Report 1 "modest" given the $432 million spent on DYFS since January 2004. Some legislators complained that goals were achieved primarily because monitoring standards were now set so low (Livio, 2007).

Notwithstanding the grousing of a shrinking, albeit important, handful, the tone of discourse around child welfare reform had changed rather dramatically in 2007. Terrible things continued to happen to children under DCF–DYFS supervision, but the media coverage of these incidents—even child fatalities—did not resonate with the outrage evident in previous years' coverage. As steadily as the vituperation over child deaths was declining, so apparently was the actual number of these deaths. Susan Livio, the *New Jersey Star Ledger* reporter who had covered DYFS extensively, reported in March 2007 that deaths due to abuse and neglect had dropped from 31 in 2003 to 23 in 2006, a drop consistent with information published on the DCF website (Livio, 2007; New Jersey Department of Children and Families, 2010). Yet in 2003, Livio wrote that deaths in 2003 from abuse or neglect had reached 37, a number that is consistent with DYFS reporting to the National Child Abuse and Neglect Data System (NCANDS) (Livio, 2003; U.S. Department of Health and Human Services, ACF, 2003). This puzzling diminution is not limited to 2003; the average number of child deaths from 2000 through 2008 reported on the DCF webpage is 25 while the average reported by New Jersey to the federal government is nearly 33.

Also disappearing from the media and general conversation were the often contentious interchanges between DYFS and the Office of the Child Advocate. Articles such as "Advocate Rips into DYFS on Three Deaths" (Livio & Hepp, 2005), commonplace during Kevin Ryan's tenure as Child Advocate from 2003 through 2005, became harder to find. DCF–DYFS and the Child Advocate's Office appeared increasingly to be collaborators, and by mid-2009 the agencies were issuing fatality and abuse/neglect reports jointly (Livio, 2009).

Under the terms of the modified settlement, DCF and DYFS looked to be making real strides in reducing the risk of abuse and neglect among New Jersey's child population. In Monitoring Reports 3 through 7, DCF scored consistently high marks in implementing Phase 1 components and exhibited a consistent, if sometimes halting, progress. The Period VII Monitoring Report, assessing the period from July to December 2009, noted that DCF had met or surpassed expectations in developing a case practice model, conducting investigations, visiting children's homes, limiting inappropriate placements, reducing abuse/neglect in foster homes, reducing caseload sizes, training its workforce, and increasing child access to healthcare (Center for the Study of Social Policy, 2010). Advances were being made on Phase 2 targets as well. Repeat maltreatment for children not removed from their homes dropped from 7.4% in 2006 to 3.5% in 2008; repeat maltreatment of children in foster care declined from 0.3% to 0.14% (Center for the Study of Social Policy, 2010, pp. 102–104).

Improvement in New Jersey's CPS was also reflected in the federal CFSR conducted in 2008–2009. Now DCF–DYFS was *not* in substantial conformity with 10 out of the 14 outcome and systems factors (New Jersey Department of Children and Families, 2008).

While New Jersey was reducing both the exposure and threat magnitude to child safety, i.e., the hazard, the state was also working vigorously to blunt the impact that outrage had been having on the perception of child risk. In July 2009 DCF announced that neither DCF–DYFS nor the Office of the Child Advocate would any longer publicly disclose the details of DYFS' prior actions when a child the agency had supervised died from abuse or neglect. Kimberly Ricketts, the new Commissioner of DCF (Kevin Ryan resigned in January 2008), declared that "reporting individual cases, children's names and detailed histories is not a useful way to assess how the child welfare system is working" (Livio, 2009, p. 1). Ricketts went on to suggest that such reporting could even hurt victims' families. DYFS had discovered a great truth: the devil is really in the details; by embargoing highly specific accounts of victims' cases, the agency could limit the public's capacity to sympathize, personalize, and yes, demonize.

NEW JERSEY AND MEGAN'S LAW

New Jersey has also sought to reform public child welfare through legislative intervention. The 1994 rape and murder of 7-year-old Megan Kanka by a repeat sex offender ignited a public outrage that shook the foundations of law enforcement and child protection throughout the entire state of New Jersey and, indeed, the nation

(Zgoba, Veysey, & Dalessandro, 2010). Within months of the death the State Assembly fast-tracked legislation that would require the registration of sex offenders with local and state police departments, notification of residents and community agencies by authorities, and civil commitment of suspected perpetrators. The registration component of New Jersey's legislation became a federal mandate in 1994 under provisions of the Jacob Wetterling Act and the public notification of sex offender home addresses became federal law in 1996.

The effectiveness of community notification and registration laws in reducing child sex abuse continues to be a topic of great discussion. A recent study of Megan's Law in New Jersey found that the law did not have a significant effect on sex offense recidivism, number of sex offenses, violent offenses, or number of children abused (Zgoba, Veysey, & Dalessandro, 2010). In a 10 state study, moreover, Vasques, Maddan, and Walker (2008) find impacts in only two states for recidivism, but broader impacts on first term offenders. In an analysis of the relative importance of the notification and registration provisions of sex offender laws, Prescott and Rockoff (2008) report a positive impact of registration on sex offense recidivism, but an effect of notification that is limited to first time offenders. The impact of sex offender laws on CPS operations remains largely unexplored; however, it is difficult to imagine how such legislation cannot inject more worry into a caseworker environment already saturated with perceptions of infinite jeopardy and zero tolerance.

NEW JERSEY AND BEYOND

The New Jersey experience with judicial and legislative intrusion into its child protective services is hardly unique. In Appendix I we show the registration and implementation dates of sex offender laws in all the states using classifications developed by Agan (2007) and Walker and associates (2005). Appendix II shows that 37 states and the District of Columbia have experienced some type of decree litigation based on the Fourteenth Amendment due process and equal protection clauses, the Adoption Assistance and Child Welfare Act of 1980, the Adoption and Safe Families Act of 1997, the federal disability act, or allegations of state law violations. In some states such as Arizona and Colorado this reform litigation sought modest goals; in others such as Missouri, Illinois, Alabama, Utah, and the District of Columbia the thrust was more expansive.

CASE STUDY INSIGHTS AND LIMITATIONS

Case studies such as the one we have presented have been the approach typically employed by social scientists and journalists in analyses of CPS reform (Golden, 2009; Gainsborough, 2010; Nelson, 1984; Mezey, 2000). In her book *Pitiful Plaintiffs*, Susan Mezey (2000) provides a case study analysis of structural reform litigation that has confronted the Illinois Department of Child and Family Services (DCFS) since 1988. Her analysis of *B.H. v. McDonald* and the retinue of related cases point up the importance of media and advocacy groups in stimulating legislative hearings and driving CPS reform, especially the "unending unfavorable news accounts" being written in the *Chicago Tribune* (Mezey, 2000, pp. 141–149) about children being "killed." Anthony Bertelli (2004) takes us back to the very early days of structural reform litigation in his examination of *G.L. v. Zumwalt*, a suit brought against the Missouri Division of Family Services (DFS) in 1982 that in some form continues to this day. Coverage of maltreated children leavened with accounts of DCF bungling and malfeasance in the *Kansas City Star* and *St. Louis Post Dispatch* allowed the public to experience continuous outrage at what was termed the worst child welfare system in America. Olivia Golden's (2009) *Reforming Child Welfare* makes it clear that proximity to federal policy makers and the *Washington Post* exerted enormous influence on CPS behavior in the District of Columbia when the agency was operating under the *LaShawn A. v. Fenty* consent decree. Golden laments how coverage of individual tragedies can serve to intensify a vicious cycle of blame, administrative and caseworker passivity, and turnover (p. 177). Noonan, Sabel, and Simon (2009) in their analysis of *R.C. v. Walley* in Alabama and *David C. v. Leavitt* in Utah also call attention to the media and "moral entrepreneurs" as both an animator and inhibitor of child welfare reform.

Although we believe that case studies have great value in helping us describe changes in child protective services processes and outcomes, we also maintain that they have clear limitations when they are employed to analyze program or policy impacts. In Figures 2.1 to 2.6 we show time series of child maltreatment rates for five states (and the District of Columbia) that have experienced CPS reform under broad consent decrees. The source of data used in these descriptions is the National Child Abuse and Neglect Data System (NCANDS) maintained as the National Data Archive on Child Abuse and Neglect (NDACAN) by Cornell University.

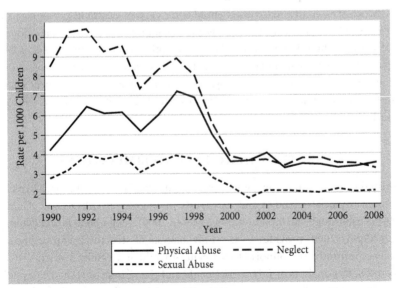

FIG 2.1 Child Maltreatment Rates. Alabama 1990–2008.

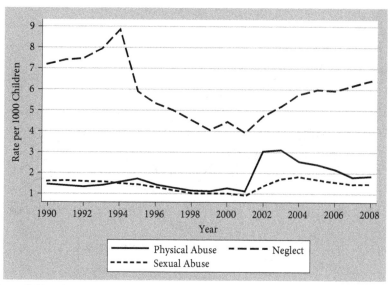

FIG 2.2 Child Maltreatment Rates, Illinois 1990–2008.

In Alabama (Figure 2.1) we see that physical abuse, sexual abuse, and neglect have all been reduced dramatically. In Illinois (Figure 2.2) sexual and physical abuse are stable whereas neglect cases have been rising steadily. Missouri (Figure 2.3) has experienced substantial declines in neglect rates while Utah exhibits stable neglect and abuse rates (Figure 2.4).

Washington, DC appears to have stabilized neglect at lower levels (Figure 2.5), whereas New Jersey's progress since 1996 seems to be quite unremarkable neglect

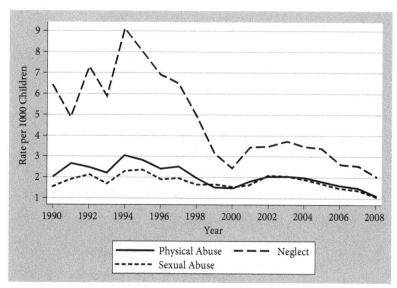

FIG 2.3 Child Maltreatment Rates, Missouri 1990–2008.

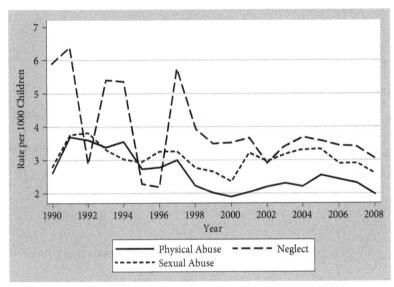

FIG 2.4 Child Maltreatment Rates, Utah 1990–2008.

rates even rising a bit (Figure 2.6). Case study analyses are suggestive; here they seem to suggest that reform litigation worked dramatically in Alabama and not so well in Washington, DC or New Jersey. The Illinois case, moreover, indicates a perverse effect.

Our presentation of these six state child outcome profiles is not meant to confuse the reader and is certainly not meant to intimate that the impact of outrage-driven CPS reform is best studied on a case-by-case basis. It suggests to us that the case study

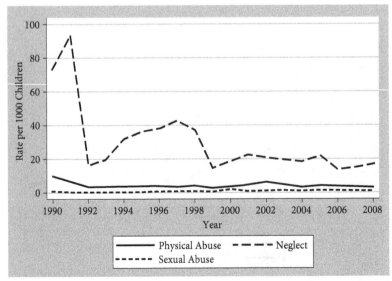

FIG 2.5 Child Maltreatment Rates, Washington, DC 1990–2008.

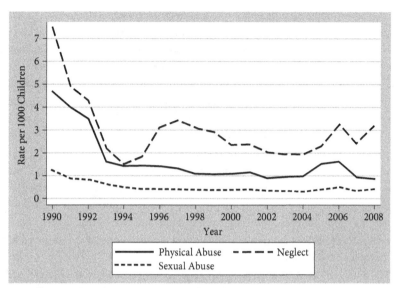

FIG 2.6 Child Maltreatment Rates, New Jersey 1990–2008.

methodology requires augmentation with more formal statistical analyses that take into consideration both within-state and across-state reasons for reform outcomes.

The case studies, consent decrees, and state legislative initiatives we have reviewed in this chapter have provided us with some valuable insights into how social outrage inaugurates and sustains change in public CPS agencies. We share these with the reader in Figure 2.7. Here we outline how we believe outrage imbues the entire CPS reform process through the actions of five principal change agents: the media, moral entrepreneurs, the courts and state legislatures, and the CPS workforce. Fatalities or

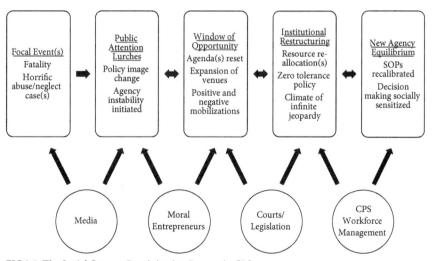

FIG 2.7 The Social Outrage Routinization Process in CPS.

severe maltreatment are sufficiently rare and horrifying events, the ideal material for compelling human interest stories prized by the media (Mezey, 2000; Nelson, 1984; Gainsborough, 2010). Our case study analyses indicate that these stories dovetail nicely with companion stories of public agency failure or scandal, another favorite media topic. Where media attention wanes on issues such as how to fix CPS or broadening the factual base of the event's public harm, policy entrepreneurs—ACNJ and Children's Rights, Inc. come immediately to mind—push to process. Whether through the creation of statistical reports, leading calls for increased government oversight, or other agenda-setting activities, these entrepreneurs drive the outrage into judicial or legislative venues by pointing up the alarming size of the problem and level of public injury. Baumgartner and Jones (2009) view windows of opportunity opening from both positive mobilizations, stemming from alarmed discovery and optimistic problem solving, and negative mobilizations, resulting from critique and "corrective" action. The case material we have reviewed indicates that negative mobilizations have dominated in the CPS outrage routinization process.

Full routinization of outrage generally requires the embrace of the judicial and/or legislative branch(es) of state government. These bodies have the power to enforce all-inclusive screening protocols, zero tolerance policies, and the like. Yet although their involvement sets the necessary condition for routinization, it is the acquiescence of the CPS workforce that provides the sufficient condition. Workforce punctuations in the forms of mass resignations and dramatic increases in new hires resulting from judicial or legislative action are critical, we believe, for understanding decisions to protect children.

3

THE RISKY BUSINESS OF RISK ASSESSMENT

We took risks. We knew we took them. Things came out against us. We have no cause for complaint.
Robert Falcon Scott (1912)
Message to the Public

In New Jersey and other Child Protective Services (CPS) agencies, decisions to protect children are built around the process of assessing risk. As we noted in Chapter 1, risk in CPS is defined as hazard, where hazard has the public health connotation of potential danger, measured by threat magnitude and probability of exposure. We saw in Chapter 2 that employing this definition of risk, New Jersey and other states have not been judged to be successful in their decision making by the general public, legislators, the courts, and the media. The basic architecture of CPS decisions has been depicted in any number of articles and texts (see, for example, Schene, 1998; English et al., 1998); we provide the rendering disseminated by the National Clearinghouse on Child Abuse and Neglect Information (2008) in Figure 3.1.

It is relatively clear from the figure that the CPS staff, case workers, and immediate supervisors need to make choices on whether or not to investigate a case, to substantiate a report(s), to remove a child from home, or to return a child home. There are also decisions on the level of services that should be provided and the critical decision on when to close a case. What isn't so transparent from the structure of the CPS decision process is the frequency with which choices are made under conditions of significant risk vis-à-vis choices made under certainty or uncertainty. The distinction is not a trivial one, especially for CPS workers who must make the decisions depicted in Figure 3.1.

Decision making under certainty, a relatively uncommon circumstance in CPS, assumes that the decision maker is able to enumerate all possible courses of action, know the strategies necessary to carry each out, and project the consequences of actions taken with complete assurance. It implies that there is a single empirical reality to which the decision maker can attach a probability of 1.0. In Figure 3.2a we show this circumstance with the state of nature designated as s_i, its associated probability $p(s_i)$, and the utility of a course of action (f) with f's consequences as $u[f(s_i)]$. For example, if a CPS worker gives a very high value (u) to substantiating cases of child abuse (f) in homes characterized by very young children and nonwhite parents who use illegal drugs and who have income below the poverty level (s_i) (see Wulczyn, 2009), and the

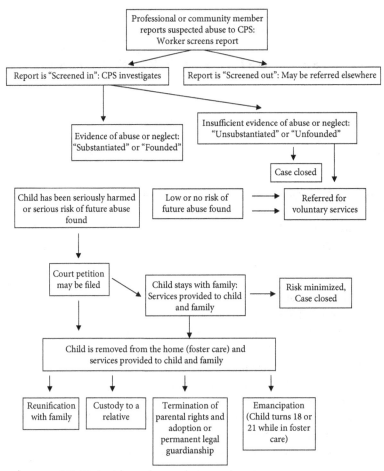

FIG 3.1 Suspected Child Abuse or Neglect.

probability of abuse $p(s_i)$ in such homes has been shown or is believed to be 100%, the worker, if rational, would always substantiate such cases. No matter what the amount of value a worker attaches to not substantiating cases for reasons of workload, personal prejudices, etc., it would be a fool's errand to do so with this type of case because the probability of no abuse, i.e., $1 - p(s_i)$, would be 0.

When decisions are made under conditions of risk, there is an assumption of multiple states of nature and probabilities assigned to each state that are derived from relative frequencies of event occurrences. If instead of a 100% likelihood of abuse (Figure 3.2a) there were a 60% chance of abuse, the decision to substantiate or not substantiate would depend on the utility a worker has for each course of action and the probabilities attached to the occurrence of each event. When, for example, a worker has a value of, say, 10 for a substantiated case of abuse, a value of 1 for being wrong (a false positive), a value of 5 for not substantiating a case that does not have abuse, and a value of 2 for being wrong under this condition (a false negative), then her two utilities can be calculated:

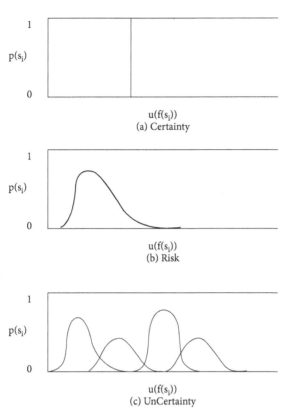

FIG 3.2 Distributions of Decisions under Certainty, Risk, and Uncertainty.
Adapted from Camerer and Weber (1992).

Substantiate = 10(0.6) + 1(0.4) = 6.4

Not substantiate = 5(0.4) + 2(0.6) = 3.2

Here the risk value of substantiating far outweighs the risk of not substantiating. Risk situations here produce probability distributions such as those in Figure 3.2b.

Decision making under uncertainty shares with risk situations the assumptions of multiple states of nature, but lacks the objective probabilities that can be attached to occurring events. It is possible, however, to identify probability distributions that emanate from subjective sources, including personal risk evaluation systems. This, of course, implies that distributions of decisions can vary greatly from person to person (Figure 3.2c) and that the variation is not simply a function of personal values but is dependent on subjective probabilities as well.

CPS workers, like many other decision makers, acquire training, knowledge, technology, and professional skills that help them as they are encouraged to transform choices made under uncertain conditions into decisions based on more clearly defined risks (Lave & March, 1975; Von Winterfeldt & Edwards, 1986). The transformation proceeds through a shaping of values around the application of best practices and/or evidence-based practice $\{u[f(s_i)]\}$ and, to a lesser extent, by providing workers with a set of objective probabilities for understanding child maltreatment occurrences $p(s_j)$. If successful, a reduction in ambiguity should be accompanied by a diminution in unacceptable and unsatisfactory child outcomes.

The child welfare literature is teeming with guidance for case workers and supervisors on how they should navigate the frequently storm-swollen decision-making flows captured in Figure 3.1 (Janchill, 1981; Hornby, 1989; Besharov, 1990; Morton & Holder, 1997; Mather et al., 2007). The Besharov book, *Recognizing Child Abuse*, comes with a 336-page training manual and "six high quality videos" (Besharov, 2009). Especially detailed advice is provided by the more than half-dozen handbooks specifically designed for CPS practice. The American Humane Association's *Helping in Child Protective Services* (Brittain & Hunt, 2004) is published as "a comprehensive desk reference that serves as both a daily guide for workers and a training tool for supervisors and administrators" (p. II). The Dubowitz and DePanfilis (2000) *Handbook for Child Protection Practice* contains over 120 chapters, most of which begin by asking a specific question—How Do I Assess Risk and Safety? or How Do I Determine If a Child Has Been Sexually Abused? and so on—followed by specific instructions on how to answer the question. Equally comprehensive handbooks and desk references have been written by the American Professional Society on the Abuse of Children (2002), the National Center for the Prosecution of Child Abuse (2004), The Annie E. Casey Foundation (Feild & Winterfeld, 2003), and the federal government's Administration for Children and Families (ACF) (Goldman & Salus, 2003; DePanfilis & Salus, 2003; Salus, 2004).

CONVERTING UNCERTAINTY INTO RISK

Despite the ongoing efforts to minimize decision making under uncertainty, the realities of child welfare work often defy categorization of events into mutually agreed upon and unambiguous probability distributions. What is more, worker attitudes about making risky choices may lead some to take unacceptable chances and cause others to avoid making any difficult decisions at all. If, for example, the expected utility of a worker for making the decision to substantiate (taking a risk) is less than the expected utility from the decision outcome, a worker can be considered risk averse. Using the utility model discussed above, the expected value of this worker for making the choice is (as a Bernoulli function): $[\log(10)]\ (0.6) + [\log(1)]\ (0.4) = 1.38$, while her expected value of the decision outcome is $\log(6.4)$ or 1.86. If, on the other hand, her value for the choice making was greater than the value received from the choice, this worker could be considered risk inclined (Wright, 1984; Von Winterfeldt & Edwards, 1986).

CPS has faced significant difficulties in its endeavors to understand risks, risk probabilities, and risk utilities and to train case workers and supervisors to become better risk takers and decision makers. The efforts have continued unabated, however, and two general strategies for amelioration have emerged. The first strategy calls on the current CPS system to provide better diagnostic, treatment, and service tools, and seems to have the support of a majority of the child welfare administrators and practitioners in the country.

An example of such reform has been termed differential response. As Lisa Merkel-Halguin of the American Humane Association describes it, with differential response or dual track response

> low and moderate-risk cases are provided a family assessment and offered timely services, without a formal determination or substantiation of child abuse or neglect. The incident-based, oftentimes perceived adversarial investigation is reserved for accepted reports that are high-risk and egregious. (American Humane Association, 2005, p. 2)

Many states employ some sort of differential response based on case severity, and do so within the structure shown in Figure 3.1. There are, however, those who advocate for more radical forms of differential response that remove duties from CPS worker and supervisor job descriptions. In what amounts to a type of addition through subtraction, it is believed that workers who shed irrelevant tasks (and cases) will become more highly focused, more expert, and make better decisions.

Task and case relevancy are in large measure a function of how the reform proponent prioritizes the family support and rescue objectives of CPS. Some, like Pelton (1989), believe child protective services should give up investigation completely so that the agency can concentrate on providing services to poor families on a voluntary acceptance basis. For Pelton "discovery, investigation and judgment of individual culpability and wrongdoing should have provenance in law enforcement and the courts" (p. 158). Lindsey (2004) also recommends that law enforcement assume responsibility for CPS investigation functions but limits that role to serious abuse cases in which intentional harm is alleged or suspected. He sees "assessments" of improper care resulting in child neglect along with the delivery of family services as critical components of a revitalized, welfare-oriented CPS system. Some, but certainly not all, of the impetus for a CPS grounded in social services delivery emanates from legislation such as the Adoption Assistance and Child Welfare Act of 1980 and from a vibrant Family Preservation movement (Wexler, 2008; Cameron et al., 1997, especially pp. 123–126; Pecora et al., 2000). Despite some substantial empirical evidence to the contrary (Schuerman et al., 1994; Heneghan, Horwitz, & Leventhal, 1996; Lindsey, 2004; Gelles, 1997), Family Preservation resonates well with both the American ethos of encouraging strong families and social work ideals of forging effective helping relationships through intensive expenditures of effort.

There are some critics of CPS who wish to narrow the agency's scope but who would proceed by embracing the rescue functions and discarding the family services components. Waldfogel (1998a, 1998b) supports a differential response that would allow CPS to work closely with law enforcement on the toughest cases of child abuse and neglect and refer less severe cases to community and family services agencies. She asserts that this approach would solve the five principal problems of the current CPS system, i.e., overinclusion, capacity, underinclusion, inadequate services, and inappropriate services (Waldfogel, 1998a, pp. 132–133). Another proponent of this investigation, or the extreme cases/safety model, is the Vera Institute of Justice. As Ross (2009) notes, the

New York City Administration for Children's Services was split out of the City's Human Resources Administration in 1996 in the wake of widely publicized child deaths and widespread concern about the system's ability to keep the city's children safe.

Although several states have pursued a type of narrowing approach to improve CPS decision making (New York, Florida, and Iowa come to mind), most states that have made significant reforms under court order have done so without circumscribing the decision flows of Figure 3.1. Instead, there has been an attempt witnessed in New Jersey, Utah, Alabama, the District of Columbia, and other states to implement what has variously been termed the social work practice model, problem-solving model, or diagnostician approach (Noonan et al., 2009). An emphasis is placed on careful triage backed by a rigorous quality service system (QSS), which, in turn, is based on explicit standards for child status and system performance success and continuous case review (pp. 532–536).

The problem with both narrowing or minimizing strategies on the one hand, and court-ordered comprehensive models on the other, is that decisions made under uncertainty and risk are not in any way obviated. Granted, some choices can be moved to police departments or community service agencies, but decisions about child safety still need to be made—hopefully by professionals with sensitivity and skill. As Myers (2006) points out, the lines separating the criminal from the noncriminal and the severe from the nonsevere are fuzzy ones, and problems will continue to overlap (pp. 176–177). Whether decisions are made in one bureaucracy or several matters less, it would seem, than whether these decisions are made competently.

UNDERSTANDING RISKS AS HAZARDS

In Chapter 1 we briefly discussed how CPS professionals and child welfare academics are trained to conceptualize risks to child safety in much the same fashion that public health professions view illness and injury, i.e.,

$$\text{Risk} = f(\text{Hazard})$$

where the hazard embodies the properties of a person, object, or event that poses a threat to personal health and safety. As noted in Chapter 1, the level of risk posed depends on the magnitude of this threat (state of nature), measured by toxicity and dosage, and the likelihood of exposure (probability assigned to these natural states).

A classical decision tree for hazard analysis helps to highlight the complexity faced by a decision maker attempting to assess and manage a risk. As shown in Figure 3.3, the initial judgment task is to determine if a hazard is present in the environment, followed by a judgment regarding probability of exposure. Exposure assessment requires the decision maker to determine how sensitive the victim has been to the stressor; for example, was she affected physically, emotionally, or financially, etc. This information permits the decision maker to make a risk calculation and a diagnosis; it also provides an opportunity to make a judgment error if a problem goes undetected—Risk #1 (false negative). Some diagnosed cases may not suffer from any actual exposure and require

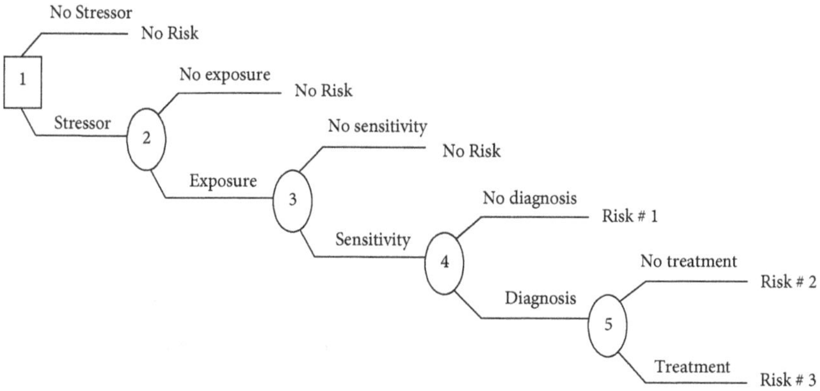

FIG 3.3 Classical Decision Tree for Hazard Analysis and Assessment of Risk.
Source: European Commission, Risk Assessment Unit
Public Health and Risk Assessment Directorate (2004).

no treatment, but could become victimized by the diagnosis itself—Risk #2 (false positives); still others could succumb to the treatment prescribed even when the diagnosis is correct—Risk #3 (iatrogenic effect).

There are three principal factors that influence decision maker success in predicting hazard: (1) the true prevalence rate of the threat, (2) the validity of the decision tool used to gauge probability of exposure, and (3) the reliability or precision of the decision tool. It is an epidemiologic fact, assuming other factors are held constant, that the higher the prevalence of a threat, the higher the likelihood that a decision maker will be able to identify these threats (Lilienfeld & Stolley, 1994). In an epidemic, for example, cases of disease are not very difficult to find. Seldom in CPS decision making are true prevalences of maltreatment known, and where they are known they can change, sometimes dramatically. In the absence of actual prevalence it is necessary to employ estimates, and these can yield decision-making mistakes.

Although the prevalence rate is generally outside the control of the decision maker, the decision tools at his or her disposal can, in principle, be manipulated and improved to ensure reliability and predictive validity. To illustrate the importance of both these measurement qualities in predicting real hazards to children, we examine a hypothetical population of 100 cases reported to CPS that have all passed through initial screening. As Figure 3.4a shows, this particular population is normally distributed (it doesn't have to be) on a measure of hazard that ranges from 0 (no threat at all) to 60 (an arbitrary number describing maximum threat). The figure also shows the normal score (z-score) conversion of threat level and three scores (0.25, 0.75, and 1.25) that workers could employ as a threshold below which real cases of child maltreatment are deemed not to occur. In the example we assume that the 0.75 decision point accurately identifies the true prevalence of child maltreatment at (14 + 9 + 5 + 1 + 1) or 30 cases. In Figure 3.4b we show this ideal scenario of a perfectly precise and accurate decision rule as two distinctive distributions of nonabuser and abuser cases. Note that in our perfect world the two distributions of cases do not overlap: if a worker adheres to the 0.75 threshold consistently, no errors in identification will be made.

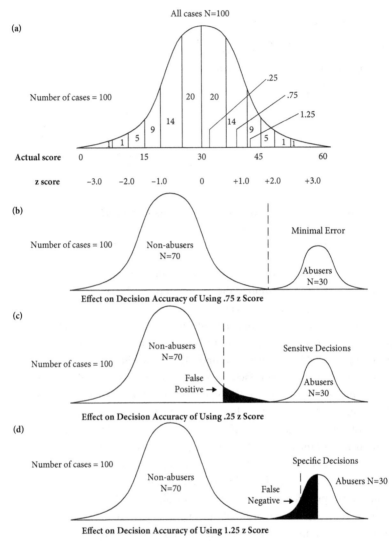

FIG 3.4 The Impact of Using Different Risk Assessment Scores to Measure Threat Levels in a Hypothetical Population of 100 Cases.

In Figure 3.4c we show what happens if a worker opts to abandon the 0.75 cutoff and use a lower score as a cutoff, in this instance 0.25. It is clear that such a choice increases the number of substantiated cases by about 20 and adds substantially to the case worker's workload. If a worker knows that 0.75 yields the optimal separation of abusers and nonabusers, why would she or he assume such a decision stance? The answer lies both within the hazard model of risk and outside it. As Thomas Scheff (1972) pointed out nearly 40 years ago, social workers and other helping professionals show a tendency to tolerate higher levels of false-positive cases, feeling that these cases can be reevaluated later if necessary. In short, there is a tendency to apply the maxim "when in doubt, diagnose." This professional tendency is exacerbated, however, in environments seeking to make CPS workers more accountable; i.e., zero tolerance environments. Anechiarico and Jacobs (1996) assert that government agencies subject to hyperscrutiny can create a panoptic vision among workers, a kind of pervasive, eclectic doubt. The description closely parallels Behn's (2001) climate of infinite jeopardy we introduced in Chapter 1.

The distribution of cases in Figure 3.4d indicates what results when a decision maker chooses a decision point of 1.25 to substantiate cases. False-positive cases disappear but the new problem of false-negative cases occurs. In our hypothetical population, a little over half (16) of the actual abuse cases are now deemed unnecessary to substantiate. In light of our assumption of a completely valid and reliable test and cutoff point of 0.75, such an action would be considered indefensible and would probably result in the employee's dismissal from CPS. Risk-inclined workers would be best advised to seek a different profession, perhaps in business where diagnoses that can ruin opportunity or lives can be made with much more panache.

Within the risk-as-hazard perspective of child maltreatment there are several ways to evaluate the validity of a decision tool, and these are listed in Figure 3.5. Test sensitivity is measured as true positives (TP) divided by true positives plus false negatives (FN). The denominator here is all the cases that have the threat. Test specificity, on the other hand, measures the proportion of true negatives (TN) divided by true negatives plus false positives (FP) and the denominator is all the cases that have not

	True Prevalence			True Prevalence			True Prevalence	
(a)	abusers	non-abusers	(b)	abusers	non-abusers	(c)	abusers	non-abusers
abusers identified								
decision threshold scores .75	30 (16) TP	0 FP (15)	.25	30 (22) TP	20 FP (28)	1.25	16 (11) TP	0 FP (5)
	FN	TN		FN	TN		FN	TN
non-abusers identified	0 (14)	70 (55)		0 (8)	50 (42)		14 (19)	70 (65)

	Decision Cutoff 0.75	Reliability 1.00 (0.25)	Decision Cutoff 0.25	Reliability 1.00 (0.25)	Decision Cutoff 1.25	Reliability 1.00 (0.25)
Test Sensitivity	$\frac{30}{30+0}$ = 100% (53%)		$\frac{30}{30+0}$ = 100% (76%)		$\frac{16}{16+14}$ = 53.3% (36%)	
Test Specificity	$\frac{70}{70+0}$ = 100% (79%)		$\frac{50}{50+20}$ = 71.4% (60%)		$\frac{70}{70+0}$ = 100% (92%)	
Positive Predictive Value	$\frac{30}{30+0}$ = 100% (51.6%)		$\frac{30}{30+20}$ = 60% (44%)		$\frac{16}{16+0}$ = 100% (68.7%)	
Negative Predictive Value	$\frac{70}{70+0}$ = 100% (79.7%)		$\frac{50}{50+0}$ = 100% (84%)		$\frac{70}{70+14}$ = 83.3% (77.3%)	

Notes and Formula:
TP = True Positives, FP = False Positives, FN = False Negatives, TN = True Negatives
1-Sensitivity = False Negative Rate   1-Specificity=False Positive Rate

Values in parenthesis indicate counts obtained by adjusting models for .25 reliability using the following formula:
$$1 - \Phi\,[(1-x)\rho\,/\,\sqrt{1-\rho^2}\,]$$
where Φ is the cumulative normal distribution function
x is the threshold level
ρ^2 is the reliability level

FIG 3.5 Test Validity and Predictive Value of Risk Assessment Score Thresholds in a Hypothetical Population of 100 Cases.

experienced the threat. When a test cutoff is set at a low level it becomes very sensitive, and when it is set high it becomes highly specific. In Figure 3.5a we show the sensitivity and specificity calculations for cutoff point 0.75, the threshold that perfectly distinguishes abuser and nonabuser groups—and, as is to be expected, the measures are both 100%.

Figure 3.5b and c provides the case counts when decision points 0.25 and 1.25 are utilized. As expected, sensitivity remains perfect and specificity drops in Figure 3.5b, and specificity remains perfect and sensitivity drops in Figure 3.5c.

Although sensitivity and specificity provide us with insight into an instrument's accuracy, they do not supply information on the instrument's predictive power. Positive predictive value measures the proportion TP/(TP + FP) in which the denominator reflects all cases with a positive result. Negative predictive value measures the proportion TN/(TN + FN) and has a denominator comprising all cases with a negative classification. As Figure 3.5 shows, both positive and negative predictive values are 100% for the optimal cutoff point of 0.75, but the former declines when the 0.25 decision rule is used whereas the later declines when 1.25 is used.

Thus far we have examined the outcomes of the risk as hazard model assuming the true prevalence is known and that it is knowable through the lens of a completely valid instrument. If, however, an instrument possesses low reliability then it, by definition, also possesses low validity. The parenthetical percentages and numbers in Figure 3.5 are an illustration of what befalls the decision-making process when an instrument has a test–retest, internal consistency or alternative forms reliability of just 0.25 instead of 1.00 (perfect reliability). The 0.25 level, as Lindsey notes, is much more in line with the actual performance of CPS risk assessment tools. Our calculations for attenuation follow the formula suggested by Lindsey (Lindsey, 1994, p. 137):

$$1-\Phi[(1-x)\rho/(1-\rho^2)^{1/2}]$$

where ρ^2 is the reliability level, x is the cutoff point, and Φ is the cumulative normal distribution function. Thus for cutpoint 0.75, instead of the 14 cases we would expect if the instrument were completely reliable, we now predict fewer cases, i.e., $1 - \Phi[(1-0.75)(0.5)/(1-0.5^2)^{1/2}] = 0.443$, and (0.443) (14) or just 6 cases.

When we apply this attenuation formula to all segments of the normal distribution in Figure 3.5a above the 0.75 cutoff we predict five cases at 1.25, three cases at 1.75, one case at 2.25, and one case at 2.75. Now instead of 30 true-positive cases we identify a total of 16. All measures of instrument validity take the expected plunge with test sensitivity and positive predictive value suffering especially.

Figure 3.5b and c shows the counts of cases and the validities that can be expected with a reliability of 0.25 and z-score cutoffs of 0.25 and 1.25. It is evident that the decision maker is faced with two entangled distributions of abusers and nonabusers and the formidable task of balancing considerations of sensitivity and specificity.

As referrals to CPS agencies across the country continue on their dramatic rise, reaching an estimated 3.3 million involving about 6 million children in 2009 (U.S. Department of Health and Human Services, ACF, 2010), decision making under uncertainty or poorly understood risk remains the stubborn reality of daily operations. A distinctive pattern has emerged as cases wend their way through the CPS decision flow: e.g., too many cases screened in, too many cases investigated, too many cases kept under supervision, and too many false positives (Spratt, 2000; Waldfogel, 1998b; Lindsey, 2004). Gibbons and his colleagues (1995, p. 51) have likened CPS to trawling for fish, "casting a tightly woven meshed net in which a large number of minnows are caught—only to be discarded later—as well as the marketable fish." Though his analogy is perhaps in poor taste, Gibbons is correct in calling attention to the consequences of overidentification—misdirected or wasted resources, trauma inflicted on blameless parents, and a distrustful public. However, it is the outrage over a child fatality or other especially egregious instance of child maltreatment, as we have seen, that quickly transforms the dialogue into a cry for an even bigger net.

HELPING CPS MAKE BETTER DECISIONS

The progress that CPS has made in converting decisions with uncertain outcomes into decisions based on calculable risks has been, at best, halting and transitory. The operationalization of risk-as-hazard has not advanced all that well either. A number of leading child welfare scholars attribute a major share of blame for the apparent stagnation on a paucity of empirically based knowledge that they claim impedes efficient assessment, precludes intelligent risk taking, and obscures effective treatment choices (Gambrill, 2008a; Lindsey, 1997; Pelton, 1989). Lindsey (1997), for example, draws this contrast between CPS and emergency medicine:

> Physicians operate from a scientifically tested and validated knowledge base that provides reliable and satisfactory intervention. Unfortunately, the same cannot be said of decision-making in child welfare. The child welfare field has yet to develop a satisfactory scientific knowledge base to inform practice, largely because the field is so new. Empirical studies essentially began only three decades ago. Further, there has not been a tradition of active research in the field as has been the case in medicine. Finally, the nature of the problems CPS workers confront may not lend themselves to resolution by the scientific method as readily as the problems, which physicians attempt to solve. (p. 123)

Lindsay goes on to call the CPS decision flows we show in Figure 3.1 a manifestation of "an atheoretical framework" for providing child safety. Equally unkind are Bauman (1997) and Wilson and Morton (1997) who see CPS as operating without "a clear and compelling etiological framework."

What these critics and others (see, for example, Littell, 2008; Gambrill, 2008b) seem to be clamoring for is a set of decision-making guidelines modeled after those found in the Cochrane and Campbell Collaborations (Petrosino et al., 2001; Boruch, 2005), i.e., the replacement of compilations of ostensible evidence found in CPS practice handbooks with information on efficacy obtained from strong research designs. Instead of the development of a robust evidence-based CPS practice, however, child welfare decision making remains enmeshed in a tangle of conceptual prescriptions and prohibitions that have served to confuse practitioners as much as enlighten them. We outline below several of the themes that we believe have been especially detrimental to progress.

THE LIMITATIONS OF NORMATIVE DECISION MAKING

It is not difficult to find discussions in the child welfare literature decrying rational choice theory and the principle of subjective expected utility (SEU) (illustrated earlier in the chapter) as a realistic base from which to make CPS decisions (Munro, 2004, 2008; Schwalbe, 2004; Gambrill & Shlonsky, 2001). The arguments employed here generally follow one of two lines of explanation, viz. individuals lack the knowledge of probabilities and the states of nature to properly calculate marginal utilities, and even when the knowledge is available, decision makers opt for nonrational shortcuts. Gigerenzer (2004), a noted authority on choice behavior and a physician by training, summarizes the problem with rational utility models in this way:

> If you open a book on judgment and decision making, chances are that you will stumble over the following moral: Good reasoning must adhere to the laws of logic, the calculus of probability, or the maximization of expected utility; if not, there must be a cognitive or motivational flaw. Don't be taken in by this fable. Logic and probability are mathematically beautiful and elegant systems. But they do not describe how actual people—including the authors of books on decision making—reason, as the subsequent story highlights. A decision theorist from Columbia University was struggling whether to accept an offer from a rival university or to stay. His colleague took him aside and said, 'Just maximize your expected utility—you always write about doing this.' Exasperated, the decision theorist responded, 'Come on, this is serious.' (p. 62)

Although discussions of social workers' poor understanding of probability has been lamented for years (Light, 1973; Gambrill & Shlonsky, 2001; Nugent, 2004; Munro, 2004), most of the critique of rational choice theory has been motivated by workers' alleged use of "heuristics" or informal rules of thumb when integrating information about probabilities and alternatives (judgments) and making choices about courses of action (decisions). Herbert Simon (1955, 1979) was among the earliest social scientists to advance the notion that individuals, because of information access and/or processing constraints, rarely maximize or optimize their utility when making choices; rather, they "satisfice," using a decision process he termed "bounded rationality." Simon (1979) remarked that

> utility maximization...was not essential...for it would have required the decision maker to be able to estimate the marginal costs and returns of a search in a decision situation that was already too complex for the exercise of global rationality...the important thing about search and satisficing theory is that it showed how choice could actually be made with reasonable amounts of calculation, and using

very incomplete information, without the need for performing the impossible—of carrying out the optimizing procedure. (p. 503)

If Simon laid the initial foundation for the examination of the role played by "cognitive imperfections" on normative models of decision making, it is the work of Tversky and Kahneman (1974, 1982; Kahneman et al., 1982) that has had the most significant impact in the field of social work. In their 1974 article that appeared in the journal *Science*, these researchers have proposed and empirically demonstrated three heuristics—-*representativeness, availability, and adjustment and anchoring*—that people employ to assess probabilities and to predict values, and enumerated the biases to which these heuristics can lead. Tversky and Kahneman showed that when people are faced with the task of assigning probability, they equate likelihood with *representativeness*, thereby judging an event to be more probable the more it represents its parent population. For example, after reading a description of a man as intelligent, but unimaginative, compulsive, and generally lifeless, having been good at mathematics in school, but not so good in social studies and humanities, subjects in an experiment assigned a high probability to his being an accountant when asked to rate the likelihood of each of several possible occupations (Tversky & Kahneman, 1982). The representativeness heuristic at play here causes the experimental subject to assess the probability that the man is an accountant according to the degree to which he is representative of or similar to the stereotype of an accountant, while ignoring prior information in the form of prevalence or "base" rates of, say, accountants in the population.

People also frequently use ease of recall, i.e., "the ease with which instances or associations could be brought to mind" (Tversky & Kahneman, 1982), as the basis for estimating how frequent a particular event is. Termed the *availability* heuristic, Tversky and Kahneman illustrated its use with the following experiment: A group of people were asked if there are more murders or suicides in New York City in any given year. Most people responded that there are more murders, when in fact there are many more suicides. Because murders receive much more publicity than do suicides, they occupy a more advantageous position in people's memory, facilitating easier recall. The same is true of people tending to assign higher weight to recent information when making decisions, simply because of its easier access.

Anchoring and adjustment calls attention to the tendency of decision makers to first form an initial impression or an anchor, and adjusting it on the basis of any additional information to yield a final answer. Kahneman and Tversky (1979) show that people's perception of the frequency of events appears to be highly sensitive to the anchoring estimate from which they begin. They demonstrate this phenomenon by asking a group of students to estimate the percentage of African countries that are members of the United Nations. Before the students began, they were asked to spin a wheel that contained numbers between one and 100. The students were then asked if their estimates were higher or lower than the number of the wheel. Then the students were asked for their numerical estimates of the percentage. Kahneman et al. (1982) found that the arbitrary numbers obtained from the spin (the anchor) had a marked effect on estimates, pulling the estimates in the direction of the anchor. For example, students who got a 10 on the wheel on average estimated the percentage of African Nations in the United Nations to be 25% and those who got a 65 estimated this number to be 45% on average.

Since the early discussion of heuristics, cognitive shortcuts, and rules of thumb by Tversky and Kahneman in the 1970s, new heuristics continue to be discovered every year. For example, there is "the numerosity heuristic" in which probability judgments are based on the number of instances of a target (Pelham, Sumarta, & Myaskovsky, 1994); "the recognition heuristic" in which alternatives with well-known and recognized labels are believed to be bigger, better, and safer than alternatives with unknown labels (Gigerenzer & Goldstein, 1999); and "the affect heuristic" that says that people tend to view objects and activities that have a positive connotation as yielding positive outcomes with higher probability and negative outcomes with lower probability, compared to objects and activities with negative connotations (Slovic et al., 2004). Von Winterfeldt and Edwards (1986) discuss the cognitive "illusions" of overconfidence and hindsight, whereas Nezu and Nezu (1989) identify the "biased search strategy." Baron (2000) discusses some 25 different biases or errors in judgment that can follow the use of heuristics.

As the list of heuristics has gotten longer, the use of the term heuristic as a synonym for error or biased decision making has become more widespread. That this confounding strays from Kahneman and Tversky's original intent is noted by social work researcher Katherine Tyson (1995):

> [Tversky and Kahneman] emphasized that although cognitive heuristics may lead to irrational judgments in some situations with some problems, the heuristics are neither intrinsically fallacious or designed for irrationality. On the contrary, cognitive heuristics facilitate problem solving in most decision situations. (p. 374)

A number of psychologists, in fact, assert that although the use of heuristics, practice wisdom, or intuition may appear to be ostensibly synthetic or irrational, they implicitly conform to normative rules of logic and probability theory (Over, 2004; Streufert & Swezey, 1985). Gigerenzer and his colleagues especially (Gigerenzer & Goldstein, 1996; Gigerenzer, 2004; Czerlinski et al., 1999) find "fast and frugal" heuristics strategies produce predictions that were comparable to (and in some cases better than) those using statistical prediction models, usually with about a third of the information inputs.

The focus on heuristics as error-prone decision making has served to heighten the skepticism that the CPS worker can ever truly engage in rational decision making (Wald & Woolverton, 1990; Howitt, 1993; Rossi et al., 1999; Lindsey, 2004). This emphasis on bias and error has obscured the fact that rational choice has never been disproved in the heuristics research, it simply shows that normative models do not apply to situations when individuals do not really care about how well they do or lack sufficient understanding of their interests and utilities (Carroll & Johnson, 1990; Goldstein & Hogarth, 1997). It has also closed the profession to promising lines of inquiry around issues such as the relative values of decision weights and probabilities in judgments (Kahneman & Tversky, 1979) and differential impacts of prejudice versus statistical discrimination in choice behavior (Knowles et al., 2001; Dharmapala & Ross, 2004). But perhaps most importantly, this error focus has confused the description of behavior with expected performance, causing us to lower our expectations around what CPS workers can be taught and what they can ever hope to achieve.

It would behoove CPS scholars and practitioners to keep in mind the distinction made by Kahneman and Tversky (1979) in their critique of rational choice theory as a descriptive theory of decision making under risk: viz. utility theory provides a useful descriptive model for economic behavior but a normative model for most choice behavior. Its expansion into more general decision making requires better knowledge of hazard base rates and exposure levels and therefore is feasible in an organization willing to make the effort.

THE RELATIVE EFFICACY OF ACTUARIAL AND CLINICAL RISK ASSESSMENT

In their introduction to a 2009 issue of *The Future of Children*, Paxson and Haskins state that "one implication that cuts across [this issue's] articles [on preventing child maltreatment] is the importance of accurate risk assessment" (p. 12). The appeal for reliable and valid risk management instruments and systems has been heard and repeated in CPS for at least 35 years. In 1986, the American Public Welfare Association together with the American Humane Association launched the First National Roundtable On Child Protective Services Risk Assessment. The proceedings from this forum of child welfare experts and from the 12 others that followed (see Fluke & Alsop, 1999 for the final volume) provided practitioners, academics, and the interested public with a mélange of research findings, commentary, risk management protocols and instruments, and training curricula. Efforts were made at each of these conferences to find areas of agreement and collaboration and propose agendas for further research and development. The four-volume report authored by the National Child Welfare Resource Center for Management and Administration (1989) and the over 800-page Symposium Report compiled by the National Center on Child Abuse and Neglect provided similar venues for discussion.

In more recent years much of the debate surrounding risk assessment and decision making under conditions of risk has devolved into what Johnson (2006) and Morton (2003) have termed "the risk assessment wars." The principal protagonists in this conflict have been the devotees of clinical judgment models and their opponents, the practitioners of actuarial risk assessment. We view this war more as a siege on the child welfare journals, punctuated by a few pyrrhic victories in which the only casualties are the children and families served by CPS.

The origin of today's controversy over the relative efficacy of these two approaches appears to be the publication in 1954 of Paul Meehl's book *Clinical versus Statistical Prediction*. The book's main thesis asserted that a linear or actuarial model that relates decision attributes directly to client/patient outcomes was invariably more accurate than clinical judgments supported by either implicit or explicit decision criteria. Meehl

(1986) reprised this claim with additional data 30 years later and offered his rationale for why a prediction model that bypasses actual decision-making processes outperforms the judges themselves: (1) sheer ignorance on the part of the decision maker regarding the relevant mathematics, science, or the state of extant knowledge reflected in the scholarly literature; (2) the threat of technological unemployment, i.e., the fear that those who are knowledgeable on the mathematics and sciences can outperform clinicians with advanced degrees; (3) difficulty in changing the self-concept of the professional, largely defined by his or her profession; (4) allegiances to and identification with classical theories within the profession; (5) an aversion within the profession to using an equation to predict human behavior and the perceived spiritual disreputability of reducing the individual to an inanimate object; (6) mistaken concepts of ethics regarding the use of actuarial models; and (7) computer phobia.

Grove and Meehl (1996) refined this explanation in 1996, removing some of the invective and distilling the principles to two primary causes: (1) the inherent limitations of the human brain to efficiently notice, select, categorize, record, retain, retrieve, and manipulate information for inferential purposes—the result is assignment of inoptimal weights to relevant factors and inconsistent application of weights they do assign; and (2) the inability of the clinician to assign weights in his or her predictions to the collective influence of unknown and unpredictable events. Actuarial prediction is believed to overcome both of these problems by (1) the derivation of optimal weights by means of applying a regression equation to the data, and once derived, offering a consistent application of these weights; and (2) control for the influence of unpredictable and unknown events through calculation of the error variance. Meehl's research has proven to be a wellspring from which the critics of clinical heuristics can drink deeply and often. Other researchers from psychology and the decision sciences have provided empirical support for Meehl's assertions (Dawes, 1979; Einhorn & Hogarth, 1981; Goldberg, 1991). It is important to note, however, that actuarial models have not always proven to be superior (Carroll & Johnson, 1990) and that their superiority in other instances has not been overwhelming (Gigerenzer, 2004; Over, 2004).

Actuarial risk assessment models were introduced to CPS from the field of juvenile justice, with researchers at the National Council on Crime and Delinquency particularly influential. Examples of the actuarial risk assessment tools that have been used in CPS work include the Wisconsin Delinquency Risk Model (Schwartz et al., 2008), the Michigan Family Risk Assessment of Abuse and Neglect (FRAAN) (Baird et al., 1991; Baird & Wagner, 2000), and the California Family Risk Assessment, a modification of FRAAN (Shlonsky & Wagner, 2005). The structure of the California instrument is provided in Figure 3.6 and illustrates a limited set of attributes, some valued more than others, added together to form an overall hazard score. The scale can be linked, usually through some type of regression analysis, to the outcomes of worker choices gleaned from records or observation. An especially appealing feature of actuarial instruments is their brevity and efficiency. A possible limitation and one that has major implications for prediction is that all the pertinent attributes are not included and subsequent regression analyses suffer from omitted variables bias. These omitted variables may be

CALIFORNIA
FAMILY RISK ASSESSMENT   c: 06/02

Referral Name: _____   Referral #: _____   County: _____

County Name: _____   Worker Name: _____   Worker ID#: _____

NEGLECT	Score	ABUSE	Score

NEGLECT

N1. Current Complaint is for Neglect
 a. No...0
 b. Yes...1 _____

N2. Prior Investigations (assign highest score that applies)
 a. None...0
 b. One or more, abuse only.......................1
 c. One or two for neglect.........................2
 d. Three or more for neglect.....................3 _____

N3. Household has Previously Received CPS (voluntary/court-order)
 a. No...0
 b. Yes...1 _____

N4. Number of Children Involved in the CA/N Incident
 a. One, two, or three.............................0
 b. Four or more....................................1 _____

N5. Age of Youngest Child in the Home
 a. Two or older....................................0
 b. Under two.......................................1 _____

N6. Primary Caretaker Provides Physical Care Inconsistent with Child Needs
 a. No...0
 b. Yes...1 _____

N7. Primary Caretaker has a Past or Current Mental Health Problem
 a. No...0
 b. Yes...1 _____

N8. Primary Caretaker has a Historic or Current Alcohol or Drug Problem. (Check applicable items and add for score)
 a. Not applicable..................................0
 b. ____ Alcohol (current or historic).........1
 c. ____ Drug (current or historic)...........1 _____

N9. Characteristics of Children in Household (Check applicable items and add for score)
 a. Not applicable..................................0
 b. ____ Medically fragile/failure to thrive....1
 c. ____ Developmental or physical disability...1
 d. ____ Positive toxicology screen at birth...1 _____

N10. Housing (check applicable items and add for score)
 a. Not applicable..................................0
 b. ____ Current housing is physically unsafe...1
 c. ____ Homeless at time of investigation....2 _____

ABUSE

A1. Current Complaint is for Abuse
 a. No...0
 b. Yes...1 _____

A2. Number of Prior Abuse Investigations (number: ____)
 a. None...0
 b. One...1
 c. Two or More......................................2 _____

A3. Household has Previously Received CPS (voluntary/court-ordered)
 a. No...0
 b. Yes...1 _____

A4. Prior Injury to a Child Resulting from CA/N
 a. No...0
 b. Yes...1 _____

A5. Primary Caretaker's Assessment of Incident (check applicable items and add for score)
 a. Not applicable..................................0
 b. ____ Blames child..............................1
 c. ____ Justifies maltreatment of a child.....2 _____

A6. Domestic Violence in the Household in the Past Year
 a. No...0
 b. Yes...2 _____

A7. Primary Caretaker Characteristics (check applicable items and add for score)
 a. Not applicable..................................0
 b. ____ Provides insufficient emotional/psychological support 1
 c. ____ Employs excessive/inappropriate discipline...1
 d. ____ Domineering caretaker(s)..............1 _____

A8. Primary Caretaker has a History of Abuse or Neglect as a Child
 a. No...0
 b. Yes...1 _____

A9. Secondary Caretaker has Historic or Current Alcohol or Drug Problem
 a. No...0
 b. Yes, alcohol and/or drug (check all applicable)...1
    ____ Alcohol   ____ Drug _____

A10. Characteristics of Children in Household (check appropriate items and add for score)
 a. Not applicable..................................0
 b. ____ Delinquency history......................1
 c. ____ Developmental disability.................1
 d. ____ Mental health/behavioral problem....1 _____

TOTAL NEGLECT RISK SCORE _____   **TOTAL ABUSE RISK SCORE** _____

SCORED RISK LEVEL. Assign the family's scored risk level based on the highest score on either the neglect or abuse instrument, using the following chart:

Neglect Score	Abuse Score	Scored Risk Level
_____ 0 – 1	_____ 0 – 1	_____ Low
_____ 2 – 4	_____ 2 – 4	_____ Moderate
_____ 5 – 8	_____ 5 – 7	_____ High
_____ 9+	_____ 8+	_____ Very High

POLICY OVERRIDES. Circle yes if a condition shown below is applicable in this case. If any condition is applicable, override final risk level to very high.
Yes   No   1. Sexual abuse case AND the perpetrator is likely to have access to the child victim.
Yes   No   2. Non-accidental injury to a child under age two.
Yes   No   3. Severe non-accidental injury.
Yes   No   4. Caretaker(s) action or inaction resulted in death of a child due to abuse or neglect (previous or current).

DISCRETIONARY OVERRIDE. If a discretionary override is made, circle yes, circle override risk level, and indicate reason. Risk level may be overridden one level higher.
Yes   No   5. If yes, override risk level (circle one):   Low   Moderate   High   Very High
         Discretionary override reason: _____

Supervisors Review/Approval of Discretionary Override: _____   Date: ___/___/___

FINAL RISK LEVEL (circle final level assigned):   Low   Moderate   High   Very High

FIG 3.6 California Family Risk Assessment Form. © 2012 by NCCD, all rights reserved. Reprinted with permission.

of two kinds, e.g., unmeasured case characteristics and/or contextual factors influencing worker choices, regardless of the case risk score computed (Shlonsky & Wagner, 2005; English et al., 1998; DePanfilis & Girvin, 2005).

Consensus or structured clinical forms of risk assessment, obversely, are compiled by panels of experts who draw upon previous research findings, literature reviews, and clinical opinion to construct rating scales anchored around distinctive sets of risk factors that can be simply added (or weighted and added in some cases) to form an overall assessment of hazard. Several of the more prominently used consensus tools are the Illinois Child Abuse and Neglect Training System (CANTS) 17B, the Washington Risk Model (WRM), the California Family Assessment Factor Analysis, and the New York Child Protection Services Risk Document (CPSRD) (Lyons et al., 1996; English et al., 2002). Consensus-based risk assessment protocols tend to be much more detailed than actuarial models and require workers to rate children and families in distinctive conceptual domains. We have included a copy of the risk assessment matrix (WRM) developed by the Department of Social and Health Services, Washington State in Appendix III. The matrix contains 37 items organized around seven distinctive risk areas—the number of items in a domain creates an implicit scale of unequal importance weights.

The risk assessment wars have led, rather surprisingly, to relatively few direct confrontations, and these skirmishes have proven to be inconclusive. Baird and Wagner (2000) and Baird, Wagner, Healy, and Johnson (1999), open advocates of actuarial instruments, compared the performance of the California Family Assessment Factor Analysis and WRM to that of Michigan actuarial system on measures of reliability and validity. Using rates of subsequent investigations, substantiations, and placements as outcome measures, Baird and Wagner report that the actuarial model risk classifications were superior in each instance. For example, whereas the Michigan instrument predicted 46% of new investigations for high-risk classified cases and 16% for low-risk cases, the percentages were 38% and 28% for the California instrument and 37% and 25% for WRM. Baird and Wagner did not report any sensitivity or specificity statistics. A British study conducted by Leschied et al. (2003), however, found that clinical judgments to place children in care were consistent with the predictions of an actuarial instrument in up to 81% of cases. In a comparison of clinical and actuarial performance, Baumann and his associates (2005, 2006) conducted two experiments with random assignment of CPS casework units into treatment groups that completed either a paper form or computerized actuarial risk form and a control group that conducted service as usual. In predictions of substantiation after investigation and reinvestigation after investigation, the control group performed about as well as the treatment groups on the substantiation criterion (validity coefficients 0.3 to 0.5) and equally poorly on the reinvestigation criterion (coefficients 0.1 to 0.2). The Baumann et al. experiments offer the reader enough information to ask a question that goes beyond invidious comparisons and straight to the issue of relative efficacy: If one method of risk assessment functions better than a second does but both lack substantial validity, what have we gained by the comparison?

As former participants in the risk assessment wars ourselves (Jagannathan & Camasso, 1996; Camasso & Jagannathan, 2000), we believe it is time for an extended truce. Many studies (Camasso & Jagannathan, 2000; Bae et al., 2007; English et al., 2002; Davidson-Arad et al., 2006) and many reviews of studies (Lyons et al., 1996; Gambrill & Shlonsky, 2001; Rycus & Hughes, 2008) have documented the low levels of validity in risk assessment systems of all kinds. The truce would mark a propitious time to abstain from repeating "the old saws" and begin work on an agenda that should significantly advance the measurement of hazard in CPS. Included on the agenda would be the following items:

1. Undertake more classical and natural experimental designs. The arguments against experimentation advanced by Johnson (2006) and some others in the social work profession apply to much weaker designs as well, and these designs have the additional problems of lower internal validity.
2. Continue the promising line of research that employs computer-aided segmentation techniques to model decision points and isolate risk groups (Schwartz et al., 2008; McDonald et al., 2001; Johnson et al., 2002; Schwartz et al., 2004). Many of these search algorithms have their roots in the multiway contingency table analyses developed at the University of Michigan in the 1960s (Andrews, Morgan, & Sonquist, 1967).
3. Develop and test the relative efficacy of structured decision making (SDM) approaches that integrate actuarial and consensus-based variables (Shlonsky & Wagner, 2005; Shook & Sarri, 2007). Factorial experimental designs would be ideal for evaluating these approaches.
4. Institute a requirement by journal editors and reviewers that all studies purporting to measure the prediction or criterion validity of risk assessment applications report both sensitivity levels and positive predictive values of the instruments/ models employed.
5. Institute an additional requirement that these studies amass sufficient data to undertake a receiver operating curve (ROC) analysis. ROC curves avoid the problem imposed by reporting a single sensitivity and specificity conditioned on one decision threshold; instead, sensitivity and specificity on an instrument are compared over a wide and continuous range of criterion levels. ROC analysis has a long history in medicine (Turner, 1978; Hanley & McNeil, 1982) and has been proposed as an important evaluative tool in CPS (National Center on Child Abuse and Neglect, 1991; Gottfredson & Moriarty, 2006).

Despite the potential of ROC for offering rigorous validity evaluations in CPS, the method has been, to our knowledge, employed only once—by us in a 1995 *Social Work Research* article (Camasso & Jagannathan, 1995). In this publication we compared the predictive validity of the WRM and Illinois CANTS 17B by plotting each instrument's sensitivity against its false-positive rate (1–specificity). The results from the series of analyses are reported in the ROC curves that appear in Figure 3.7. The principal diagnostic for validity in ROC analysis appears as areas under the curve measured as the area between the diagonal line of no information and the curve's left and top trajectory. Curves that trace closely to the diagonal line indicate less or no power to discriminate between real hazard and no hazard. Using Hanley and McNeil's (1982) rank order method it is possible to compute an area under the curve (AUC) probability that provides a measure of an instrument's overall prediction accuracy.

In our analysis we found that WRM yielded overall prediction accuracies of 68% for case recidivism, 69% for case closings, and 68% for case substantiations. The accuracies for the Illinois instrument were 58%, 74%, and 66%. To contrast these results with higher validity tests we ask the reader to review the ROC curves reported by Murphy

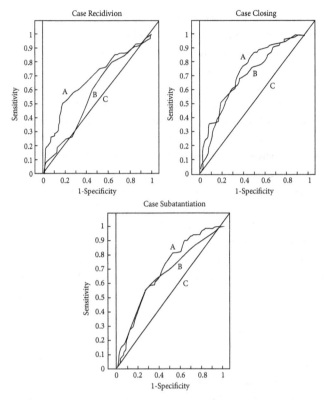

Note: ROC = receiver operating characteristics; A = Washington instrument; B = Illino is instrument; C = line of no information
Source: Camasso and Jagannathan (1995)

FIG 3.7 ROC Curves.

et al. (1987) in their analysis of three sets of scoring rules used on the Health Opinion Survey. Here the prediction accuracy for distinguishing the psychiatrically well and ill range from 90% to 97%. Such levels of accuracy are commonplace in the medical and public health literature.

As these particular (and possibly invidious) comparisons indicate, CPS risk assessment has a long way to go to reach respectable levels of accuracy. Nevertheless, if CPS does not undertake the rigorous analyses that are needed to gauge validity, it is hard to imagine how any real progress can be made.

DECISIONS MADE OUT OF CONTEXT

In our introduction to the limits of modeling risk to children as a function of hazard (Chapter 1) we pointed up the reality that the social context in which CPS decisions are made, particularly decisions made in a climate in which zero tolerance, infinite jeopardy, and punctuated equilibrium reign, has the potential to dramatically change assessments of child risk. In Chapter 2 we provided multiple instances in which CPS decision flows were significantly altered in the wake of child fatalities and/or egregious cases of maltreatment. In the parlance of decision theory, risk analyses in these and similar situations require the inclusion of characteristics of the decision maker as well as characteristics of the decision (i.e., the choice alternatives) as a prerequisite to any real understanding of choice behavior (Hoffman & Duncan, 1988; Camasso & Jagannathan, 2001). The need for such contextual analyses should become quite evident after the examination of some state-level data provided by Lindsey (2004).

In his book *The Welfare of Children*, Lindsey (2004, p. 147) provides a table showing the rates of substantiated child abuse in 24 states for the year 2000. These rates range from 1.9 per 1000 in Pennsylvania to 37.1 per 1000 in Alaska. The author then queries:

> Why is it that the rate of substantiated child abuse in Pennsylvania is less than 10 times the rate found in the bordering state of Ohio? North Carolina and Virginia share a long border and would seem to be similar, yet the rate of substantiated child abuse in North Carolina is more than three times greater than Virginia. Likewise the rate of abuse in Kentucky is three times greater than the abuse reported in Tennessee.

Lindsey goes on to examine large state differences in rates of child removal and placement in foster care.

> Children are removed at a rate ten times greater in California compared to New Jersey. What is the explanation? There is no credible reason to explain how child abuse can be substantiated at a rate ten times greater in California in comparison to New Jersey.... Victims of child abuse in Oregon are removed from their family at a rate seven times greater than in Colorado. These are all children who have been victimized. It is just that in some states the decision to remove is far more frequent—by several fold—than in others. (pp. 172–173).

How can we explain these truly astonishing differences in the diagnosis and treatment of children under CPS care? Lindsay believes that some of this variation may arise from the manner in which states report administrative data. We concur and see reporting differences as the sequela of differential capacities of states to (1) identify and analyze actual hazards to children, (2) estimate the degree to which worker perception and self-interest have augmented hazard in decision making, and (3) determine the levels of organizational and broader societal factors that have an impact on (1) and (2). But although the capacity of states to accurately analyze hazard to children does undoubtedly vary, we view this contribution to be relatively small—states, after all, receive much the same federal technical assistance, are subject to much the same social work training and curriculum, and work with more or less the same low validity risk assessment technology. We believe the contributions of (2) and (3) are considerably larger; after all, it is here that the routinization of outrage is manifest.

An important literature has been growing in the decision sciences on the comparative importance of risk as hazard vis-à-vis risk as perception in settings where good science and political concerns clash (Slovic, 1987; Slovic et al., 2004; Sjoberg, 2000; Taylor-Gooby & Zinn, 2006). Slovic (1987) points out that risk perceptions tend to come from news media reports that "rather thoroughly document mishaps and threats" (p. 236) but lead readers to overestimate threat potentials.

We would expect that CPS workers and agency managers subjected to social outrage and committed to its routinization would exhibit an increased likelihood to incorporate an affective/political dimension into their risk deliberations. How intense and/ or extensive this integration is and its duration are conditioned by characteristics of the organizational task environment (i.e., degree of workforce punctuations, turnover, worker training, workload, quality control, information feedback) and extraorganizational factors (minority populations, poverty rates, social policies, etc.).

Increasingly, the field of child welfare is recognizing the importance of organizational climate and social context for CPS decisions. Discussions by DePanfilis and Girvin (2005), Brintall (1981), and English et al. (1998) on caseload sizes and time pressures and those by Gambrill (2008a), Gambrill and Shlonsky (2001), and Rzepnicki and Johnson (2005) on task environments have increased our understanding of how the immediate work environment affects decisions to protect. These discussions, however, have provided us with little insight into how bounded rationality and analytic assessments of risk metamorphose into forms of contextual rationality filled with high levels of organizational affect, worker fear, and risk aversion. They tell us even less about how procedural rationality (O'Reilly, 1983) evolves in climates where hazard takes a backseat to outrage considerations.

4

AGENCY OPERATIONS IN AN OUTRAGE ERA

Seal up the mouth of outrage for a while,
Till we can clear these ambiguities
Shakespeare (1595)
Romeo and Juliet

The institutional accountability introduced by consent decrees or new legislation can push child protective services (CPS) agencies for performance even while it exacerbates risk-averse and other overly cautious behavior (Golden, 2009; Behn, 2001; Sandler & Schoenbrod, 2003). Any number of observers have advanced the notion that institutional reform litigation sets up an interminable conflict between rule-of-law values and bureaucratic needs for flexibility that can serve to thwart organizational performance. Noonan, Sabel, and Simon (2009), for example, describe the struggle in CPS to balance performance with legal compliance, Sandler and Schoenbrod (2003) see a broader dilemma in a simultaneous pursuit of aspirations and responsibilities, and Carbonara, Parisi, and von Wangenheim (2008) call attention to litigation that triggers a social response by opening a social divide. Golden (2009) is perhaps most on point, however, when she calls attention to what appears to be a kind of Marcusian "active-passivity" among workers, supervisors, and even CPS top management.

Although court orders and some legislation in CPS share with other social reforms a focus on fairness and needed resources, they also have been aggressive in pursuing a performance-oriented regime, complete with enforceable elements, time frames, benchmarks, and measurable system indicators. A content analysis that we performed of the complaints and court orders of more than 30 states that faced major CPS litigation sometime from 1991 through 2010 (see Appendix II) reveals language calling for improvement in one or more of these areas, viz. managerial efficiency, worker quality, caseload management and sizes, information and data system operations, funding amounts or resource reallocation, worker training and decision-making strategies, and the evaluation and monitoring of foster care utilization. Directives targeting specific child outcomes are somewhat less common, appearing when they do, in the final years of the consent decree.

Many of the operations, personnel, and financial problems addressed in CPS litigation, and in legislative reforms as well, have demonstrated a stubborn resiliency.

Linked to this resilience and perhaps to some extent its cause is the variability in state and local CPS policies and practices that have also complicated efforts to distill a set of evidence-based best practices. In a 2003 study conducted by the Department of Health and Human Services-ACF (2003) on CPS systems and reform efforts, the authors conclude that the extensive variation from state to state in policies addressing screening and intake, investigation, and alternative response is "potentially of great concern" (p. 65). The report goes on to identify six components of decisions to protect children in which the impact of variation on child outcomes is poorly understood or unknown entirely, e.g., mandated reporters, investigation objectives, standards of evidence, maltreatment definitions, required timeliness, and due process requirements (p. 6). The issue of the unmeasured or unintended consequences of CPS policy and procedures variability has also been a subject of discussion in several U.S. General Accountability Office Reports (United States Government Accountability Office, 1995, 1997).

Variation in management policies and procedures makes its way throughout authority, work activity, information, and decision-making flows of CPS. It exerts an influence on who and how many will comprise the frontline workforce and how well paid and protected these workers will be. Variation in policies can also lead to distinctive styles of case management, differences in quality assurance systems, particularly worker training priorities, and variation in how technology and data are valued and utilized in an agency. All this variation, in turn, can affect levels of child safety and well-being. In this chapter we examine several features of CPS agency operations that almost always appear in treatments of child welfare reform and we begin where most of these discussions begin—with the condition of the child welfare labor force.

THE CRITICIZED MASS—CHILD PROTECTIVE SERVICES WORKERS

In our conceptual model, we specify risk-to-child as a function of actual hazard to the child and risk to the CPS worker where worker risk comprises outrage pressures and components identifying worker competence and insulation from personal and/or career harm (Eqs. 4, 5, and 6 in Chapter 1). It follows from this specification that workers with more professional skills and/or protections have the resources to offset the influences of outrage when making decisions to protect.

Questioning the competence of the typical CPS worker has been a favorite parlor and seminar game, played unceasingly by politicians, the media, and many social work scholars. In a 1997 U.S. General Accountability Office report (United States Government Accountability Office, 1997) the federal evaluators identify four long-standing weaknesses within CPS that hamper the organization's capacity to protect children (p. 10), and at the very top of this list is CPS difficulty in maintaining a professional and skilled workforce. In 2003, two national studies on the "condition of the public sector, human services labor force" by the Annie E. Casey Foundation and the Brookings Institution observed that the current workforce lacks confidence in their organizations' capacity to spend program dollars wisely and believe the public, and many clients have unfairly judged workers as uncaring or incapable. This sentiment, captured in statistical summaries of large-scale surveys, is much more poignantly expressed in focus groups and personal interviews with CPS workers. Westbrook, Ellis, and Ellett (2006, p. 48) report that a pressing issue among workers in Georgia is the deterioration of the public image of child welfare and of child welfare staff in particular. Ellett et al. (2007) find much the same in their study of 58 focus groups, noting that workers see themselves trying to function in a culture of tension and fear—fear of legal liability, fear of making a mistake, fear of a ruined reputation or career, and fear of public ridicule. Geen and Tumlin's (1999, p. 9) interviews with caseworkers in 13 states find a consensus that highly publicized child death cases profoundly affect the day-to-day decision making of these workers. So, too, do Smith and Donovan (2003) in their interviews with Illinois CPS workers. A caseworker's worst nightmare is this media account quoting a government official: "Every year we get more and more [social workers] who can't do the job...There are horrible social worker decisions made by some goofy social workers" (p. 545). To CPS workers across the country, the dream always ends the same way: This month's award for incompetence goes to Mr./Ms. *(fill in my name)*!

The ongoing criticism of CPS workers has had serious consequences for organizational operations, especially the contribution it makes to employee turnover. In a 1995 U.S. General Accountability Office report, low morale together with hiring freezes, low pay, and poor working conditions are viewed as the causes of CPS failures to both recruit and retain high-quality caseworkers. This report concludes:

> These factors, in turn, led to staff shortages, high caseloads, and high burnout and turnover rates among caseworkers. In some jurisdictions, caseloads have reached 100 cases per caseworker, well above the 25 per caseworker recommended by the National Association of Social Workers. In New York City, annual turnover rates for caseworkers have been as high as 75%, so that each year most foster children, who have suffered from unstable families, get a new caseworker. (p. 3)

Subsequent General Accountability Office reports affirm the obstinacy of the turnover problem, estimating a rate in public child welfare at between 30% and 40% per year (United States Government Accountability Office, 2003a). Caseloads well above the Child Welfare League of America (CWLA) standard of 12–15 families per worker, along with caseworker pay, paperwork requirements, and breakdowns in supervision, are promulgated as the principal factors affecting a state's ability to retain workers (United States Government Accountability Office, 2006). Numerous studies conducted by social work researchers have also examined the correlates of CPS turnover and have found organizational conditions including pay, benefits, workload, caseload size, and job stress to be related (Zell, 2006; Nissly et al., 2004; American Humane Association, 2002; Malm et al., 2001; Moynihan & Landuyt, 2008). Demographic factors, especially agency tenure, which is negatively related to turnover, and education, which has a positive association, have been shown to be consistent associates of turnover as well (Freund, 2005; Mor Barak et al., 2001; Light, 2003; Moynihan & Landuyt, 2008). Moynihan and Pandey (2007, p. 211) have likened the pull and push of tenure and education to the combination of sticky webs that keep employees with the same organization and the trampolines that vault employees onto their next job.

One correlate of turnover in public human services agencies that has also been empirically linked to worker competence and performance is organizational and professional commitment to agency values and mission. Following the expectancy theory of motivation developed by Vroom (1960), commitment can be operationalized as a subjective expected utility (SEU) optimized as a function of three distinctive beliefs:

$$C = P(\text{Expectancy}) \cdot P(\text{Instrumentality}) \cdot \text{Valence}$$

where C is Commitment Level and Expectancy is the belief that effort will result in a good performance. Instrumentality is the perception that performance yields clear rewards, Valence is the value that the worker places in the reward, and P is probability associated with expectancy and instrumentality.

Low levels of commitment, unfortunately, have been shown to be much too common in public human services (DeParle, 2004; The Annie E. Casey Foundation, 2003; Jagannathan & Camasso, 2006; Hagen, Lurie, & Wang, 1993), and in CPS these low levels have exacerbated the turnover problem (Freund, 2005; Mor Barak et al., 2001; Moynihan & Landuyt, 2008). And although the evidence is very thin, there are some indications that committed workers are more likely to make realistic assessments of risk and are better able to integrate the emotional and rational elements of decision making (Cash, 2001; English et al., 1998; Rossi et al., 1999).

The Government Accountability Office (GAO) studies cited above taken together with the social work research offer us a profile of the CPS workforce that is both unflattering and blameworthy. The typical CPS worker has an agency tenure of less than 2 years (United States Government Accountability Office, 2003a), manages a caseload several times the recommended Child Welfare League of America (CWLA) or National Association of Social Workers (NASW) standard, and holds a bachelor's degree in a field other than social work (Child Welfare League of America, 1999; Ryan et al., 2006). We believe that we broaden this profile a bit with the state level CPS workforce data that are presented in Table 4.1.

In columns (a) and (b) of Table 4.1 we attempt to shed some light on variation in volume (and perhaps indirectly on stress) experienced by CPS workers in the country. It is clear that both the ratios of front-line workers per 1000 screened-in cases and per 1000 child population at risk exhibit an extraordinary divergence across the United States. The mean number of CPS workers in 2008 was 21.85 per 1000 reports and 0.54 per 1000 children, with ranges of 6.5 to 128 and 0.15 to 1.73, respectively. Such variation begs the obvious questions: why do such differences exist? Are they empirically related to worker turnover, competence, stress, or commitment? Do they predict child outcomes? If the currently available research is correct, we would expect that states with high ratios of workers (and hence lower cases per worker) would have more time to spend on individual cases, leading to better decisions and performance.

Table 4.1 Child Protective Services Workers in Organizational Context: State Comparisons on Adjusted Workforce Size, Expenditures, and Union Protection—2008

State	Front-Line Workers per 1000 Screened-in Cases (a)	Front-Line Workers per 1000 Child Population (b)	Federal Expenditures per Number of Workers (c)	State Expenditures per Number of Workers (d)	Percent of Unionized Public Sector Workers (e)
Alabama	34.37899	0.6028622	232420.3	238037.2	29.8
Alaska	33.64772	1.466667	205637	283142	55.6
Arizona	37.33261	0.6374134	279326	254577.4	19.2
Arkansas	15.5621	0.6133144	148035.4	96576.96	16
California	19.02176	0.4937812	486323.2	274657.1	57.3
Colorado	.	.	.	.	22
Connecticut	11.67602	0.3484108	1947653	1642310	63
Delaware	15.30124	0.4615385	87519.87	506267.1	38.7
District of Columbia	40.26417	1.733945	588379.9	1021698	21.1
Florida	10.9977	0.4738806	270795.9	313129.3	28
Georgia	17.80882	0.2285477	1372665	670238.4	8.7
Hawaii	35.48644	0.3111888	752081.3	738826.8	54.3
Idaho	40.54253	0.6610577	126539.2	45484.74	16.7
Illinois	14.6372	0.3084906	535794.3	727741.8	50.3
Indiana	8.307093	0.3490863	447830.3	342842.8	27.4
Iowa	10.295	0.3136428	975998.3	685873.6	31.3
Kansas	20.98318	0.5050071	95970.58	890301.6	16.6
Kentucky	33.85625	1.675248	120020.4	151630.2	16.3
Louisiana	11.07218	0.2119857	558089.7	411197.7	13.3
Maine	25.2574	0.5772059	300806.6	978020.5	45.2
Maryland	.	0.4381095	443389.3	527760.1	30.9
Massachusetts	8.147696	0.2482806	705914.3	1456724	61
Michigan	6.544138	0.1982286	1058052	602189.3	57.3
Minnesota	23.10834	0.3493095	313939.8	216148.8	55
Mississippi	23.44856	0.5738126	144266.6	44773.83	9.4
Missouri	9.505588	0.3328582	299319.4	331734.9	23.3
Montana	23.91087	0.8842593	200667.5	204271.1	38.5
Nebraska	9.381014	0.2588496	926182	800428.4	27.3
Nevada	15.28049	0.3263786	295830.3	230661.1	36.5

(continued)

Table 4.1 *(Continued)*

State	Front-Line Workers per 1000 Screened-in Cases (a)	Front-Line Workers per 1000 Child Population (b)	Federal Expenditures per Number of Workers (c)	State Expenditures per Number of Workers (d)	Percent of Unionized Public Sector Workers (e)
New Hampshire	8.840742	0.2398649	843186.8	173684.1	47.8
New Jersey	19.48233	0.5159705	314759.5	583959.1	62.1
New Mexico	15.06669	0.4299803	263539.9	0	16
New York	.	.	.	.	70.5
North Carolina	15.29642	0.46194	218669.3	85879.72	11
North Dakota	26.42732	0.7361111	343660.7	128431.6	16.3
Ohio	17.71506	0.5415755	623077.6	109387.7	40.6
Oklahoma	9.988552	0.3882091	416365	425383	18
Oregon	15.89958	0.5022988	664677.3	450579.7	59.9
Pennsylvania	128.3781	1.166062	12787.43	346717.7	52.9
Rhode Island	9.282568	0.2521368	1429751	2315661	61.9
South Carolina	17.08228	0.2922932	916882.2	214190.3	10.9
Tennessee	19.52858	0.824501	235903.9	260160.8	16
Texas	21.25828	0.5331953	206387.8	119579.9	15
Utah	6.676036	0.1542923	419287	700624.5	15.5
Vermont	26.28232	0.488189	880553.1	661473.3	40.2
Virginia	16.39684	0.255102	272321.9	164878.4	9.3
Washington	11.5709	0.2669683	634372.5	646408.8	51
West Virginia	20.12726	1.210938	245556.6	255947.1	25.3
Wisconsin	15.01023	0.2988679	408916.3	288889	47.7
Wyoming	52.54379	0.9545454	102307	109586.2	13.2
Mean	21.85/1000 reports	0.540 per 1000 children	485968.20	473067.60	33.09%
SD	18.76	0.365	390330.60	439442.50	18.53%
Min	6.54	0.154	12787.43	0	8.7%
Max	128.37	1.73	194765.30	2315661	70.5%

In columns (c) and (d) of Table 4.1 the ratios of federal and state expenditures for CPS services per number of frontline workers are given. The ratio is an attempt to compute a standardized measure of the state CPS organization's resources supporting workers as they perform their duties. Here again, the cross-state variation is extraordinary. Total federal expenditures per state worker averaged about $486,000 in 2008 while state contributions averaged approximately $473,000. These amounts of course include foster care and institutional placement costs as well as CPS administrative and daily operations costs. As might be expected, the variance in state expenditures is greater than the federal contribution, but both are substantial. Does this variability reflect state differences in true prevalence of child maltreatment or simply distinctive state priorities? Do higher resourced states achieve superior results? Are there optimal spending levels yielding optimal benefit-to-cost ratios?

As important as cross-state variability in workforce and expenditure rates (ratios) may be for our understanding of CPS decision outcomes, we believe that simply examining changes in resource size (and quality, if such information were available) reflect only part of the story. Much more critical, we believe, are abrupt within-state changes in workforce size and experience that characterize the punctuated equilibriums in agency policies and practices produced by outrage-directed change. It is the mass exodus of workers following negative media coverage of an archetypical case and/or the mass hiring of new workers subsequent to consent decrees or sweeping new statutes that are critical. Frontline workers and their immediate supervisors are, after all, responsible for almost all case decisions. Volatile within-state fiscal levels may also indicate punctuated equilibria, but we believe these sudden changes are blunted by existing bureaucracy (Robinson, 2004; Bess et al., 2001; Geen, Boots, & Tumlin, 1999). Column (e) of Table 4.1 examines the percentage of public sector workers in a state (2008) that are represented by a union. The subject of unionization has been discussed sparsely in the social work literature; nevertheless, it has been linked in the broader human services literature to employee empowerment and lower worker turnover (Moynihan & Landuyt, 2008; Hirsch & Macpherson, 2003). As in the instances of standardized worker numbers and CPS expenditures, union representation varied greatly across the states in 2008, ranging from a low of 8.7% in Georgia to over 70% in New York. Do unionized CPS workers produce outcomes superior to their nonunionized counterparts? Our risk model (Eqs. 4, 5, and 6) would suggest they do—if the protections that unions offer can shield workers from the manifestations of social outrage.

The remedy-crafting phase of CPS institutional reform litigation and legislation almost always contains language requiring the hiring of additional, high-quality workers. And this, in turn, has required states to increase CPS budgets (Cooper, 1988; Noonan et al., 2009; Sandler & Schoenbrod, 2003). New Jersey and other states have complied with consent decrees and court orders, albeit at times reluctantly, hoping that these new resources will influence worker competence, commitment, caseload, workload, turnover, and, ultimately, CPS organizational performance. Unfortunately, we have yet to see definitive evidence of a strong input–output connection emanating from these interventions.

ACCOUNTABILITY IN CASE MANAGEMENT, ONCE AGAIN

A central component of CPS reform has been the call for a reinvigorated and account-able case management system. Although many definitions of the case management function can be found in the social work literature, the description offered by Roberts and Greene (2002) is perhaps the most thorough:

> Case Management is a service that links and coordinates assistance from insti-tutions and agencies providing medical, psychosocial, and concrete support for individuals in need of such assistance. It is the process of social work interven-tion that helps people to organize and use the supports, services, and opportuni-ties that enable them to achieve life outcomes that they value. Additionally, it is a direct practice method that involves skills in assessment, counseling, teaching, and advocacy that aims to improve the social functioning of clients served. A service concept in which clients are provided both individualized counseling and linkage to other needed services and supports. In summary, the case manager is respon-sible for developing a plan with the client, organizing and coordinating services, mediating differences among providers, sustaining and empowering client partici-pation, and evaluating outcomes. (p. 831)

In CPS practices, case management includes intake information processing, initial assessment, investigation of allegations, family assessment, developing a case plan complete with targeted outcomes, goals and tasks, service provision, monitoring fam-ily/child(ren) progress, and responsible case closure (Brittain & Hunt, 2004; DePanfilis & Salus, 2003). Case management often requires close coordination with the family and juvenile court system as well.

As we noted in Chapter 3, one model of case management that has been "rediscovered" in reform litigation is the traditional case practice model or the "social-work based prac-tice model" (Golden, 2009; Noonan et al., 2009). To the many skeptics of CPS reform this would appear to be a case of new wine in the same old bottles, or even the same old wine in the same old bottles. There is, however, a new ingredient: case quality assessment and comparison. In Alabama, Utah, Washington, DC, New Jersey, and other states, each case managed is viewed as a unique and valid test of the CPS system, a principle that serves to bundle case management, case record review, and quality assurance into an integrated monitoring and improvement management tool (New Jersey Department of Human Services, 2004; Utah Division of Child and Family Services, 1999; Golden, 2009).

The integration of case management and quality control has proven to be no mean feat in any state, however. Just how difficult this integration can be is observable from the results of the Child and Family Services Reviews (CFSRs) conducted in 2001–2004 and again in 2010 by the United States Department of Health and Human Services–Administration for Children and Families (USDHHS–ACF). These results are sum-marized in Table 4.2. Substantial conformity with "Case Review System" standards, i.e., case plans developed with families, periodic reviews of plans, etc., was achieved by 13 states in the first CFSR administration and by only one state in the second administration.

Table 4.2 Number and Percentage of States Achieving Substantial Conformity on Seven CPS Systemic Performance Indicators in Round 1 and Round 2 of Child and Family Services Reviews (CFSR)

Systemic Performance Factors	Round 1 States Achieving Substantial Compliance (%) (N = 51)	Round 2 States Achieving Substantial Compliance (%) (N = 49)	States Noncompliant in Rounds 1 and 2	With Positive Change	With Negative Change
Statewide Information System	45 (88%)	38 (76%)	4	4	7
Case Review System	13 (25%)	1 (2%)	35	3	13
Quality Assurance System	35 (69%)	39 (80%)	4	13	6
Worker Training	34 (67%)	34 (69%)	6	11	9
Service Array	23 (45%)	10 (20%)	22	6	17
Responsiveness to Community	48 (94%)	48 (98%)	0	5	1
Foster/Adaptive Parent Licensing and Recruitment	42 (82%)	36 (73%)	4	7	9

Sources: CFSR Database 2001–2004 and CFSR Database 2007–2010.

http://www.acf.hhs.gov/programs/cb/cwmonitoring/index.htm#cfsr.

Conformity with quality assurance standards, on the other hand, was much higher, occurring in about 70% of the states in the first administration and 80% of the states in the second administration. A key item on which quality assurance conformity is judged (Item 3 on the CFSR Review Form) reads as follows:

> The State is operating an identifiable quality assurance system that is in place in the jurisdictions where the services included in the CFSP (Child and Family Services Plan) are provided, evaluates the quality of services, identifies strengths and needs of the service delivery system, provides relevant reports, and evaluates program improvement measures implemented.

How the quality assurance standard can be met so often in light of the dearth of case reviews is hardly intuitive.

Our reading of legislation, court orders, and monitoring reports reveals significant, albeit scattered, connections of the case practice model to three of social work's most sacred contemporary shibboleths: viz. (1) structured decision making (SDM), (2) continuous quality improvement, and (3) evidence-based best practices. SDM marks an attempt to integrate actuarial and clinical decision-making approaches in CPS case practice (Shlonsky & Wagner, 2005; Kim et al., 2008). Workers typically complete an actuarial risk assessment and complement this with a more open-ended assessment of family strengths and needs. According to Kim et al. (2008) SDM provides the structured tools "to assist social workers in making accurate and consistent decisions about the levels of risk for maltreatment found in families, to provide guidance about service provision and to assist with reunification and permanency planning" (p. 6). In New Jersey, the adoption of SDM in late 2003 (Cotton, 2003) was met with a good deal of derision. One media outlet titled the endeavor as "Assessing Families by the Numbers" and summarized the bottom line of SDM as "Don't trust your gut" (Livio, 2004, p. 1).

Although social work has long trumpeted the virtues of continuous quality improvement (CQI), citing the classics such as Crosby's *Quality Without Tears* (1995) and Peters and Waterman's *In Search of Excellence* (1982, 2004), examples of functioning CQI in social work continue to be drawn from the health profession (see, for example, Yeager, 2004; Silimperi et al., 2004). Quality improvement systems that have the best chance of working in CPS appear to be sets of circumscribed practices that (1) provide a source of clinical training for caseworkers, (2) use peer review at all levels of the organization, and (3) employ quality review data as a measure of performance and as a diagnostic tool of systemic reform (Utah Division of Child and Family Services, 1999; Golden, 2009; Noonan et al., 2009). More often than not, however, state CPS agencies adopt broad, all-encompassing approaches that can overwhelm the implementers as well as the workers. In New Jersey the CQI component of the Case Practice Model is described in Figure 4.1.

FIG 4.1 Continuous Quality Improvement Component of the Case Practice Model.

Although the Plan-Do-Check-Act figure is not referenced in the Department's Case Practice Model manual (New Jersey Department of Children and Families, 2007) it is clear that the chart is borrowed from W. Edwards Deming (Deming, 1986). A more faithful and functional representation could have included the operational indicators, assessment tools, control charts, and task assignments rather than the simply broad concepts that are displayed.

Without doubt it is the implementation of evidence-based practice (EBP) in CPS that has presented the most challenges. As defined in Roberts and Yeager (2004, p. 984), EBP is an approach to practice that requires the examination of research findings from systematic clinical research (e.g., randomized controlled clinical research) in making decisions about the care of a specific population with a specific problem. Agencies wishing to incorporate EBP into their case practice system find that evidence of efficacy and effectiveness of CPS care is weak and contradictory (Lindsey, 2004, pp. 53–55; Littell, 2008; Gambrill, 2008). It can also be quite elusive, as the following excerpt from New Jersey's Period III Monitoring Report seems to indicate. Confronted with criticism concerning the state's progress in operationalizing data and evidence-guided performance, a full 6 years after the publication of "A New Beginning" (New Jersey Department of Human Services, 2004), the Department of Children and Families "agreed to spend January through June 2010 researching the best practices of managing by data from child welfare agencies throughout the country…DCF has scheduled individual [telephone] calls with a number of states to learn about their work…" (Center for the Study of Social Policy, 2010, p. 164).

The effect of the case practice model on child safety outcomes remains indeterminate. Perhaps it will go the way of earlier case management approaches, which in Schorr's (2000) words "were subverted and swallowed up in a pathological system" (p. 130). In the meantime, however, prudence calls for treating the case practice model as both a consumer *and* a target of EBP research.

TECHNOLOGY UNPLUGGED

A cursory examination of web pages disseminated by the Administration for Children and Families (ACF)–Children's Bureau reveals what appears to be a veritable treasure trove of data and information sources created to support decision making in child protective services (U.S. Department of Health and Human Services, Children's Bureau, Administration for Children and Families, 2011). There is the state level adoption and foster care database provided through the Adoption and Foster Care Analysis and Reporting System (AFCARS). AFCARS was established in 1993 under Section 479 of the Social Security Act to ensure that states could more accurately gauge children's experiences in foster care and adoption and determine how sensitive those experiences were to changes in state policies. Several years earlier (in 1988) the Child Abuse Prevention and Treatment Act (CAPTA) had been amended to direct USDHHS to establish a national database and analysis program to make available state-level information on child abuse and neglect reporting. The National Child Abuse and Neglect Data System (NCANDS) began operations in 1990, accepting case-level and aggregated summary data from states on a voluntary basis (U.S. Department of Health and Human Services, Children's Bureau, Administration for Children and Families, 2011). In 1993 under provisions of the Omnibus Budget Reconciliation Act, an enhanced Match for Statewide Automated Child Welfare Information System (SACWIS) was made available to state child protective services agencies. If a state accepts SACWIS monies, it is expected to use SACWIS as its "sole case management automation tool." In addition,

> Staff are expected to enter all case management information into SACWIS so it holds a State's "official case record"—a complete, current, accurate, and unified case management history on all children and families served by the Title IV-B/IV-E State agency. By law, a SACWIS is required to support the reporting of data to the Adoption and Foster Care Analysis Reporting System (AFCARS) and the National Child Abuse and Neglect Data System (NCANDS). Furthermore, a SACWIS is expected to have bi-directional interfaces with a State's Title IV-A (Temporary Assistance for Needy Families), Title XIX (Medicaid), and Title IV-D (Child Support) systems. (U.S. Department of Health and Human Services, Children's Bureau, Administration for Children and Families, 2011, p. 1)

The Children's Bureau also widely publicizes data resources that focus on child outcomes. In 1994, Amendments to the Social Security Act authorized USDHHS to review state child and family service programs to ensure conformity to Title IV-B and IV-E requirements. On January 25, 2000 this review authority was expanded to include federal assessments of system performance conformity in seven areas (see Table 4.2) and on seven child outcomes, viz.:

Safety
- Children are, first and foremost, protected from abuse and neglect.
- Children are safely maintained in their homes whenever possible and appropriate.

Permanency
- Children have permanency and stability in their living situations.
- The continuity of family relationships and connections is preserved for children.

Family and child well-being
- Families have enhanced capacity to provide for their children's needs.
- Children receive appropriate services to meet their educational needs.
- Children receive adequate services to meet their physical and mental health needs.

Readers will, of course, recognize this early effort at child welfare monitoring as the inchoate form of the CFSRs system. Data from CFSR have been used by USDHHS–ACF and the states in concert with monitoring reports from SACWIS and AFCARS (U.S. Department of Health and Human Services, Children's Bureau, Administration for Children and Families, 2007–2010). Another source of child outcome data listed by the Children's Bureau originates in the National Incidence Study of Child Abuse and Neglect (NIS) first mandated by Congress in 1974 under Public Law 93–247 (Sedlak et al., 2010). NIS gathers case level data from across the United States from CPS and non-CPS sources in an effort to establish a true child maltreatment prevalence rate.

Amid this apparent gush of management information systems and cascade of data, we do not have to dive very deep to find evidence that child welfare data and data management need substantial improvement. One source of support for this contention can be found in the collection of complaints, consent decrees, and court orders that document institutional reform litigation cases. In New Jersey, for example, the state, under *Charlie and Nadine H. v. Corzine*, agreed to rectify major deficiencies in data collection and management including (1) buying the necessary computer hardware and hiring the personnel essential to implement the SACWIS system (New Jersey Department of Human Services, 2004, p. 10); (2) creation of a research and analysis unit within CPS that could support quality assurance and case management functions (p. 164); and (3) creation of an internal audit capacity capable of conducting CFSR style reviews (p. 157). Problems with CPS state data management systems have been an often-repeated refrain in litigation in Washington, DC, Illinois, California, Missouri, Colorado, and a dozen other states (Gainsborough, 2010; Malm et al., 2001; Golden, 2009; Noonan et al., 2009). Problems with CPS data and information management systems have been a frequent subject of U.S. General Accountability Office reports (United States Government Accountability Office, 1997, 2003a, 2003b). One report entitled "States Face Challenges in Developing Information Systems and Reporting Reliable Child Welfare Data" (United States Government Accountability Office, 2003a) documents the difficulties states have confronted in their efforts to maintain AFCARS and NCANDS reporting systems, including insufficient worker training, inaccurate and incomplete data entry, lack of technical support from USDHHS, and the state's inability to locate qualified vendors. Another report issued in 2003 entitled "Most States are Developing Statewide Information Systems but the Reliability of Child Welfare Data Could Be Improved" (United States Government Accountability Office, 2003b) calls attention to barriers limiting full implementation of SACWIS in many states. Here again, worker training, lack of oversight on data entry and quality, and the location of qualified computer hardware and software vendors are listed as major obstacles to successful implementations.

Insufficient and poor quality data much as a poor-functioning workforce or an unaccountable case management system could be expected to hamper CPS effectiveness in the security, safety, and well-being outcomes for children and families. Hence, it is troubling when state data systems such as SACWIS or AFCARS are alleged to increase rather than decrease paperwork (Malm et al., 2001; Golden, 2009). English, Brandford, and Coghlan (2000) trace some of this paperwork increase to workers who do not support the transition from paper to electronic case files, but find that the cumbersome nature of the computer systems also contributes to the problem. Yet as

Brittain and Hunt (2004) are correct to remark, case workers must be at the center of any beneficial management information system (MIS):

> The usefulness of a SACWIS system depends on the accuracy of the data it contains. It is essential that the frontline CPS worker enters accurate data so that management staff will have accurate information to use in deciding where to assign limited resources or to defend the actions of the agency in terms of achievement of required outcomes. If management is unable to present the work of the agency accurately, then it is less likely to obtain necessary funding resources to relieve workload pressures for the frontline worker. If the data in the automated system are unreliable, or if the data are reliable but no one values or uses the information, it is unlikely that the system will have long-term viability. The caseworker's role in the input of case data is a key aspect of agency accountability. (p. 506)

The NCANDS data reporting system, which began as a voluntary management information tool, was modified by USDHHS–ACF in 1996 to require state reporting of 12 essential CAPTA items (National Child Abuse and Neglect Data System, 2002). We reproduce these items in Figure 4.2 to show the reader how very basic this information is to CPS daily operations. Even as late as 2011, however, some states failed to report required items.

Notwithstanding this new required reporting status, our analysis of state reporting of required CAPTA items revealed that, on average, states reported about 80% of the items with only New Hampshire reporting all 12 items to USDHHS–ACF. Rather

(1) The number of children who were reported to the State during the year as abused or neglected.
(2) Of the number of children described in paragraph (1), the number with respect to whom such reports were –
    a. substantiated;
    b. unsubstantiated; or
    c. determined to be false.
(3) Of the number of children described in paragraph (2) –
    a. the number that did not receive services during the year under the State program funded under this section or an equivalent State program;
    b. the number that received services during the year under the State program funded under this section or an equivalent State program; and
    c. the number that were removed from their families during the year by disposition of the case.
(4) The number of families that received preventive services from the State during the year.
(5) The number of deaths in the State during the year resulting from child abuse or neglect.
(6) Of the number of children described in paragraph (5), the number of such children who were in foster care.
(7) The number of child protective services workers responsible for the intake and screening of reports filed in the previous year.
(8) The agency response time with respect to each such report with respect to initial investigation of reports of child abuse or neglect.
(9) The response time with respect to the provision of services to families and children where an allegation of abuse or neglect has been made.
(10) The number of child protective services workers responsible for intake, assessment, and investigation of child abuse and neglect reports relative to the number of reports investigated in the previous year.
(11) The number of children reunited with their families or receiving family preservation services that, within five years, result in subsequent substantiated reports of child abuse and neglect, including death of the child.
(12) The number of children for whom individuals were appointed by the court to represent the best interests of such children and the average number of out of court contacts between such individuals and children.

FIG 4.2 Required CAPTA Data Items.

Source: U.S. Department of Health and Human Services, Children's Bureau, Administration for Children and Families, NCANDS, 2009.

ironically, Maryland, the home of the Annie E. Casey Foundation, did not report any of the required items in 2008. No doubt, complete reporting is hampered by a demurrer statement that appears in the 1996 CAPTA amendments, declaring that

> All states that receive funds from the Basic State Grant program [are required] to work with the Secretary of the Department to provide specific data, *To the Extent Practicable*, on children who have been maltreated. (U.S. Department of Health and Human Services, Children's Bureau, Administration for Children and Families, 2002, p. 1)

It is not clear in SACWIS, AFCARS, or NCANDS legislation and/or administrative rules what sanctions states face for reporting incomplete or inaccurate data or even for nonparticipation. Withholding Title IV-B or IV-E monies is certainly an option, but the actual denial or reduction in funds portends a level of public and media outrage that few if any politicians have the stomach for. We could not find any states penalized for an NCANDS, AFCARS, or SACWIS data management or reporting transgression, and as Table 4.2 shows, according to CFSR compliance with statewide information system mandates declined by 12 percentage points from 2004 to 2010.

The CFSR monitoring system has also been subject to its own share of criticisms. Courtney, Needell, and Wulczyn (2004) assert that the performance measures employed in CFSR are not risk adjusted and therefore do not consider between-state differences in the characteristics of children and families in the formulation of conformity standards. These researchers point out, moreover, that samples from different administrations (waves) cannot be linked in any meaningful fashion. Noonan, Sabel, and Simon (2009, p. 552) grouse that CFSR performance definitions confound process and outcome measures and are based on insufficient numbers of case reviews. Golden (2009, p. 147) complains that the CFSR reviews in Washington, DC were hampered by computer connection glitches, outdated hardware, spotty staff training, and no technical assistance.

As we have seen in New Jersey and in other states under court order as well, states' lack of compliance with CFSR standards has been substantial and embarrassing (Pear, 2004; Price, 2005). It is remedies for the problem that continue to frustrate CPS policy makers.

THE SOCIAL WORK ELIXIR—TRAINING

If Alexander Pope (1733) is correct and hope springs eternal in the human breast, its corporeal form in social work must be training. Child welfare reform efforts, whether administrative, legislative, or litigated, are almost unanimous in their cry for better training for CPS workers and supervisors. Nothing less than institutional reform, moreover, calls for nothing less than transformational training, or so it would seem from the language of some legislation and many consent decrees. One popular form of transformative training seeks to increase CPS case worker competence by developing a set of core values, knowledge, and skills. This training can be quite encompassing, as the inventory drawn from DePanfilis and Salus (2003) in Figure 4.3 indicates.

CORE VALUES	CORE KNOWLEDGE	CORE SKILLS
Belief that:	**Understanding of:**	**Ability to:**
• All people have a reservoir of untapped, renewable, and expandable abilities (mental, physical, emotional, social, and spiritual) that can be used to facilitate change.	• Family systems, the family's environment, the family in a historical context, diverse family structures, and concepts of family empowerment.	• Identify strengths and needs and engage the family in a strength-based assessment process.
• Each child has a right to a permanent family.	• Individual growth and development with particular attention to attachment and bonding, separation, loss, and identity development.	• Take decisive and appropriate action when a child needs protection.
• Each child and family member should be empowered to work toward his or her own needs and goals.	• Child abuse and neglect dynamics.	• Analyze complex information.
	• Cultural diversity, the characteristics of special populations, and the implications for assessment and intervention.	• Be persistent in approach to CPS work.
Commitment to:		• Employ crisis intervention and early intervention services and strategies.
• Using a strength-based, child-centered, family-focused practice.	• Continuum of placement services including the foster care system, the residential care system, kinship care, placement prevention, familial ties maintenance, family reunification, and adoption.	• Assess a family's readiness to change and employ appropriate strategies for increasing motivation and building the helping alliance.
• Assuring the safety of children in the context of their family.	• Services including crisis intervention, parenting skills training, family counseling, conflict resolution, and individual and group counseling.	• Function as a case manager and a team member, and collaborate with other service providers.
Commitment to:		• Assess for substance abuse, domestic violence, sexual abuse, and mental illness.
• Practicing complete confidentiality.	**Command of:**	• Work with birth families to create a permanent plan for a child in foster care, kinship care, or group care.
	• Case management issues and responsibilities.	**Aptitude for:**
	• Child welfare and child protection programs and models.	• Developing and maintaining professional relationships with families.

- Ensuring accountability and an end-results orientation.
- Implementing quality professional practice.
- Continuing pursuit of knowledge and skills to effectively accomplish the mission of CPS.

Respect for:

- Persons of diverse racial, religious, ethnic, and cultural backgrounds, and a belief that there is strength in diversity.
- Each person's dignity, individuality, and right to self-determination.

- Principles of permanency planning for children and the role of out-of-home care.

Familiarity with:

- Special problems of poverty, oppression, and deprivation.
- Substance abuse issues and their effect on children and families.
- Dynamics of community and family violence, including partner abuse and the impact of trauma.
- Direct services available to children and families in the mental health, health care, substance abuse treatment, education, juvenile justice, and community systems.
- Wraparound services available for families through the economic security, housing, transportation, and job training systems.
- Legal systems related to child welfare practice.
- Political and advocacy processes and how they relate to funding and acquiring services.

- Listening.
- Remaining flexible.
- Working with involuntary clients, including those who are hostile or resistant.
- Working with legal systems, including documentation and court testimony.
- Empowering the child and family to sustain gains and use family and community supports.

Expertise in:

- Assessing for abuse, neglect, and the safety of the child and others in the family setting.
- Negotiating, implementing, and evaluating the case plan with the family.
- Working with the family and key supports to accomplish the service agreement goals.
- Applying knowledge of human behavior and successful intervention methods with children and adolescents at various developmental stages.

FIG 4.3 CPS Worker Values, Knowledge and Skills Essential to Professional Competence

Source: DePanfilis and Salus, 2003

In New Jersey, under the modified settlement, newly hired workers are required to undertake preservice training, all workers are mandated to take concurrent and in-service training, and supervisors are required to undertake ongoing supervisory training in an effort to elevate core competencies (Center for the Study of Social Policy, 2007). Much of this training is provided by the state's New Jersey Child Welfare Training Academy, although universities and private sector consultants have been retained to do CPS training as well (New Jersey Department of Children and Families, 2006; Mahon, 2008; Nolan, 2007; ACTION for Child Protection, 2007).

Related to core competency training is training that attempts to teach social workers how to engage in critical thinking (Gambrill, 1997; Graef & Potter, 2002; Gibbs & Gambrill, 1999). In the words of Gibbs and Gambrill, critical thinking

> involves the careful examination and evaluation of beliefs and actions. It requires paying attention to the process of reasoning, not just the product. In this broad definition, critical thinking is much more than the appraisal of claims and arguments. Well-reasoned thinking is a form of creation and construction. Reasoning has a purpose. (p. 3)

Gambrill (1997) points out that social workers are often flooded by information and emotion that decrease their capacity to make wise decisions. Faced with the overload, they often rely on heuristics, hunches, preconceptions, and dogmatism to help them get through work days, accumulating errors of omission and commission along the way.

We are not usually told in the social work training literature just how difficult it is to teach critical thinking. The cognitive psychologist, Daniel Willingham (2007) maintains, as does a recent publication of the National Research Council (2007), that inquiry methods such as critical thinking, absent knowledge of professional or science content, is not likely to lead to more proficient thinking. In other words, seeing both sides of an argument, being open to new evidence, deducing and inferring conclusions from available facts, solving problems, or even understanding what evidence *is* requires that a CPS decision maker have a solid knowledge base in child development, family dynamics, environmental hazards, etc. This, of course, brings us full circle, back to the quality of the workforce being trained. Steib and Blome (2003) argue that this issue has not received anywhere near the attention it deserves in institutional reform litigation settlements or in the adoption of new child protective services legislation.

If knowledge of child development, family dynamics, predator behavior, etc. is indeed an essential prerequisite for any real training impact, our current child welfare workforce appears to start from a point of considerable disadvantage. The Annie E. Casey Foundation (2003, pp. 2–3) study, introduced earlier, describes a CPS workforce with low SAT scores and low class rank in college with education and training that do not match the roles and demands of the job. There is some evidence that workers with BSWs or MSWs do possess significantly more relevant knowledge (Booz-Allen & Hamilton, 1987; Albers et al., 1993); however, as we noted earlier, approximately 80% of CPS workers do not hold these degrees (Ryan et al., 2006).

Vastly outnumbering the occasional reports of "effective" CPS training (Howing et al., 1992; Preston, 2004) are the spate of research articles and commentaries documenting training shortcomings and failures (Rosenthal & Waters, 2006; Zell, 2006; Mor Barak et al., 2001; American Humane Association, 2002). Using data from the first administration of the CFSR, Milner and Hornsby (2004) identify a number of problems in state CPS training regimens including inconsistent intrastate training requirements, insufficient time devoted to training, lack of standardized or core requirements for ongoing training, the poor quality of some training content, and lack of training reinforcement. In our analysis of CFSR data on training (see Table 4.2) we find that about 70% of states achieved substantial compliance with federal standards. CFSR compliance here means

- The State is operating a staff development and training program that supports the goals and objectives in the Child and Family Services Plan (CFSP), addresses services provided under Titles IV-B and IV-E, and provides initial training for all staff who deliver these services.
- The State provides for ongoing training for staff that addresses the skills and knowledge base needed to carry out their duties with regard to the services included in the CFSP.
- The State provides training for current or prospective foster parents, adoptive parents, and staff of State licensed or approved facilities that care for children receiving foster care or adoption assistance under title IV-E that addresses the skills and knowledge base needed to carry out their duties with regard to foster and adopted children.

There are indications that CFSR compliance may be somewhat ephemeral with 11 states moving from noncompliance to compliance status between 2004 and 2010 even as nine other states fell out of compliance (Table 4.2).

It is important to note here that although many millions of dollars continue to be spent on CPS training, we lack any rigorous research or data to confirm that training increases core competencies, critical thinking, or any other important work performance outcome (see, for example, Dickinson & Gil de Gibaja, 2004). Although we patiently wait for such evidence, CPS continues to go to work each day (much in the manner of former Secretary of Defense Donald Rumsfeld) with the workforce it has rather than the well-prepared workforce it wished it had.

CPS OPERATIONS AND CHILD OUTCOMES

In the institutional reform litigation around the country, performance timeframes, benchmarks, and enforceable elements have generally targeted changes in CPS operations and management. Improvements in child outcomes are treated, more or less, as an ineffable—the implicit and natural consequence of CPS structure and process reform. This reticence to specify the anticipated child outcomes of a CPS intervention is not simply an oversight; it has deep, historical roots. Halting efforts to delineate the changes in child and family functioning that could be expected from an efficient, professionally run CPS agency can be traced back to the creation of the U.S. Children's Bureau in 1912 (Bremner, 1971). Since that time, a multitude of conceptual and operational definitions had emerged even as the prospects for an overall consensus dimmed (American Humane Association et al., 1993).

As criticism of the quality and accessibility of public social services mounted in the 1960s, 1970s, and 1980s, public tolerance for a CPS agency with a vague and often equivocal mission shrank as well. In 1993, the first national roundtable on CPS outcome measures was convened by the American Humane Association and the National Association of Public Child Welfare administrators in San Antonio, Texas. The purpose of this professional gathering was summed up succinctly in the opening remarks of Donald Schmid (1993), a CPS director from North Dakota:

> As public child welfare systems, we often do not say what the desired outcome of our intervention is—perhaps because there is no consensus as to what it should be. And instead, we just absorb the verbal onslaught. (p. 2)

The work of this roundtable, nine subsequent roundtables and a consortium of national organizations, led by the American Humane Association and the Annie E. Casey Foundation, helped produce the first nationwide consensus on CPS child welfare outcomes (Alsop & Winterfeld, 1999; McDaniel, 2004; Fisher et al., 1999). Figure 4.4 displays the three general domains and 23 outcome indicators articulated by the American Humane Society and Annie E. Casey Foundation to form the concept of CPS-influenced, child outcomes.

The indicators are wide ranging and include measures of maltreatment recurrence, family preservation, general health, academic performance, and cultural sensitivity. If the architecture of this outcome categorization looks familiar to readers, it is because these domains and measures have been incorporated, mutatis mutandis, into USDHHS–ACF's CFSR child outcome standards, which are now employed nationwide. As Figure 4.5 shows, CFSR utilizes a three-domain 23-indicator structure like the earlier conceptualization but attempts to reduce the amount of child outcome–system outcome obfuscation evident in the AHA/Casey formulation.

The specification of CPS-induced, child and family functioning outcomes can be a risky enterprise in light of the paucity of evidence that CPS actions significantly impact safety, permanency, or well-being. Lindsey (2004), for example, concludes after his review of empirical results that "on balance, it is fair to say that there has been limited evidence of the effectiveness of casework intervention" (p. 53). A 2006 report issued by the U.S. General Accountability Office concluded that there was little evidence that Title IV-B services had any impact on children's outcomes. One damning indication of the fragility of the CPS service-outcome connection can be found in the CFSR data on child impact. We summarize, in Table 4.3, the numbers and percentage of states that achieved substantial compliance on the safety, permanency, and well-being standards promulgated by USDHHS–ACF.

Domain 1	Outcome Indicators	Domain 2	Outcome Indicators	Domain 3	Outcome Indicators
Family Support	Change in parents' application of knowledge of children's physical and developmental needs as measured by an appropriate instrument.	Permanency	Post-finalization adoption disruption.	Well-Being	General physical health functioning as measured by an appropriate instrument or program such as EPSDT.
Safety	Recurrence of substantiated or indicated child abuse or neglect (while open for child welfare services).	Permanency	Length of stay between the placement date of the first temporary out-of-home placement and the date of permanent placement.	Well-Being	Child is drug and alcohol free.
Safety	Recurrence of substantiated or indicated child abuse or neglect (within a specified period of time following case closure).	Permanency	Children placed in out-of-home care who are placed with providers who are relatives or kin.	Well-Being	Caregiver is drug and alcohol free.
Safety	Recurrence of substantiated or indicated child abuse or neglect (for families involved in a prior unsubstantiated report of child abuse and neglect).	Permanency	Children placed in out-of-home care who are placed with siblings.	Well-Being	Safe and adequate housing.

FIG 4.4 General Domains and Outcome Indicators of CPS-Influenced Child Outcomes

Domain 1	Outcome Indicators	Domain 2	Outcome Indicators	Domain 3	Outcome Indicators
Safety	Post-reunification disruptions.	Permanency	Children placed in out-of-home care who are placed within the school district of origin.	Well-Being	Basic needs (food and clothing) are provided.
Decision Making	Ratio of percentage of children by race or ethnicity in caseload to percentage in general population.	Permanency	Children placed in out-of-home care who are reunified with family.	Well-Being	Academic performance of children in an appropriate school setting (while open for child welfare services)
Decision Making Satisfaction	Satisfaction of children with quality and effectiveness of services.	Well-Being	Change in frequency of positive child-caregiver interactions and/or attachment measured by an appropriate instrument.	Well-Being	Appropriately identifies with own ethnic or racial background.
		Well-Being	Children's cognitive, physical, and mental functioning in relation to developmental milestones.	Well-Being	Number of school suspensions/expulsions for children (while open for services).

FIG 4.4 (*Continued*)

SAFETY OUTCOMES	PERMANENCY OUTCOMES	WELL-BEING OUTCOMES
Safety Outcome 1: Children are first and foremost, protected from abuse and neglect	**Permanency Outcome 1:** Children have permanency and stability in their living situations	**Well-Being Outcome 1:** Families have enhanced capacity to provide for children's needs
Item 1: Timeliness of investigations	Item 5: Foster care re-entry	Item 17: Needs/services of child, parents, and foster parents
Item 2: Repeat maltreatment	Item 6: Stability of foster care placements	Item 18: Child/family involvement in case planning
Safety Outcome 2: Children are safely maintained in their homes when possible and appropriate	Item 7: Permanency goal for child	Item 19: Worker visits with child
Item 3: Services to prevent removal	Item 8: Reunification, guardianship, and placement with relatives	Item 20: Worker visits with parents
Item 4: Risk of harm	Item 9: Adoption	**Well-Being Outcome 2:** Children receive services to meet their educational needs
	Item 10: Other planned living arrangement	Item 21: Educational needs of child
	Permanency Outcome 2: The continuity of family relationships and connections is preserved	**Well-Being Outcome 3:** Children receive services to meet their physical and mental health needs
	Item 11: Proximity of placement	Item 22: Physical health of child
	Item 12: Placement with siblings	Item 23: Mental health of child
	Item 13: Visiting with parents and siblings in foster care	
	Item 14: Preserving Connections	
	Item 15: Relative Placement	
	Item 16: Relationship of child in care with parents	

FIG 4.5 CFSR Three-Domain 23-Indicator Structure

We are struck immediately by the almost unimaginably low levels of compliance during the first administration of CFSR that only drop lower at the second administration. The juxtaposition of Tables 4.2 and 4.3 can effectively change astonishment into bewilderment: Why do such high levels of compliance on quality assurance, worker training, computer technology, and community relations, all important organizational inputs, coexist with such incredibly low levels of outcome compliance?

The CFSR reviews provide CPS administrators and policy makers with a small window into the impact of agency interventions. As a management tool, however, CFSR data are of limited utility due to the small number of observations, the use of case cohorts instead of panels, and the infrequency of reviews.

The NCANDS database offers an alternative means of linking operations to outcomes, especially after 1996 when the reporting of many CAPTA items was made mandatory. This database comprises 146 child-level data elements and 25 agency-level elements. As we noted earlier, however, NCANDS reporting has not been uniform or

Table 4.3 Number and Percentage of States Achieving Substantial Conformity on Seven CPS Child Outcome Measures in Round 1 and Round 2 of Child and Family Services Reviews (CFSR)

Child Outcome Measures	Round 1 States Achieving Substantial Compliance (%) N = 51	Round 2 States Achieving Substantial Compliance (%) N = 49	States Noncompliant in Rounds 1 and 2	With Positive Change	With Negative Change
Safety Outcome 1 Child Protection	6 (12%)	0 (0%)	43	2	6
Safety Outcome 2 In-home safety	6 (12%)	0 (0%)	44	2	5
Permanency Outcome 1 Living Situations	0 (0%)	0 (0%)	49	2	0
Permanency Outcome 2 Family Preservation	7 (14%)	0 (0%)	42	2	7
Well-Being 1 Family Capacity	0 (0%)	0 (0%)	49	2	0
Well-Being 2 Services	16 (31%)	10 (20%)	28	8	11
Well-Being 3 Health Needs	1 (2%)	0 (0%)	48	2	1

Sources: CFSR Database 2001–2004 and CFSR Database 2007–2010.

complete. Our examination of reporting patterns since 1992 indicates that required CAPTA items documenting response time with respect to investigations (eight items), response time with respect to services (nine items), and families who received preventive services (four items) were the most often unreported, whereas required items documenting child outcomes tended to be more consistently reported.

NCANDS data have been used by the Children's Bureau to help evaluate its own management and performance (U.S. Department of Health and Human Services, Children's Bureau, Administration for Children and Families, 2010). Among the measures it employs for the purpose are the following:

> Improvement in States' average response time between maltreatment report and investigation. This is based on the median of States' reported average response time, in hours, from screened-in reports to the initiation of the investigation as reported in the NCANDS Agency File. The objective is to improve the efficiency of child protective services and to reduce the risk of maltreatment to potential victims (CAPTA). (U.S. Department of Health and Human Services, Children's Bureau, Administration for Children and Families, 2010, p. 3)

Given the widespread underreporting of response times by states, the Children's Bureau management report must be incomplete as well. Inasmuch as the Children's Bureau appears to view NCANDS more as "a critical source of information for many publications, reports and activities of the federal government and other groups" (U.S. Department of Health and Human Services, Children's Bureau, Administration for Children and Families, 2009, p. 9) than as a state CPS management tool, the latter function has not received much nurturing and remains in a primitive state.

A third source of information on the influence that CPS operations and services exert on child outcomes comes from the periodic research effort called the National Incidence Study of Child Abuse and Neglect (NIS). Four NIS studies have been commissioned by Congress since 1980 with the most recent data collection, NIS-4, taking place in 2005 and 2006. Unlike CFSR and NCANDS information, which is gathered by federal and state CPS authorities, NIS is the work of private consultants working under federal contract. NIS employs a methodology for detecting the incidence of child maltreatment termed the "sentinel approach." In addition to CPS agencies, which serve as the community's official sentinel, unofficial "sentinels" comprise professionals from agencies such as police departments, public schools, day care centers, hospitals, social service agencies, mental health services, public housing and shelters, public health departments, and county probation who encounter children on a daily basis and in the course of their job duties serve as lookouts for victims of child abuse and neglect (Sedlak et al., 2010, pp. 2–4). NIS-4 design included data on 6,208 children identified by sentinels and 10,677 reported to CPS agencies during a 3-month period gleaned from a nationally representative sample of 122 U.S. counties. Child abuse and neglect definitions followed the same standards of harm used by NCANDS and CFSR.

The release of the NIS report in February 2010 occurred with little federal and professional fanfare; it did, however, capture some media attention. The principal finding of the report that the incidence of child abuse in America had dropped from 1,553,800 children in 1993 to 1,256,600 in 2006, or 26%, was indeed a major news story (The Associated Press, 2010; Crary, 2010). Another finding from NIS-4, which did not receive extensive press coverage and which the authors of the report referred as an "enigma" (Sedlak et al., 2010, p. 82), disclosed that only 32% of the children who were found by the research team to have met the harm standard had their cases investigated by CPS. This low proportion of CPS investigations repeated a pattern that had occurred in NIS-1 conducted in 1980 (33%), NIS-2 in 1986 (44%), and NIS-3 (28%).

The consistently low levels of CPS investigation in the face of tangible child maltreatment hazard reported by sentinel organizations present a second and perhaps larger enigma than either the researchers or the press acknowledged. Why do CPS investigations, when measured against professionally defined harm standards (hazard), remain consistently low while child maltreatment rates experience dramatic rises and falls? Between 1986 and 1993, child maltreatment cases are estimated to have risen from 931,000 to 1,553,800, or 56% (Sedlak et al., 2010), followed by a precipitous decline between 1993 and 2006. Our examination of NCANDS data reveals that from 1990 to 2006 CPS investigations/assessments did not remain stable nor did they experience major peaks and valleys. Investigations, in fact, rose steadily from 36.1 per 1000 children to 47.9 per 1000 (U.S. Department of Health and Human Services, Children's Bureau, Administration for Children and Families, 2006, 2010). It would appear that CPS has been busy investigating a mix of cases that is distinctive from those inspired by epidemiological criterion—a mix we believe is in large part outrage driven.

In his commentary on the NIS-4 report, David Finklehor, a well-respected child welfare researcher, attributed declines in substantiated child maltreatment to "mobilization around the issue" of child abuse and neglect and more CPS workers being hired (The Associated Press, 2010). Linda Spears, a vice president at the Child Welfare League of America, linked the results to more public awareness and public intolerance around child abuse (Crary, 2010). "Mobilized intolerance" is perhaps just another way of labeling socially outraged risk expression.

CHILD FATALITIES AS OUTRAGE GENERATORS

The child outcome seen by the general public, politicians, and the media as the most important indicator of CPS performance is, without question, death from exposure to abuse or neglect (Lindsey, 1994, 2004; U.S. Department of Health and Human Services, Children's Bureau, Administration for Children and Families, 2006). And although it is accurate to categorize some child fatalities as a consequence of child maltreatment, the proportion of these deaths that could have been prevented remains controversial. Duncan Lindsey (2004, p. 144) calls child fatalities an "outlier," sharing with Jane Waldfogel (1998) the opinion that child deaths are rare events that shed little light on CPS decisions to protect children. If by outlier Lindsey and Waldfogel mean that child deaths are poor or inappropriate indicators of CPS safety or well-being outcome, we concur. Child fatalities, however, are not merely inappropriate outcome measures; in our opinion, they are *major causes* of the key decisions that comprise the CPS decision flow, viz. screening cases in or out, investigation, substantiation, placement, and closing.

Treating child deaths from abuse and neglect as an exogenous variable and not as an endogenous outcome is the logical extension of an outrage perspective on CPS risk assessment and management. Institutional reform litigation and sex offender registration/notification laws can be hypothesized to absorb some of the influence that the archetypical fatality has on CPS operations, but deaths themselves can have a profound and lasting impact. Malm et al. (2001) cite the beating death of Kayla McKean as the biggest impetus for changes in the Florida child welfare system; Westbrook, Ellis, and Ellett (2006) recall a 1998 death in Georgia that did the same in that state. We have witnessed the aftermath of child deaths in New Jersey, Illinois, Washington, DC, New York, and California (Therolf, 2010; Rutenberg & Kaufman, 2006) and the story lines here are similar. Gustavsson and MacEachron (2002) and Geen and Tumlin (1999) have shown us that child deaths have profound and sometimes devastating effects on CPS workers. Their effects on entire organizations should not be underestimated.

Since the early 1990s, child fatalities have risen at a slow and steady rate from about 1.65 per 100,000 to 2.35 per 100,000 in 2007 (U.S. Department of Health and Human Services, Children's Bureau, Administration for Children and Families, 2010). During this same period, overall child maltreatment rates have dropped whereas CPS investigation rates have risen. Do some children have to die before sufficient decisions are made to protect children? In Chapter 6 we try to answer this question with a bit of econometric modeling.

5

SOCIETAL FACTORS AFFECTING
CHILD WELFARE
POVERTY, INCOME SUPPORT, AND RACE

"The greatest of evils and the worst of crimes is poverty. Our first duty—a duty which every other consideration should be sacrificed—is not to be poor."
George Bernard Shaw (1901)
Major Barbara (Preface)

In Chapter 4, our focus was placed on the workforce, financial, and other factors internal to the child welfare system that researchers and child welfare experts have linked to child protection decisions. We now turn our attention to the psychological, ecological, and broad social environmental influences that have often been viewed as causes of child maltreatment. We take longer looks at the roles attributed to poverty, income support policies, and race.

CHILD AND FAMILY DEFICIENCIES

Early theories of child maltreatment placed the blame squarely on the perpetrating individual, and sometimes even on the child victim, pointing to a psychopathological etiology (Kempe et al., 1962; Galdston, 1965; Steele & Pollock, 1968; Shorkey, 1980; Polansky et al., 1981; Wolfe, 1985). This "psychopathological" perspective assumes that the parent or the caretaker suffers from some form of psychological malady or deficiency that is at the root of maltreatment. Some have traced the illness to a "role reversal" belief the perpetrator may hold (Morris & Gould, 1963; Holder & Corey, 1995), whereas others claim that the illness can also be the result of the perpetrator's own history of abuse or neglect (Kempe, 1973; Brown & Daniels, 1968; Steele & Pollock, 1968; Green, Gaines, & Sandgrun, 1974; Newberger et al., 1975; Zalba, 1967). Where role reversal is at work, the perpetrator holds a distorted perception of the nature of childhood in which the parent views the child as a source of emotional support rather than a dependent organism that must be cared for and nurtured (Morris & Gould, 1963). This, in turn, leads to unrealistic or grossly inaccurate assumptions on the part of the parent regarding the child's developing competencies, e.g., attainment of developmental milestones such as walking, talking, and bladder and bowel control, believing these to take place at a much earlier age than is usual (Green, 1976; Paulson & Blake, 1969; Steele & Pollock, 1968).

That the perpetrators' psychological defects can also arise from his or her own history of maltreatment has a long history itself in the child welfare literature (Kempe, 1973; Brown & Daniels, 1968; Steele & Pollock, 1968; Green, Gaines, & Sandgrun, 1974; Newberger et al., 1975; Zalba, 1967). The mechanisms through which childhood abuse translates to abusive behavior in adulthood have been tied to observational learning, i.e., simply imitating our parent's abusive behavior (Young, 1964; Baker & Ball, 1969; Owens & Strauss, 1975), or emotional deprivation resulting from not experiencing warmth, love, and nurturance from our own parent (Green, 1976; Brown & Daniels, 1968; Melnick & Hurley, 1969). Belsky (1978) asserts that abuse and neglect and early rejection hamper personality development of young children, who can turn out to be aggressive, insensitive, and noncaring adults.

The psychopathological model, with its focus on "kinds of people" theories (Iverson & Segal, 1990), has identified specific characteristics of maltreating parents that distinguish them from nonmaltreating parents. These characteristics include impulsivity, immaturity, substance abuse, depression (Steele & Pollock, 1968; Kempe et al., 1962; Bennie & Sclare, 1969; Chaffin, Kelleher, & Hollenberg, 1996), poor emotional control and inadequacy (Bennie & Sclare, 1969), self-centeredness, hypersensitivity, aggression (Kempe et al., 1962), pervasive anger (Zalba, 1971), dependency, egocentricity, narcissism, and insecurity (Steele & Pollock, 1968).

Other theories that explain child maltreatment at the individual (ontogenetic) level include "the effect of the child on caregiver model" (Belsky, 1978), which traces the causes of maltreatment to the physical and psychological characteristics of the child victim (Gil, 1971; Birrell & Birrell, 1969; Johnson & Morse, 1968; Schneider-Rosen & Cicchetti, 1984; Wolfe & Mosk, 1983; Burrell, Thomson, & Sexton, 1994). Some empirical evidence exists that supports the claim that maltreated children tend to be atypical, difficult to manage, and are often "whiny, fussy, listless, chronically crying, demanding, stubborn, resistive, negativistic, pallid, sickly, emaciated, fearful, panicky, unsmily..." (Johnson & Morse, 1968). Other characteristics of abused children identified in the literature include low birth weight and early gestational age (Martin et al., 1974; Fontana, 1971; Elmer & Gregg, 1967).

Psychopathological theories, whether parent or child oriented, according to Iversen and Segal (1990) are more helpful for predictive, rather than explanatory purposes. These theories have been subject to extensive empirical testing, however (Iversen & Segal, 1990), and the evidence that has emerged provides less than convincing support for psychopathology as fully explaining abusive behavior. The research shows that many of the characteristics that identify maltreating individuals are not unique to them; in fact, they are also shared by nonmaltreating parents. And in an environment increasingly sensitive to social justice and macropolicy influence, individual and/or family psychopathology now seems quaint or even victim blaming.

ECOLOGICAL APPROACHES TO CHILD ABUSE

The idea that child maltreatment is a result of forces that reside outside the individual—in the larger social environment—can be traced to the work of David Gil (1970,

1974), Urie Bronfenbrenner (1977, 1979), and James Garbarino (1981). In Gil's (1970) view, child maltreatment is the result of a complex interaction of multidimensional factors. He uses two broad conceptual components to organize his social model. One specifies the "levels of manifestation," in which different forms of maltreatment are believed to occur at the interpersonal level (e.g., abuse at home), at the institutional level (e.g., corporal punishment in the school), and at the societal level (e.g., social policies that are child unfriendly). The second component contains a three-tiered "levels of causation," which organizes the social and environmental factors that contribute to child maltreatment through (1) the dominant social philosophy and the value system emanating from it, e.g., a value system that is consistent with child maltreatment, (2) the social definition of children's rights and the extent to which society sanctions or condones violence, especially toward children, and (3) the environmental factors such as stress or frustration triggered by poverty, which in turn may cause maltreatment.

In 1977, Urie Bronfenbrenner (1977, 1979) proposed an ecological theory of maltreatment, specifying that the etiology of maltreatment resides amid complex interactions between the individual child, his or her family, the community, and the social and cultural environment in which the child lives. Bronfenbrenner's "systems approach," in fact, identified four "elements": the microsystem, comprising the individual child and the family, the mesosystem, composed of the interactions among the different social spheres such as home and school where the child participates, an exosystem, in which decisions that could have a bearing on the child's quality of life are made but where the child does not participate (e.g., school boards, parents' workplace), and the macrosystem, which provides a broad ideological, political, social, and cultural framework within which all the other systems operate. The ecological approach posits that maltreatment occurs when one or more of these systems experience failure.

Garbarino (1981) uses Bronfenbrenner's ecological framework as a guide in identifying "situations in which the conditions of life conspire to compound rather than counteract the deficiencies and vulnerabilities of parents" (p. 232) and identifies solutions that focus jointly on social support and social control, instead of solutions that focus on individuals. Garbarino identifies the mesosystem as the main culprit, however, and claims that social isolation of maltreating families is the linchpin that binds individualistic and ecologic exegesis. Garbarino and Gilliam (1980) note that

> social isolation is the weak link that is responsible for abuse and neglect. Isolation from potent, prosocial support systems places even the strong and competent in jeopardy, and often sends the weak or incompetent over the edge when stresses from within and outside the family conspire. (p. 31)

It is this isolation, moreover, contends Garbarino (1981), that generates the destructive emotional climate so prevalent in the home life of abused and neglected children. There is quite a bit of empirical support for Garbarino's contention—general isolation of the abusive or neglectful family from the community is an often reported finding in child abuse and neglect cases (Elmer, 1967; Lauer et al., 1974; Polansky et al., 1981; Schneider et al., 1976; Ten Broeck, 1977. It has also been argued that social isolation itself is a function of the level of economic resources and social supports (e.g., the amount of tangible goods and intangible emotional resources) available in a community, as well as the degree of residential mobility evidenced in the community (Camasso & Wilkinson, 1990). The social isolation–resource depletion hypothesis proposes that child maltreatment may be the result of a family living under poor economic circumstances in highly transient neighborhoods with the attendant inadequate social supports.

Iverson and Segal (1990) point out that the principal advantage of ecological theory—its breadth—may also be its major disadvantage. The theory's test requires capturing the dynamic interplay and/or reciprocal influence of factors at the individual, family, school, peer group, community, and society level. Empirical investigations of such "tangled web of pathology" models are typically confronted by statistical issues such as unidentified and/or untestable systems. Over the past 25 years, attempts have been made to isolate key components from this tangled web, most notably poverty, public welfare, and race.

ECONOMIC AND POVERTY APPROACHES

No matter the *causes* of poverty and regardless of whether the explanation centers on the individual or societal opportunity structures, there is broad consensus in the scholarly community that poverty and child maltreatment are strongly related. This consensus has emerged from numerous correlational studies that show that children who live in poor households are much more likely than nonpoor children to be the subject of both actual and reported maltreatment (see, for example, Gil, 1970; Brown, 1984; Pelton, 1989; Gelles, 1992; U.S. Department of Health and Human Services, 1981, 1994; Coulton et al., 1995; Courtney et al., 1996; Bartholet, 1999; Drake & Pandey, 1996; Drake et al., 2003; Fluke et al., 2003; Sedlak et al., 2010).

Pelton (1989), in his book *For Reasons of Poverty*, traces this poverty–child welfare relationship back to 1880, arguing that "the really fundamental problems of child welfare in this country do not lie within the child welfare system, but within the larger economic and social welfare systems of our society....the issue that must be addressed is poverty itself, not merely some of its by-products" (p. 176). Pelton goes on to blame the psychodynamic medical model for depicting child maltreatment as an epidemic that is "classless," thereby diverting attention from real causes of abuse and neglect. Pelton sees a direct link between poverty, adoption, and lack of preventive support and says that despite official and public outcries to preserve families, the child welfare system continues to remove children from their homes and place them in adoptive or foster care for reasons of poverty alone (p. 52). Lindsey (1994) concurs based on his own review of studies on the reasons for child removal: "Overall the data examined....clearly demonstrate that child abuse is not the major reason children are removed from their parents. Rather, inadequacy of income, more than any other factor, constitutes the reason that children are removed...More and more the variables we thought had some bearing in deciding the issue appear a smoke screen masking the real issue, which is poverty" (p. 155).

The four National Incidence Studies (NIS) offer evidence that appears to support Pelton and Lindsey's assertions. Table 5.1 summarizes the family income findings from the NIS reports. All the NIS reports have consistently found a robustly significant relationship between low socioeconomic status and child maltreatment. The first study, the NIS-1 (U.S. Department of Health and Human Services, 1981) (Table 5.1a), reported that there was "a very strong measured relationship between family income and recognized maltreatment: the estimated overall incidence for children in families with income under $7,000 (27.3 children per 1000) is ten times higher than the estimated incidence for children in families with annual incomes of $25,000 or more" (p. 21) and that the relationship is substantially more pronounced for neglect than abuse. Moreover, the study found that 43% of the child victims lived in families with income less than $7,000 whereas the comparable number for the general U.S. child population was only 17%. Similarly, although 45% of U.S. children lived in families with income under $15,000, 82% of victims of maltreatment fell in this income category.

The NIS-2, conducted between 1986 and 1987, again found "profound" effects of income on child maltreatment (U.S. Department of Health and Human Services, 1988). Table 5.1b shows that the overall rate of maltreatment was more than five times higher among children from families with annual incomes lower than $15,000 (in 1986). In addition, the rate of physical abuse was four times higher and the rate of neglect was nearly eight times higher for children in these lower income families, compared to children in families with incomes of $15,000 or above.

The third study in the series (Table 5.1c), NIS-3, yet again showed "significant and pervasive" differences in maltreatment incidence with respect to family income (Sedlak & Broadhurst, 1996). Children living in families in the lowest income category experienced the highest rates of maltreatment incidence. For example, children who lived with family incomes of under $15,000 had more than twice the maltreatment rate of children with family incomes between $15,000 and $29,999, and 22 times the incidence rate of the highest income group. The abuse rate for the lowest income group was 14 times the abuse rate of the children in the highest income category and their incidence of neglect was 45 times higher!

The NIS-4 uses two measures of poverty—the parent's employment status and a composite socioeconomic status (SES). The latter measure combines information on household income, parent's education, and participation in a poverty program. Families who fall at the low end of each of these variables (household income under $15,000, parent is a high school dropout, and family participates in a poverty program) are classified as low SES and the others are classified as not of low SES. The study reports a strong association between parental employment and incidence of maltreatment. Children whose parents were either not in the labor force or unemployed were at a significantly higher risk of maltreatment compared to children with employed parents (22.6 and 15.9 per 1000 compared to 7.6). The study also finds that children from low-SES families experienced a maltreatment rate that is five times that of children in families that are not categorized as low SES. These children's neglect rate was nearly eight times higher, and their abuse rate was more than three times higher.

Table 5.1 Poverty Evidence from the National Incidence Study of Child Abuse and Neglect (NIS)

(a) Study: NIS-1 (1979–1980)

Income Level	Abuse	Neglect	Total
< $7,000	34	53	43
$7,000–$14,999	44	34	39
$15,000–$24,999	15	10	13
$25,000 or more	7	4	6

Numbers shown are percentage of children in each income group

(b) Study: NIS-2 (1986–1987)

Income Level	Abuse	Neglect	Total
< $15,000	16.6	17.3	32.3
$15,000 or more	4.1	2.2	6.1

Numbers shown are rates per 1000 children

(c) Study: NIS-3 (1993–1995)

Income Level	Abuse	Neglect	Total
< $15,000	22.2	27.2	47
$15,000–$29,999	9.7	11.3	20
$30,000 or more	1.6	0.6	2.1

Numbers shown are rates per 1000 children

(d) Study: NIS-4 (2005–2006)

Parent's Employment Status	Abuse	Neglect	Total
Parent not in labor force	9.6	14.8	22.6
Parent unemployed	4.8	12.1	15.9
Parent employed	3.9	4.1	7.6
Socioeconomic Status	*Abuse*	*Neglect*	*Total*
Low SES	7.7	16.1	22.5
Not low SES	2.5	2.2	4.4

Numbers shown are rates per 1000 children

Sources: U.S. Department of Health and Human Services (1981, 1988), Sedlack and Broadhurst (1996), and Sedlak et al. (2010).

A second source of national data on child maltreatment is the National Child Abuse and Neglect Data System (NCANDS). These data also indicate robust relationship between state poverty level and incidence of child maltreatment. In Table 5.2 we present a comparison of various CPS outcomes among the 10 states with the highest child poverty rates and those with the lowest child poverty rates in 2008. Maltreatment reporting rates in high-poverty states range from 17 to 49 for an average of 30 reports

Table 5.2 Poverty and Child Maltreatment, 2008

Top 10 Poverty States

State	Reporting Rate	Maltreatment Rate	Substantiation Rate	Number of Fatalities	Fatality Rate
District of Columbia	43.06	24.27	0.88	8	0.073
Arizona	17.07	2.03	0.19	11	0.006
New Mexico	28.54	11.16	0.42	19	0.037
Kentucky	49.48	18.07	0.32	22	0.022
Alabama	17.54	8.24	0.49	20	0.018
Mississippi	24.48	10.24	0.46	17	0.022
Indiana	42.02	13.77	0.35	34	0.021
Louisiana	19.15	9.1	0.48	30	0.027
Texas	25.08	10.49	0.47	223	0.033
Oklahoma	38.87	12.42	0.34	31	0.034
Average	30.529	11.979	0.44	41.5	0.0293

Bottom 10 Poverty States

State	Reporting Rate	Maltreatment Rate	Substantiation Rate	Number of Fatalities	Fatality Rate
New Hampshire	27.3	3.81	0.17	0	0
Utah	23.11	15.29	0.69	15	0.017
Alaska	43.59	25.12	0.55	2	0.011
Vermont	18.57	5.33	0.29	1	0.008
Maryland	N/A	N/A	N/A	N/A	N/A
Connecticut	29.84	11.79	0.43	6	0.007
Wyoming	18.17	5.52	0.31	1	0.008
Wisconsin	19.91	4.37	0.24	30	0.023
Washington	23.07	4.36	0.2	23	0.015
Delaware	30.16	10.95	0.59	2	0.01
Average	25.97	9.62	0.39	8.89	0.011

Notes: Reporting rate = (number of children reported and investigated by CPS/state child population) • 1000

Maltreatment rate = (number of child victims/state child population) • 1000

Substantiation rate = fraction of investigations that results in a child victim

Fatality rate = (number of fatalities/state child population) • 1000

Sources: Child maltreatment data are from the NCANDS retrieved from the National Data Archive on Child Abuse and Neglect (NDACAN), Cornell University; data on poverty and state child population are from the U.S. Census Bureau, Current Population Survey, Annual Demographic Supplement.

Table 5.3 Correlation of Child Poverty Rate and CPS Outcomes—2000–2008

Year	Reporting Rate	Maltreatment Rate	Fatality Rate
2000	0.18	0.15	0.13
2001	0.13	0.03	0.49**
2002	0.23	0.14	0.49**
2003	0.27*	0.14	0.37**
2004	0.34**	0.17	0.40**
2005	0.43**	0.31**	0.46**
2006	0.44**	0.27*	0.41**
2007	0.36**	0.33**	0.37**
2008	0.26*	0.19	0.53**

Note: ** $p < 0.05$, * $p < 0.1$.

per 1000 children compared to low-poverty states in which they range from 18 to 43, with a lower average rate of 24. Maltreatment rates and the fraction of reports that are substantiated also follow a similar pattern. The child fatality rate is about three times higher in high-poverty states.

In Table 5.3 we show the bivariate correlation between state child poverty rates and the rate at which maltreatment reports are investigated, incidence of maltreatment, and the fatality rate during the most recent decade reported to NCANDS. The correlation between poverty and two of the three child maltreatment outcomes shown in Table 5.3—the number of maltreatment reports investigated by Child Protective Services (CPS) and the child fatality rate—is strong and consistently significant overtime.

Going beyond examinations of the zero-order relationship between poverty and child welfare, a multitude of studies have provided evidence for this relationship in a multivariate context using a variety of data sources both at national and local levels. Some recent examples include studies by Paxson and Waldfogel (1999, 2002, 2003), Berger (2004), Slack et al. (2004), Mersky et al. (2009), and Jonson-Reid et al. (2009). Using data from the NCANDS, Paxson and Waldfogel (1999, 2002) construct state-level panels for the years 1990 to 1996, and examine how the number of maltreatment reports, specific forms of child maltreatment (neglect, physical abuse, and sexual abuse) and foster care placement are affected by parental resources using regressions with state and year fixed effects. These researchers use a broadly conceptualized definition of parental resources that encompasses income, parental time, and quality of parental time and operationalize the latter two concepts with parental work status and single parenthood. Their 1999 study showed that parental employment and family structure have a stronger link to child maltreatment than family income. Specifically, they find that children who live with a working mother and an absent father were at significantly higher risk of maltreatment (especially physical abuse and neglect) compared to children with a nonworking mother and a working father. Paxon and

Waldfogel (2002) expand on their 1999 work and include a direct poverty measure of the fraction of children who live in extreme poverty (family incomes less than 75% of the poverty line) and confirm their earlier findings on the effects of single parenthood and mother's work status. In addition, they report substantial effects of poverty on all types of maltreatment. When Paxon and Waldfogel (2003) conduct still another analysis to include two more years of data (from 1990 to 1998) they again find that (1) higher poverty rates were indicative of higher substantiated maltreatment; an increase in the fraction of children in extreme poverty of 5% increased substantiated maltreatment by 3.8%; and (2) increases in the fraction of children living with working mothers and absent fathers predict higher rates of substantiated maltreatment.

Lawrence Berger (2004) uses the National Longitudinal Survey of Youth (NLSY) to examine the effect of family income, family structure, and public policies on risk of child maltreatment. His dependent variables include five different measures of "maltreatment risk" in three categories: routine medical care (medical checkup and dental visits in the previous 12 months), the home environment (cognitive stimulation and emotional support), and spanking behavior as well as an overall index of maltreatment risk. Berger finds that income is significantly and positively related to dental visits and quality of the home environment, and negatively related to overall risk of maltreatment. Moreover, he finds that children in single mother families, especially where the mother works, are at higher risk of having poorer caregiving environments, and may also have an overall higher risk of maltreatment.

Slack and her colleagues use longitudinal survey and administrative data from the Illinois Family Study and look at the direct effect of poverty (as measured by perceived material hardship and sporadic employment) on child neglect, as well as its indirect effect mediated by parenting characteristics (measured by low parental warmth, use of physical discipline, and allowing the child to watch television frequently) (Slack et al., 2004). Although these researchers find that poverty and parental characteristics predict child neglect, they also show that parental factors do not mediate the poverty–neglect relationship and that poverty exerts a direct and independent effect on neglectful behavior.

In another longitudinal study conducted in a Midwestern metropolitan area, Johnson-Reid and her colleagues use administrative data from child and public welfare agencies along with data from the Census and other social service agencies over the period 1993–2006 and compare poor children reported to child welfare to those not reported, and to nonpoor children who were reported to the system (Jonson-Reid et al., 2009). They state that poor children who were brought to CPS attention had a substantially higher risk for a range of negative outcomes (e.g., unintentional injuries, delinquency, mental health problems) compared to either children who are poor but not reported or those who are reported for maltreatment but are not poor.

Mersky and his colleagues investigate the poverty–child maltreatment association using the Chicago Longitudinal Study involving primarily disadvantaged minority children (Mersky et al., 2009). With the aid of data from two administrative sources—the child welfare system and the juvenile court system—they construct three outcome variables that indicate the occurrence of any maltreatment and more specific

occurrence of physical abuse or neglect, and use welfare receipt as their primary poverty measure. Mersky et al. find that receipt of public assistance exerts a significant
influence on multiple maltreatment outcomes. They conclude that despite using a
rough-hewn measure of poverty, viz. welfare receipt, their "findings suggest that the
relationship between poverty and maltreatment is discernible, even in a highly disadvantaged sample" (p. 82).

As the preceding review illustrates, there is considerable agreement in the social science community that poverty is a leading indicator of child maltreatment. Less clear,
however, is how poverty matters to the etiology of child maltreatment. There are lin-
gering questions as to whether the relationship is a causal one and there have been
persistent efforts undertaken to understand the mechanisms through which poverty
exercises its ill effects on children. It has not been an easy undertaking, however, given
the complexities involved in empirically disentangling the effects of poverty from other
correlates of poverty such as race, social exclusion, family structure, and other problems such as mental illness or substance abuse. The National Society for the Prevention
of Cruelty to Children (NSPCC), a U.K.-based organization, sums up the problem as
follows: "It is difficult, if not impossible, to unravel how these different variables may
influence, interact or contribute towards the increased risk of child maltreatment...the
causative pathways are complex and many inter-related variables at work, and disentangling the relative influence of different variables is problematic" (NSPCC, 2008, p.
8). Pelton (1989) states that "the most reasonable conclusion that can be drawn from
the nature of the relationship between poverty and child abuse and neglect is that
poverty is often a contributing factor, a partial determinant that often provides the
context for abuse and neglect, and that there must be other *mediating* factors between
poverty and these resultants" (p. 41, emphasis in original). Dorothy Roberts, in her
book *Shattered Bonds: The Color of Child Welfare,* traces out three types of associations
between poverty and child abuse and neglect: maltreatment may be *caused* by poverty,
it may be *detected* because of poverty, or it may be *defined* by parental poverty (Roberts,
2002). And in a synthesis of research on disproportionality in child welfare, Robert
Hill (2006, p. 17) concludes that poverty is not a cause of maltreatment but, rather, it
appears to interact with other risk factors such as depression, domestic violence, teen
pregnancy, unemployment, substance abuse, and isolation.

We conclude this discussion of the hypothesized impact of poverty on child
maltreatment with two observations. First, although direct measures of poverty or
extreme poverty (e.g., percentage of people/families with incomes under the official
poverty level) are common, researchers have also used other (and some rough-hewn)
markers of poverty such as receipt and duration of public assistance, family structure
(e.g., single parenthood), and parental employment (Mersky et al., 2009; Paxson &
Waldfogel, 2002; Slack et al., 2003, 2004; Fryer & Miyoshi, 1995; Courtney et al., 2001;
Fein & Lee, 2003) to study whether poor economic circumstances per se are correlated
with the incidence and prevalence of child abuse and neglect. It is quite possible that
some of these poverty measures contain a substantial amount of measurement error,
distorting the real impact of poverty or even masking the importance of conceptually
distinctive influences. Second, poverty may be confounded with the scrutiny given to

poorer children by media promulgating social justice agendas and by moral entrepreneurs pressing for equal treatment by public institutions. This potential for significant social selection bias has been discussed by Geen et al. (1999), Gainsborough (2010), Mezey (2000), and others.

WELFARE REFORM, INCOME SUPPORT, AND CHILD WELFARE

Public welfare and child welfare have been historically viewed by the general public as intertwined and inseparable systems. No doubt the stated goals of the two programs are different; the goal of the public welfare system is to attempt to bolster the provider role of parents by promoting economic self-sufficiency, whereas the goal of the child welfare system is to focus on the parent's role as a caregiver and provide assessment and supportive services to increase child safety and decrease the risk of child maltreatment (Berrick et al., 2006). Often, however, there is considerable overlap in the families served by the two systems; viz. families that tend to be characterized by poverty, low education, and single parenthood.

About 50% of the families that come to CPS attention receive public assistance at the time of referral to CPS and "a great majority" have been welfare recipients in the past (U.S. Department of Health and Human Services, 2000; Pelton, 1994; Lindsey, 1994; American Association for the Protection of Children, 1987). A qualitative study using focus group methods conducted by the Urban Institute reports that child welfare workers estimated that between 70% and 90% of families receiving support services at home from the child welfare system were on public assistance (Tumlin & Geen, 2000). A reasonable working hypothesis is that changes made to the public welfare system will likely affect child welfare outcomes. This is all the more likely when sweeping changes were made to the public welfare system that were aimed at profoundly influencing parental attitudes and behaviors.

The U.S. public welfare system has undergone a considerable transformation beginning in the early 1990s that significantly altered the terms under which poor women receive public assistance. At the center of this overhaul is the Personal Responsibility and Work Opportunity Reconciliation Act (PRWORA) passed in 1996, which changed the welfare program from Aid to Families with Dependent Children (AFDC) to Temporary Assistance to Needy Families (TANF), and in doing so, abolished "entitlement" to public assistance. TANF also required reciprocal responsibilities on the part of the aid recipient by making cash and other in-kind assistance conditional on the expectation that the recipient be engaged in some type of human capital development or labor force attachment activities, i.e., training or work.

State efforts to overhaul the welfare system started in the early 1990s, enabled by the Section 1115 waiver program under the Social Security Act (49 *Stat.* 620 [1935]; 42 USC 1315(a) [2006]; Levin-Epstein, 2003). There were 81 distinct waiver programs approved by Presidents Bush and Clinton that were operating in 44 states during the period 1992–1996 (Harvey et al., 2000). These waivers contained both carrots and sticks, and ranged from relatively minor modifications to AFDC program, such as changes in the limits on assets and earned income that a household could maintain and still remain eligible for welfare, to very radical innovations that aimed to influence social behaviors. The net intent of all the reform provisions was to reduce welfare dependency by making work attractive to single mother families. The most noteworthy among the waivers are (1) work requirements, which focused on imposing obligations to work in exchange for assistance; (2) time limits, which imposed a lifetime cap on welfare benefits; (3) the family cap, which denied cash benefits to families for children born while the mother received public assistance; (4) work incentives, which allowed recipients to keep more of their earned income while maintaining eligibility for public assistance; and (5) sanction policy, which penalized recipients for program rule infractions, especially noncompliance with work requirements.

As welfare reform unfolded, many policy makers, policy analysts, and moral entrepreneurs were fearful of significant negative impacts on children and families. Scholars predicted that the new rules would increase actual and reported child maltreatment and out-of-home placements (Aber et al., 1995; Allen, 1996; Child Welfare League of America, 1998; Knitzer & Bernard, 1997; Courtney, 1997; Waldfogel, 1998). There were also concerns that in view of the sheer size of the welfare system relative to the child welfare system, even a fairly small change in the former could have substantial impacts on the latter (Geen et al., 2001; Waldfogel, 2004). If family poverty is strongly related to child maltreatment, as consensus indicated, and if welfare reform increased family poverty, reform could be hypothesized to result in large increases to the child welfare caseload. Waldfogel (2004) summarizes the expectations and the uncertainties of welfare reform as follows:

> Overall, there was good reason to expect that welfare reform might have some effects on the child welfare system. Welfare reform, and the associated changes in work supports and the strong economy, resulted in major changes in families' welfare reliance and in single mothers' participation in the labor market. Given that historically such a large share of the child welfare population came from the welfare population, and given the major changes being experienced by welfare recipients (and potential recipients), it made sense to think that families in the child welfare system, or at risk of entering the child welfare system, would have been affected. However, the likely direction (and magnitude) of those effects was not so clear. If families were financially better off and also functioning better at home, or if families were simply less visible to reporters, child welfare involvement might decrease. Conversely, if families were financially worse off or under more stress at home, or if at-risk families became more visible to reporters, child welfare involvement might increase. (p. 925)

Frame (1999) predicted an "institutional response to TANF, not only because of increased demand for services, but also in terms of the relative roles and functions of welfare and child protection as systems of intervention. The historically symbiotic relationship between welfare and child protection means that both programs must change the way they operate under TANF (just as they have during prior periods of reform), perhaps signaling a sort of institutional rapprochement crisis" (p. 720).

Some arguments for carefully monitoring the welfare reform–child maltreatment connection center on the altered financial circumstances of parents emanating from changes in welfare benefits or employment resulting from various reform elements. Fein and Lee (2003) present a comprehensive framework in which welfare reform components (work requirement, time limits, sanctions, family cap, earnings disregards, child care, and work supports) filter their effects through two main pathways—employment and welfare payments—on two principal channels—parent's psychological well-being and quantity/quality of adult supervision—which then translate to acts of child abuse or neglect (and eventually out-of-home placement). If some of the welfare reform components result in increased employment (e.g., work requirements, work incentives) and if such employment is of good quality, then parents may experience increased income, self-esteem, self-efficacy, life satisfaction and decreased stress, depression, and substance abuse. All of these positive outcomes could potentially promote higher psychological well-being, better parenting, and therefore fewer instances of abuse or neglect. The converse is also likely to occur if welfare reform does not promote employment or if the nature of the employment is poor. Welfare reform components can also be hypothesized to reduce welfare benefits (e.g., family cap, sanctions), thus reducing available family income. Increased economic hardship may reflect negatively on the parent's psychological health and parenting capabilities and result in higher instances of child maltreatment. Fein and Lee (2003) admit that "The number and nature of different pathways of potential influence are such that we cannot predict the net impacts of welfare reforms on child maltreatment with any confidence. The net effects will depend on the relative strength of varying causal associations, as well as on a number of state-specific factors, including policy design and implementation, caseload characteristics, and socioeconomic environment. Thus it is by looking carefully at the experiences in individual states that we may be most likely to glean insights into more generally applicable principles" (p. 87).

Did welfare reform influence child maltreatment? Though not extensively studied, empirical evidence is slowly accumulating on a possible connection between welfare reform and child welfare. Because this connection impinges mostly on employment and related financial circumstances, the first question that needs to be addressed is whether welfare reform has reduced dependency and enabled more welfare recipients to join the workforce. The answer here appears to be a "yes." Studies concur that even after accounting for booming economic times, work support policies such as Earned Income Tax Credit (EITC) and minimum wage, welfare reform has contributed to massive reductions in welfare dependency (Council of Economic Advisors, 1999; Figlio & Ziliak, 1999; Moffitt, 1999; Schoeni & Blank, 2000; Ziliak et al., 2000; Blank, 2002, 2007; Grogger & Karoly, 2005; Jagannathan, 2011). Between 1992 and 2005, welfare recipients as a percentage of the population fell from 5.2% to 1.6% and caseloads fell by nearly 70%, with researchers attributing the majority of the decline to welfare reform (Council of Economic Advisors, 1999; Rector & Youseff, 1999; Fang & Keane, 2004; Blank, 2007; Danielson & Klerman, 2008; Jagannathan, 2011).

There is also evidence that labor force participation of single mothers increased during the reform period (Waldfogel et al., 2002; Cancian et al., 1999; Blank, 2002;

Coley et al., 2007) and that poverty rates of children living in single-parent families fell throughout the 1990s. Some women appear to have made substantial gains in income whereas others, who remained on welfare or who left welfare but did not work, were worse off (Primus et al., 1999). A recent investigation of the direct effect of welfare reform on poverty concludes that welfare reform has been a significant driver of poverty reductions over the period 1992–2005 (Camasso & Jagannathan, 2012). It has also been argued that for poor single women in the labor force incomes actually fell, plunging these women and their children into deeper poverty (Haskins, 2001; Blank, 2002; Zedlewski et al., 2002), and that welfare reform has led to significant increases in poverty (McKernan & Ratcliffe, 2006).

Direct assessments of welfare reform effects on child maltreatment are just emerging. The results from the only study based on a randomized experiment in the state of Delaware are troubling. Fein and Lee's (2003) 3-year evaluation of Delaware's A Better Chance (ABC) indicates that the treatment group that was exposed to a "quick employment, Work First" strategy and tough sanctions for noncompliance had higher rates of overall substantiated maltreatment in the third year of follow-up and higher neglect rates in years 1 and 3 relative to a control group subject to traditional AFDC rules. These findings were especially strong in economically disadvantaged subgroups—nonwhites, high school dropouts, long-term welfare recipients, and women with a previous history of abuse or neglect—and among recipients who were sanctioned. The ABC program, however, did not have any demonstrable or consistent effect on physical/emotional/sexual abuse rates or foster care placements.

Kristen Shook (1999) also provides some early evidence of welfare reform effects in her quantitative, observational study of 173 single mothers on welfare in the state of Illinois. Using administrative data from the child and public welfare systems and survey data, Shook examines the effect of income loss from welfare sanctions on families' involvement in the child welfare system. She finds that women who did not have employment income subsequent to being sanctioned faced a higher risk of child welfare involvement compared to women who were not sanctioned and those who were sanctioned but were able to cushion such income loss with earned income. However, Derr and Cooley (2001) contradict these findings in their study of TANF families in Utah. Comparing 187 sanctioned families with a nonsanctioned sample of TANF recipients in Utah, they find that sanctioned families were no more likely to have CPS involvement than their nonsanctioned counterparts.

Researchers from the Urban Institute provide a more aggregate perspective of early welfare reform effects on child welfare caseloads using a case study methodology. Geen et al. (2001) used structured interviews and focus groups with a broad range of child welfare stakeholders and professionals in 12 states a short time after PRWORA was passed, and report that "despite widespread fears, we found no evidence to suggest that welfare reform has significantly increased the number of families referred to child welfare agencies" (p. 2). They go on to state that a large majority of the case study respondents, however, believed that "welfare reform is still likely to have a significant negative impact on child welfare caseloads" but that "it's too early to tell" because they believed that welfare families were yet to feel the brunt of the reforms, for example, when time limits begin to matter (Geen et al., 1999).

Paxson and Waldfogel used data from NCANDS and the Current Population Surveys covering the period 1990–1996 (Paxson & Waldfogel, 2002) and 1990–1998 (Paxson & Waldfogel, 2003) to conduct two studies of the impact of welfare reform on child maltreatment. Their first study (Paxson & Waldfogel, 2002) found a mixture of good news and bad news. They reported that a 10% reduction in welfare benefit levels increased foster care placements by 24%; and time limits increased overall substantiated maltreatment by 14% and neglect by 17%. Conversely, they also found that work incentives reduced these two outcomes by roughly the same order of magnitude. Their second study (Paxson & Waldfogel, 2003) found that reductions in welfare benefits, family cap, shorter time limits, stricter work requirements, and tougher sanctions all contributed to increases in out-of-home placements. Paxson and Waldfogel also found that time limits and sanctions increased instances of substantiated maltreatment whereas family caps reduced them. These researchers conclude that overall their findings "provide some evidence that the recent welfare reforms in the United States may have increased child maltreatment" (p. 1), but warn the reader that "because most of the welfare reforms examined have been in effect only a short time, these results should be considered preliminary" (p. 1).

With welfare reform now a decade and a half old, it is time to take a fresh look at whether ties between the public welfare and child welfare systems have indeed become stronger. In Table 5.4, we show selected child welfare outcomes pre- and post- PRWORA; the trends indicate positive and negative associations. It appears that reports of maltreatment, which were on the rise across all 50 states prior to PRWORA, began to slow down a bit in the late 1990s through the early 2000s but gradually climbed back to pre-PRWORA levels. The rate of (actual) substantiated maltreatment, however, decreased from a prereform average of 12.41 to 11.33 in the postreform period. Physical abuse rates show a clear pattern of reduction although both neglect and fatality rates have trended upwards compared to prereform era.

We examine selected welfare reform components in Figures 5.1–5.6. Inasmuch as welfare reform is hypothesized to filter its effects on child welfare outcomes through the recipients' economic circumstances, we examine those elements of PRWORA that have the potential to alter recipient employment and earnings. Following Blank and Schmidt's (2001) typology, we label states as more and less generous with respect to benefit levels, earnings disregards, sanctions, and time limits. Blank and Schmidt (2001) rate each state along these four dimensions and formulate an overall rating of the strength of the work incentives the state offers. In this typology, states that provide unambiguously strong work incentives are characterized by low benefit generosity, high earnings disregards, strict sanctions, and strict time limits. At the other end of the spectrum lie states with the weakest work incentives—states that provide generous benefits, low earnings disregards, lenient sanctions, and lenient time limits. States that do not fall into either of these categories are labeled as "mixed"; these are states that mix the strongest and weakest incentives or those that are entirely in the middle.

The figures show that although states with the weakest and strongest work incentives do not differ much in their reporting rates, strong work incentive states exhibit

Table 5.4 Welfare Reform and Trends in Child Welfare Outcomes

Year	Reporting Rate	Maltreatment Rate	Physical Abuse Rate	Neglect Rate	Fatality Rate
1990	25.94	12.16	2.9	5.28	0.017
1991	26.56	12.67	3.1	5.56	0.0163
1992	27.73	13.36	2.92	6.32	0.0151
1993	27.97	12.63	3.17	6.46	0.0149
1994	28.22	12.24	3.29	7.21	0.0159
1995	27.88	11.41	3.35	7.22	0.014
1996	27.87	11.3	3.18	6.98	0.0132
1997	22.55	9.38	2.74	6.13	0.0138
1998	19.64	10.68	2.76	6.48	0.0154
1999	21.26	10.91	2.34	6.13	0.0152
2000	23.64	12.06	2.34	7.21	0.0171
2001	24.31	12.56	2.34	7.19	0.0173
2002	24.53	12.34	2.3	7.22	0.0173
2003	24.78	12.24	2.26	7.54	0.0161
2004	25.03	11.91	2.08	7.43	0.0189
2005	25.9	12.06	1.99	7.6	0.0187
2006	25.68	11.8	1.88	7.59	0.0186
2007	24.8	10.01	1.59	7.03	0.0215
2008	26.73	10.05	1.61	7.16	0.022

Source: Child maltreatment data for the years 1990–2008 are from the NCANDS retrieved from the National Data Archive on Child Abuse and Neglect (NDACAN), Cornell University.

a much higher rate of maltreatment victims overall as well as higher rates of physical abuse, neglect, and fatalities relative to weak states.[1] Physical abuse appears to be declining consistently among all types of states. Weak work incentive states have experienced quite a bit of decline in their neglect rates, although they exhibit an upward trend beginning in 2007; fatalities on the other hand, are on the rise in the "strong" and "mixed" states in recent years. Taken as a whole, the descriptive evidence provided in these figures offers inconclusive evidence of a relationship between maltreatment and welfare generosity. Figure 5.6 shows the trends in poverty rates by state grouping; these rates are slowly climbing back up to prereform levels in states of all types.

RACE AND CHILD WELFARE

Long a matter of debate and concern is the large numbers of minority children, especially black children, on the rolls of CPS. For example, in 2008, the NCANDS data

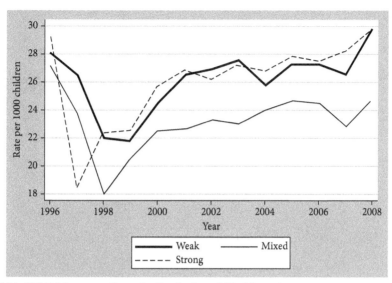

FIG 5.1 Child Maltreatment Reporting Rate by Overall Work Incentives.
Source: Welfare reform state typology follows Blank and Schmidt (2001).
Data are from NCANDS for 1996–2008.

show that black children who comprised 15% of the United States child population accounted for 22% of total child maltreatment victims. In comparison, white children who comprised 58% of the child population accounted for only 45% of the child welfare caseload. Since the issue was brought into prominence by Billingsley and Giovannoni (1972) in their book *Children of the Storm: Black Children and American*

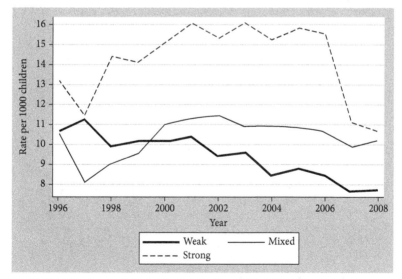

FIG 5.2 Child Maltreatment Victimization Rate by Overall Work Incentives.
Source: Welfare reform state typology follows Blank and Schmidt (2001).
Data are from NCANDS for 1996–2008.

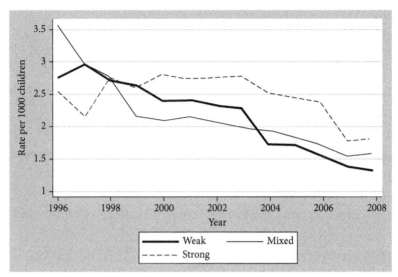

FIG 5.3 Physical Abuse Rate by Overall Work Incentives.
Source: Welfare reform state typology follows Blank and Schmidt (2001).
Data are from NCANDS for 1996–2008.

Child Welfare, the overrepresentation of black children in CPS has continued to be the subject of both research and controversy. There is empirical evidence both supporting and contradicting the importance of race in decisions to protect children .

The phenomenon of minority presence in CPS caseloads is often demonstrated using the concepts of "disproportionality" and "disparity" (Hill, 2006). The

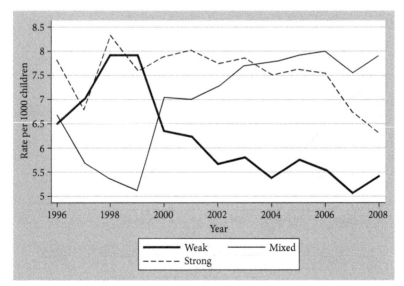

FIG 5.4 Neglect Rate by Overall Work Incentives.
Source: Welfare reform state typology follows Blank and Schmidt (2001).
Data are from NCANDS for 1996–2008.

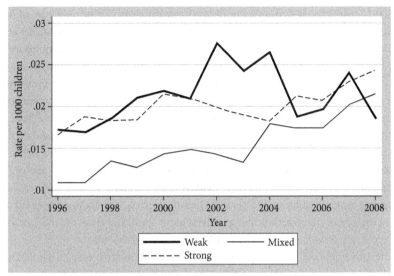

FIG 5.5 Child Fatality Rate by Overall Work Incentives.
Source: Welfare reform state typology follows Blank and Schmidt (2001).
Data are from NCANDS for 1996–2008.

disproportionality measure compares the proportion of children in each race that experiences a child welfare incident to the proportion of children of the *same* race in the general child population. Disparity measures facilitate comparison *across* different racial groups by contrasting proportions of children with a CPS event of a particular race (e.g., black) to the proportion of such children of another race (typically whites

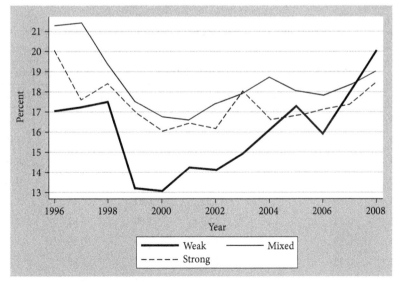

FIG 5.6 Child Poverty Rate by Overall Work Incentives.
Source: Welfare reform state typology follows Blank and Schmidt (2001).
Data on child poverty are from the U.S. Census Bureau, Current
Population Survey, Annual Demographic Supplement, 1996–2008.

are used as the reference group). The disparity measure can also be indicative of ineq-
uitable treatment or outcomes of some racial/ethnic groups compared to whites at the
various CPS decision stages (Hill, 2006). Values close to 1 for both the disproportionality and disparity indices are considered to be consistent with the assumption of no
disproportionality or disparity. Numbers that are greater than 1 (less than 1) are indicative of disproportionate overrepresentation (underrepresentation) of the particular
group compared to the norm or compared to whites. Table 5.5 presents these two indices for the years 2000–2008 for cases of substantiated maltreatment. These data show
that in the most current decade, black children were not only disproportionately overrepresented among victims of maltreatment relative to their numbers in the general
population, they were also nearly twice as likely to be victims of reported abuse/neglect
compared to white children. Whites and Hispanics are equally underrepresented relative to their respective fractions in the general population, and Hispanic children are at
or nearly on par with white children with respect to victimization.

The other major national data source on child maltreatment—the National
Incidence Study (NIS)—does not, however, reveal significant differences between
blacks and whites in the maltreatment rates for any of the first three waves. The NIS-3
results also show that after controlling for other relevant risk factors such as family
structure and income, maltreatment rates among blacks were significantly *lower* compared to white rates (Sedlak & Broadhurst, 1996; Sedlak & Schultz, 2005). The juxtaposition of findings from the NCANDS and NIS implies that the disproportionality and
disparity in substantiated maltreatment could not derive from *inherent* differences in
rates of maltreatment between blacks and whites, but must be a function of differential
treatment after entry into the CPS system. This is in fact what the authors of the NIS-3
report conclude as they attempt to reconcile the differences between the NIS and the

Table 5.5 Disproportionality and Disparity Indices for Child Maltreatment Victims,
2000–2008

	White Children		Black Children		Hispanic Children	
Year	Disproportionality	Disparity	Disproportionality	Disparity	Disproportionality	Disparity
2000	0.81	1	1.59	1.97	0.83	1.03
2001	0.81	1	1.60	1.99	0.81	1.01
2002	0.82	1	1.56	1.90	0.66	0.80
2003	0.84	1	1.56	1.87	0.82	0.98
2004	0.85	1	1.55	1.84	0.85	1.00
2005	0.83	1	1.50	1.80	0.87	1.04
2006	0.83	1	1.49	1.80	0.89	1.08
2007	0.80	1	1.42	1.77	0.98	1.23
2008	0.78	1	1.43	1.82	0.94	1.20

Source: NCANDS and the U.S. Census Bureau, Current Population Survey, Annual Social and
Economic Supplement, 2000–2008.

NCANDS findings on race: "The lack of any race differences in maltreatment incidence may be somewhat surprising in view of the disproportionate representation of
children of color in the child welfare population. This underscores the fact that the NIS
methodology identifies a much broader range of children than those who come to the
attention of child protective service agencies and the even smaller subset of those who
subsequently receive child protective services. The NIS findings suggest that [children
of] different races receive differential attention somewhere during the process of referral, investigation, and service allocation and that their differential representation in
the child welfare population does not derive from inherent differences in their rates of
abuse and neglect. It is also important to recognize that the NIS-3 reiterates the NIS-2
findings in this regard ....the NIS-2 and the NIS-3 have both consistently failed to
uncover any evidence of disproportionate victimization in relation to children's race"
(Sedlak & Broadhurst, 1996, pp. 4–30). Offering support to the NIS findings on race
is the study by Drake, Lee, and Johnson-Reid (2009). These researchers use statewide
data on Missouri for the years 1999–2001 and conclude that once poverty is controlled
for, they do not find evidence for racial disproportionality.

The NIS studies have drawn criticism for their apparent inability to detect race
bias (Ards et al., 2003; Barth, 2005). Reanalyses of these data have shown that NIS
results suffer from aggregation bias, a bias that is believed to have occurred because of
combining poor (i.e., welfare recipients) and nonpoor families and different forms of
maltreatment (i.e., abuse/neglect) during statistical analyses (Ards et al., 2003). If the
analyses were conducted separately for welfare recipients and nonwelfare recipients,
the black-to-white maltreatment ratio is only 0.33 for welfare recipients, whereas this
ratio is 2.06 among the nonwelfare cases; similar differences also emerge when physical
abuse and neglect are disaggregated and analyzed (Ards et al., 2003).

Results from NIS-4 show "strong and pervasive race differences in the incidence of
maltreatment," with rates of maltreatment for black children being significantly higher
than rates for white and Hispanic children (Sedlak et al., 2010). The authors of the
report attribute their current finding on race to (1) the greater precision of NIS-4
estimates compared to the previous three waves, and to (2) the differentially declining
rates of maltreatment across the racial/ethnic categories in which white rates declined
more than black and Hispanic rates since NIS-3 (Sedlak et al., 2010).

A systematic examination of the disproportionality phenomenon at each stage of
the CPS decision-making process described in Chapter 3 (Figure 3.1) was undertaken
by the Race Matters Consortium,[2] a think tank founded to address racial disparity
and disproportionality in child welfare. Hill (2006) used the Consortium model and
synthesized findings from various research studies conducted to identify disproportionality at reporting, investigation, substantiation, out-of-home placement, exit from
out-of-placement, and reentry into placement. His review concluded that "Despite differences in study design and methodology, this summary of the literature revealed much
consensus about disproportionality. While there were conflicting results among the
earlier studies, there is much more consensus among the more recent ones. Moreover,
many of the recent studies examined the impact of race on CPS decision making while
controlling for various risk factors. Thus, there was widespread agreement about the

role of race at most stages of CPS decision making. Most of the studies reviewed here identified race as one of the determinants of decisions at the stages of reporting, investigation, substantiation, placement, and exit from care. The only stage where no racial differences were identified concerned rates of reentry into the child welfare system" (p. 34).

In addition to disproportionate representation, Hill (2006) also found that the existing literature showed "overwhelming evidence about the existence of racial disparities" and that "most of the studies reviewed reveal that minority children more often have negative experiences in the child welfare system than white children. Children of color are more likely to be removed from their families, receive fewer vital services and lower financial support, remain in care for longer periods of time, and are less likely to be reunified with parents" (p. 34). Hill's own analyses of two national data sets [the NCANDS and the Adoption and Foster Care Analysis and Reporting System (AFCARS)] largely confirm his earlier literature review on the disproportionate representation of black children at the investigation, substantiation, and foster care placement level (Hill, 2007).

Most of the research published in more recent years since Hill's (2006) synthesis has continued to show evidence that CPS has remained disproportionally black and brown (Magruder & Shaw, 2008; Church, 2006; Wulczyn et al., 2006; Wulczyn & Lery, 2007; Harris & Hackett, 2008), with a few studies finding null or contradictory effects at least at some decision points (Johnson et al., 2007; Wulczyn & Lery, 2007; Drake et al., 2009). One of the knottiest problems in this research is the difficulty involved in disentangling race/ethnicity effects from its other close correlates such as poverty or single parenthood. John Poertner of the Race Matters Consortium admits that "People who discuss this issue from a research point of view have an incredibly difficult time understanding it. The African-American experience in this country, and other risk factors for abuse and neglect, are so intertwined, it's almost impossible to disentangle it" (cited in Green, 2006). Accepting the preponderance of research that shows that minority children are overrepresented and are treated differentially at various CPS stages, it is important to understand why this happens. One explanation is family poverty, with the relationship articulated as follows: because minority children are overrepresented among the poor and because poverty both amplifies the risk of maltreatment and disproportionately increases the need for services, minority children tend to have disproportionate representation in CPS (Hill, 2006; Barth, 2005; Schuck, 2005; Chibnall et al., 2003; Drake et al., 2003; Chaffin, Kelleher, & Hollenberg, 1996; Wells & Tracey, 1996). Consistent with this explanation, the disproportionality/disparity shown in Table 5.5 for the year 2008 can be partially explained by the fact that black (Hispanic) children experienced a 34% (30%) poverty rate compared to white children, who encompassed about 15% of the children who were poor (U.S. Census Bureau, 2011). Thus, the greater representation of minority children in CPS is simply an appropriate CPS response to the greater need for services.

A second explanation given for the disproportionality phenomenon is community risk factors. The argument here states that because minority children are more likely than white children to live in communities with a variety of risk factors such as high levels of poverty, unemployment, street crime, welfare assistance, and homelessness, they may become involved in multiple service systems (e.g., public welfare, law enforcement) and this increases their "visibility" or "exposure" to surveillance and reporting by public authorities, which in turn accounts for their overrepresentation (Coulton & Pandey, 1992; Hill, 2006; Freisthler et al., 2007; Roberts, 2007).

Finally, there is a contention that race per se is the reason that children of different races with identical risk factors are reported differentially to CPS (Chibnall et al., 2003; Roberts, 2002; Morton, 1999; Chasnoff et al., 1990; Turbett & O'Toole, 1980) and are treated differently in the CPS during the various decision points (Barth, 2005; Sedlak & Schulz, 2005; Hill, 2006; Roberts, 2002; McCabe et al., 1999). Dorothy Roberts (2002), for example, claims that "It is time to face the inescapable reality: America's child welfare system is a racist institution" (p. 99). Roberts reprises the opening passage of Billingsley and Giovanonni (1972), asserting that it still rings true today: "The racism that characterizes American society has had tragic effects upon black children. It has given the black child a history, a situation, and a set of problems that are qualitatively different from those of the white child. In a narrower context, American racism has placed black children in an especially disadvantaged position in relation to American institutions, including the institution of child welfare" (Billingsley & Giovanonni, 1972, p. vii).

In summary, poverty, welfare reform, and race have all been shown to influence rates of child maltreatment and the decisions of CPS workers who create those rates. These factors, however, at best explain only a small portion of the variance in the numbers and rates of child maltreatment.

NOTES

1. An F-test reveals these differences to be statistically significant.
2. The Race Matters Consortium is a joint effort of Westat, Casey Family Programs, and the Children and Family Research Center (CFRC) at the University of Illinois. The Consortium was formed as a national multisystem initiative to address racial and ethnic disproportionality in the child welfare system.

6

CHILD PROTECTIVE SERVICES DECISION OUTCOMES AND THE ROLE OF OUTRAGE

AN EMPIRICAL TEST

When angry, count to four; when very angry, swear.
Mark Twain
Pudd'nhead Wilson (1894)

In this chapter we provide a quantitative assessment of the impact that social outrage has on Child Protective Services (CPS) decision outcomes. Our analyses are guided by the general statistical equation (Eq. 7) presented in Chapter 1 and by the outrage routinization process articulated in Chapter 2. In this conceptualization, fatalities (and other horrific cases of maltreatment) are viewed as initial process drivers, and media, social entrepreneurs, courts, legislators, and CPS workforce are identified as the principal change agents responsible for "punctuations" in CPS agency equilibrium.

In addition to our focus on child fatalities, we examine the specific effects that child safety legislation, institutional reform litigation, and workforce punctuations exert. We do not measure the impacts of media coverage or the influence of moral entrepreneurs. In the latter instance, systematic data are not available on a state-by-state basis and simply counting statistical and policy documents could greatly understate the importance of these individuals and organizations. Counting media reports from *The New York Times* Index, *Readers' Guide*, or newspapers themselves, as some researchers have done (Nelson, 1984; Mezey, 2000; Gainsborough, 2010), has its own problems. Coverage of events is correlated with the number of media outlets and their competition level. As Baumgartner and Jones (2009) note, media attention is less than a perfect indicator of agenda status because "it does not necessarily correspond to the concerns of the mass public, weighted or otherwise" (p. 246). Gainsborough (2010) did find a significant correlation between media coverage of child welfare scandals in a state and passage of child protection legislation; however, the association was quite small. Nelson (1984), Mezey (2000), and a number of other researchers report a relationship between level of media coverage and the initiation of reform litigation—these observations tend to be impressionistic and case specific.

A common thread underlying the four indicators of outrage we employ in our analyses is their general availability, their verifiability, and their capacity to capture disruptions or punctuations in CPS agency operations. In the language of econometrics we see fatalities as a proxy measure of social outrage that can manifest itself in legislation, litigation, and/or workforce disruption. These three mechanisms, in turn, are believed to channel outrage along three distinctive stability–disruption continua with legislation providing the most long-term stability and smallest punctuation and workforce disruption yielding the least stability and most punctuations.

ECONOMETRIC APPROACH

Data and Methods

The data we use contain state- and year-specific information from 1992 through 2008 from all 50 states and the District of Columbia on key child welfare decisions, child and family risk characteristics, outrage measures, CPS task environment, reform characteristics of the closely allied public welfare system, and the overall economy. The number of state-year observations totals 867 ($= 51 \times 17$). We should note here that our use of state-level data enables us to identify relationships only at an aggregate level. For example, absent child- or household-level data, if we find that the percentage of children who live in households with unemployed parents are significantly related to substantiation rates, it does not allow us to conclude that a particular child is at a higher risk of being abused or neglected if he or she lives in such a household. Such a conclusion would suffer from an "ecological fallacy." Nonetheless, as Paxson and Waldfogel (2003) point out, aggregate relationships that are uncovered by the use of state-level data can identify potentially important state policies and/or other indicators that affect child maltreatment or CPS work.

Variable Measures

Dependent Variables: We examine three CPS decision outcomes: viz. (1) screened-in referrals of alleged child maltreatment, (2) substantiations of child maltreatment, and (3) out-of-home child placements. In addition to these performance outcomes we also look at three child outcomes: viz. classification rates of physical abuse, sexual abuse, and child neglect. It is important to keep in mind that tremendous variability exists across states in not only the incidence of maltreatment, but also how states define and handle cases of suspected child abuse and neglect through different policies, programs, and resource allocation. For example, during our study period 1992–2008, the number of maltreatment referrals accepted for investigation by Pennsylvania (Screened-in referrals or Report Rate) ranged from 4.6 to 9.1 per 1000 state child population, with substantiation rates (Percentage of reports substantiated) ranging from 16% to 32%. Alaska, on the other hand, had between 23 and 72 reports per 1000 state child population during the same time period, of which 34–94% were substantiated. No doubt part of the explanation for this contrast lies in differences in demographic and economic characteristics of these states; however, heterogeneity across states in their institutional and legal requirements and/or standards for accepting a referral for investigation or substantiation, and the number and nature of maltreatment occurrences receiving wide publicity all no doubt play a significant role as well.

Data that provide information on state variation are available from the National Child Abuse and Neglect Data System (NCANDS) established by the U.S. Department of Health and Human Services under the Child Abuse Prevention and Treatment Act (CAPTA). The numerators for all of our dependent variables can be found on NCANDS; the denominators used for rate standardization are derived from the U.S. Census. We run our statistical analyses on eight specific variables:

> *Report Rate* Number of screened-in reports per 1000 state child population
>
> *Substantiation Rate* Number of substantiated child victims per 1000 state child population
>
> *Substantiation Percent* Number of child victims expressed as a percentage of the number of children identified in maltreatment investigations
>
> *Physical Abuse Rate* Number of physical abuse victims per 1000 state child population
>
> *Neglect Rate* Number of neglect victims per 1000 state child population
>
> *Sexual Abuse Rate* Number of sexual abuse victims per 1000 state child population
>
> *Out-of-home Placement Rate* Number of children removed from the home and placed out of home per 1000 state child population
>
> *Out-of-home Placement Percent* Number of child placements expressed as a percentage of children subject to an investigation

Independent Variables—Set I: Our principal set of independent variables operationalizes the concept of *"outrage."* We employ four indicators of outrageous events in the state: (1) child fatality rate, measured as the number of child deaths reported by CPS per 1000 state child population and lagged by 1 year (*fatal_rate*); (2) implementation of sex offender registration and notification laws, coded as a dummy variable where the year of implementation (and subsequent years) is coded as a "1" (*sexoffender_law*) and lagged by 1 year; (3) two dummy variables indicating CPS involvement in litigation: an active court case, coded as "1" for years in which the state had an ongoing class action lawsuit (*current_courtcase*); and a court order, coded as "1" for years in which the state CPS agency had a formal court order (*CPS_courtorder*); (4) two variables that measure abrupt changes in the state's CPS workforce level: if the difference in the number of workers between year t and $t - 1$ is greater than 10 per 1000 reports a positive equilibrium shift is coded at "1" for time t, otherwise it is coded as 0 (*positive_equil_chg*); if the difference between year t and $t - 1$ is less than 10 per 1000 reports for time t a negative equilibrium shift is coded "1" for time t (*negative_equil_chg*). Inclusion of lagged fatalities and sex offender legislation in the modeling reflects the reality that CPS adjustments in operations require time for an initial shock to be absorbed by the system.

Independent Variables—Set II: This set contains variables that measure *hazard*, many of which appear on risk assessment measures used by CPS decision makers. Here we include the child poverty rate measured as the percentage of state children who live in poverty (*p_chil_pov*); percentage of minority children in the state population (*p_blk_chpop, p_hisp_chpop*); the percentage of children in age groups 0–3, 4–7, 8–11, and 12–15 in the state population (*p_age03_chpop, p_age47_chpop, p_age811_chpop,* and *p_age1215_chpop*); the percentage of male children in the state population (*p_male_chpop*); and the family structure as indicated by the percentage of children who live in single-parent households (*p_chil_singparhh*) and the percentage of children who live in households in which neither parent is employed (*p_chil_noparentemp*). Based on the literature we reviewed in Chapter 5, we expect child poverty rate, minority race/ ethnicity, and family structure to have a positive relationship with the dependent variables, and age and gender to have a negative relationship.

Independent Variables—Set III: We also employ a set of CPS organizational input: number of workers per 1000 child welfare caseload (*wkrs_1000caseload*); federal and state expenditures on child welfare expressed in 2008 constant dollars lagged by 1 year and adjusted to 1000 child welfare caseload (*fedex_caseload, statex_caseload*); two measures of state CPS agencies' information processing/information reporting capability—the percentage of CAPTA-required items reported by the state (*p_capta*) and whether or not the state reports child-level data to NCANDS (*rep_chlevel_data*); and an indicator of job security measured by the percentage of state's public sector covered by a union's collective bargaining agreement (*p_union_cov*). Our attempt here is to operationalize all the factors discussed in Chapter 4 for which data are available.

Independent Variables—Set IV: We add policies implemented by states to reform the public welfare system, measures of welfare reform. We focus on four specific policies identified as the most salient and controversial components of welfare reform (Lieberman & Shaw, 2000; Soss et al., 2001; Schiller, 1999; Kaushal & Kaestner, 2001): (1) work requirements, which focused on imposing obligations to work in exchange for assistance; (2) time limits, which imposed a lifetime cap on welfare benefits; (3) the family cap, which denies cash benefits to families for children born while the mother is receiving public assistance; and (4) sanction policy, which penalized recipients for program rule infractions.

The two dummy variables that represent work requirements (*work_req*) and time limits (*time_limit*) distinguish states with Personal Responsibility and Work Opportunity Reconciliation Act (PRWORA)-era rules that have more rigorous work requirements than the federal standard or time limits that are shorter than the 5-year limit imposed by the PRWORA, and/or stricter work requirements or time limits under the Section 1115 waiver program. The variables are coded as "1" when this is the case, following the coding protocol used by Fording (2003) and Soss and colleagues (2001). The family cap variable (*famcap*) is measured as a dummy variable with "1" indicating states with a cap in a given year and 0 otherwise. Although many studies have classified sanctioning policies as weak, moderate, or severe, results consistently show that stronger sanctions (Council of Economic Advisors, 1997, 1999; Soss et al., 2001) have more significant impacts on welfare exits relative to weak sanctions. We use a dummy variable that is coded as "1" when most severe sanctions such as imposition of loss of full benefits immediately or in a delayed fashion or closing of the case as a punishment for noncompliance (*severe_sanction*). In addition to welfare reform, we also include logged per capita welfare caseload (*ln_caseload*) and the generosity of welfare benefits for a family of three expressed in 2008 constant dollars (*real_maxben*).

It is not a simple matter to state *a priori* the direction of the relationship of the welfare state measures we use and child maltreatment. Any actions of the welfare state that raise family income through recipients' employment (e.g., less generous welfare benefits, work requirements, or time limits) or affect family structure by reducing nonmarital births (e.g., family cap) can be expected to reduce poverty and therefore child maltreatment; however, such actions may also increase child maltreatment if the mother's employment increases stress and work-related expenses and decreases the amount of quality time spent with the child.

Independent Variables—Set V: Finally, we add two measures of the state's economic environment. Our study period captures 8 years of booming economic expansion (1992–2000) as well as 9 years of much-below normal economic expansion character-ized by weak private sector growth (2001–2008). We use two measures of the busi-ness cycle to capture the state of the economy: the annual state level unemployment rate (*unemp*) and the female labor force participation rate (*fem_lfp*), measured as the percentage of the female population that is attached to the labor force. The unemploy-ment rate is expected to have a positive effect on child maltreatment whereas the effect of female labor force participation rate is ambiguous for the same reasons mentioned previously.

Table 6.1 provides a summary of how the study variables are measured as well as their source. We note that all monetary variables are adjusted for cost of living and inflation using the Consumer Price Index-Urban (CPI-U).

Analytic Methods

Our statistical framework is summarized in this general regression equation:

$$Y_{st} = \beta_0 + \lambda \, \mathbf{Outrage}_{st} + \gamma \, \mathbf{Hazard}_{st} + \zeta \, \mathbf{CPS}_{st} + \theta \, \mathbf{Welfare}_{st}$$
$$+ \mu \, \mathbf{Economy}_{st} + \beta_1 \, \mathbf{Trend} + \beta_2 \, \mathbf{Trend}^2 + \sigma_s + \varepsilon_{st} \qquad \text{(Eq. 8)}$$

This general model is estimated six times, each time with a different measure of social outrage. Model 1 employs fatality rate lagged by 1 year, Model 2 uses the presence or absence of sex offender registration laws lagged by 1 year, Models 3 and 4 utilize our litigation status measures and Models 5 and 6 employ our workforce equilibrium measures.

The subscripts *s* and *t* denote, respectively, each of the 50 states and District of Columbia and a specific year from 1992 to 2008. *Y* represents one of the eight depen-dent variables listed in Table 6.1 for state *s* in year *t*. **Trend** represents national linear and national quadratic functions of time, a specification deemed prudent because of the length of the time series. Trend captures otherwise smoothly occurring changes across all states over time. **Outrage** represents one of the six outrage measures. λ represents the coefficient vector of conceptual interest. **Hazard** is a vector of child risk variables (percentage of children in poverty, percentage of black and Hispanic

Table 6.1 Description of Variables Measurement and Data Sources

Variable Category	Variable	Measurement and Source
Dependent Variables	**Total Screened-in Reports Rate**	Number of total reports screened in by Child Protective Services (CPS) divided by the state's total child population expressed per 1000 children. Numerator: National Child Abuse and Neglect Data System (NCANDS) retrieved from the National Data Archive on Child Abuse and Neglect (NDACAN), Cornell University, combined aggregate files. Denominator: U.S. Census Bureau, Current Population Survey, Annual Social and Economic Supplement, various years.
	Substantiation Rate per 1000 Children	Number of child victims divided by the state's total child population expressed per 1000 state child population. Numerator: NCANDS; Denominator: U.S. Census Bureau.
	Substantiation Percent	Number of child victims expressed as a percentage of the number of children identified in maltreatment investigations. Numerator: NCANDS; Denominator: NCANDS.
	Physical Abuse Rate	Number of victims of physical abuse divided by state's total child population, expressed per 1000 children. Numerator: NCANDS; Denominator: U.S. Census Bureau.
	Neglect Rate	Number of victims of neglect divided by state's total child population, expressed per 1000 children. Numerator: NCANDS; Denominator: U.S. Census Bureau.
	Sexual Abuse Rate	Number of victims of sexual abuse divided by state's total child population, expressed per 1000 children. Numerator: NCANDS; Denominator: U.S. Census Bureau.
	Out-of-Home Placement Rate	Number of children removed from home divided by state's total child population, expressed per 1000 children. Numerator: NCANDS; Denominator: U.S. Census Bureau.
	Out-of-Home Placement Percent	Number of children removed from home as a percentage of children who are the subject of an investigation. Numerator: NCANDS; Denominator: NCANDS.

Independent Variables		
Set I: Outrage	Child Fatality Rate (Lagged)	Number of CPS child fatalities divided by state's total child population, expressed per 1000 children. Numerator: NCANDS; Denominator: U.S. Census Bureau.
	Sex Offender Registry Implementation (Lagged)	Year in which states implemented sex offender registration and notification laws. *Source:* Vasques, B. E., Madden, S., & Walker, J. T. (2008). The influence of sex offender registration and notification laws in the United States: A time series analysis. *Crime and Delinquency, 54,* 175–192.
	Class Action Lawsuit	Involvement of state CPS agency in a class action lawsuit, 1 = yes; 0 = no.
	Court Order	State CPS agency has a court order in effect, 1 = yes; 0 = no. *Sources:* Bilchik, S., & Davidson, H. (2005). *Child welfare consent decrees: Analysis of thirty-five court actions from 1995 to 2005.* Washington, DC: Child Welfare League of America and The American Bar Association Center on Children and the Law; *Child welfare: Class action reform.* Washington, DC: Center for the Study of Social Policy; *Reforming Child Welfare.* New York: Children's Rights; *Foster care reform litigation docket.* Oakland, CA: National Center for Youth Law.
	+ Workforce Equilibrium Δ	Positive state workforce change if the number of CPS frontline workers increases by >10 per 1000 reports in a 1-year period.
	− Workforce Equilibrium Δ	Negative state workforce change if the number of CPS frontline workers decreases by >10 per 1000 reports in a 1-year period. Numerator: NCANDS. Denominator: NCANDS. Equilibrium change counts for states are listed in Appendix IV.

(continued)

Table 6.1 (*Continued*)

Variable Category	Variable	Measurement and Source
Set II: Hazard	**Child Poverty**	Percentage of children living in poverty. *Source:* U.S. Census Bureau, Current Population Survey, Annual Demographic Supplement, various years.
	Child Race/Ethnicity	Percentage of children who are white, black, Hispanic. *Source:* U.S. Census Bureau. Data downloaded from http://www.census.gov/popest/.
	Child Age	Percentage of children in age groups: 0–3, 4–7, 8–11, 12–15, 16–17. *Source:* U.S. Census Bureau. Data downloaded from http://www.census.gov/popest/.
	Child Gender	Percentage of children who are males, females. *Source:* U.S. Census Bureau. Data downloaded from http://www.census.gov/popest/.
	Family Structure	
	Single Parent Households	Percentage of children who live in single-parent households. Data extracted from Kids Count Data Book (The Annie E. Casey Foundation), various years.
	No Employed Parent	Percentage of children who live in households in which no parent is employed. Data extracted from Kids Count Data Book (The Annie E. Casey Foundation), various years.
Set III: CPS Task Environment	**CPS Workers Adjusted for Caseload**	Number of CPS workers divided by total screened-in reports, expressed per 1000 reports. Data imputed for years 1992–1997.
		Numerator: NCANDS; Denominator: NCANDS.
		Numerator: NCANDS; Denominator: U.S. Census Bureau. Data imputed for years 1992–1995, 1997, 1999, 2001, 2003, 2005, 2007, 2008.
	Child Welfare Expenditure	
	Federal	Total federal dollars for child welfare activities, expressed in 2008 constant dollars, and lagged by 1 year.
	State	Total state dollars for child welfare activities, expressed in 2008 constant dollars, and lagged by 1 year. *Source:* State Child Welfare Policy Database, Child Trends. Data downloaded from http://www.childwelfarepolicy.org/.
	States Reporting of CAPTA Items	Percentage of total items (required under the Child Abuse Prevention and Treatment Act) reported by state.
	States Reporting of Child-Level Data	States providing child-level data to NCANDS: 1 = yes; 0 = no. *Source:* Child Maltreatment, Department of Health and Human Services, Administration for Children and Families, reports from various years.
	Union Coverage	Percentage of state public sector employees who are covered by a collective bargaining agreement. *Source:* Hirsch, B. T., & Macpherson, D. A. (2003). Union membership and coverage database from the Current Population Survey: Note. *Industrial and Labor Relations Review,* 56(2), 349–354. Data downloaded from http://unionstats.gsu.edu.

Set IV: Welfare Reform	Family Cap	States with an operating family cap. Data downloaded from http://anfdata.urban.org/wrd/databook.cfm. The Urban Institute's Welfare Rules Database.
	Work Requirement	States with stringent work requirements. Data downloaded from http://anfdata.urban.org/wrd/databook.cfm. The Urban Institute's Welfare Rules Database.
	Time Limit	States with stringent time limits. Data downloaded from http://anfdata.urban.org/wrd/databook.cfm. The Urban Institute's Welfare Rules Database.
	Sanction	States with the most severe sanction policy for noncompliance with work requirements. Data downloaded from http://anfdata.urban.org/wrd/databook.cfm. The Urban Institute's Welfare Rules Database.
	Welfare Caseload Size (Per Capita) (Logged)	The number of welfare recipients divided by the total state population. Numerator: Annual Report to Congress: Various years—Data downloaded from http://www.acf.hhs.gov/programs/ofa/data-reports/index.htm. U.S. Department of Health and Human Services, Administration for Children and Families. Denominator: Annual Estimates of the Resident Population for the United States, Regions, States, and Puerto Rico—Various years—Data downloaded from http://www.census.gov/popest/data/historical/index.html. Population Division, U.S. Census Bureau.
	Aid to Families with Dependent Children (AFDC)/Temporary Assistance to Needy Families (TANF) Benefits	Maximum monthly benefit for a family of three with no income. Data downloaded from http://anfdata.urban.org/wrd/databook.cfm. The Urban Institute's Welfare Rules Database.
Set V: Economic Environment	Economy Unemployment Rate	Percentage of the labor force that is unemployed. Data downloaded from http://www.bls.gov/lau/tables.htm. U.S. Department of Labor, Bureau of Labor Statistics.
	Female Labor Force Participation	Percentage of the female population attached to the labor force. Data downloaded from http://data.bls.gov/lau/. U.S. Department of Labor, Bureau of Labor Statistics.
	Consumer Price Index—All Urban Consumers	All monetary variables (monthly AFDC/TANF cash benefits and child welfare expenditures) are adjusted for cost of living and inflation using the Consumer Price Index-U for Northeast Urban, Midwest Urban, South Urban, and West Urban. Data downloaded from http://data.bls.gov/PDQ/servlet/SurveyOutputServlet?data_tool = latest_numbers&series_id = LNS11300000. U.S. Department of Labor, Bureau of Labor Statistics.
Cost of Living Adjustment for All Monetary Variables		

children, percentage of children in various age groups, percentage of male children, percentage of children who live in single-parent households, and percentage of children who live in a household in which neither parent is employed), with γ designating the associated coefficients. **CPS** captures a vector of child welfare worker's organizational environment and resources (number of workers per 1000 caseload, federal and state expenditures standardized per 1000 caseload and lagged by 1 year, reporting of required CAPTA items and child level information to NCANDS, and percentage of public sector workers in the state covered by a union) and ζ represents the associated coefficients. **Welfare** is a set of welfare reform measures (family cap, work requirement, time limit, and sanction), state monthly welfare benefits in constant 2008 dollars, and the welfare caseload in logged form. θ represents the respective coefficients. **Economy** is the state economic climate captured by the state employment rate and the female labor force participation rate. In addition, σ designates a vector of state fixed effects, which account for unobserved characteristics of states that are assumed to be time invariant. We include these state fixed effects to guard against omitted variables bias that may result if otherwise unmeasured between-state differences that influence CPS decisions are correlated with the variables measured in our models. These omitted factors may include unobserved child care costs, parental attitudes, and state differences in harm standards for definition and enforcement of CPS guidelines (Paxson & Waldfogel, 2002). Lastly, ε is the idiosyncratic random error term that varies by state and year.

Our panel regression analyses were conducted using XTREG in STATA 10.0, with robust standard errors calculated by clustering on state and assuming heteroskedastic and serially correlated errors.

RESULTS FROM OUR ANALYSES

In Table 6.2 we show the distribution of all study variables over the 17-year period. As expected, the dependent variables exhibit considerable variability across states and over time. For all qualitative independent variables (e.g., *current_courtcase*, *sexoffender_law*), the means represent the proportion of state-years in which the particular independent variable is observed.

Figures 6.1–6.3 portray the trend in the eight dependent variables. Figure 6.1 shows that during the study period child maltreatment report rates (screened-in referrals) in the United States declined during the late 1990s, stayed stable through half of the previous decade, and started to inch up in 2007. Substantiation rates have declined over time, whereas placement rates display little change.

Figure 6.2 shows that although physical and sexual abuse rates have been steadily declining over the years, rate of neglect has shown much more variability in the last two decades and has begun a decline since 2006 after trending upward through earlier years.

Figure 6.3 shows a steady and strong decline in the number of substantiated maltreatment as a percentage of children who were the subject of an investigation. Placements as a fraction of investigations, however, have remained quite stable since 1999.

Table 6.2 Distribution of Study Variables Across State-Year Observations

Variable	Obs	Mean	Std. Dev.	Min	Max
Dependent Variables					
report_rate	864	27.45028	10.54644	4.626053	71.76041
substan_rate	867	13.01074	7.605412	1.470268	83.05729
substan_percent	827	30.86503	15.17205	5.235337	95.78658
phyabuse_rate	849	2.805303	2.018843	0.3484848	18.34896
neglect_rate	849	7.677317	5.65608	0.0407617	48.57813
sexabuse_rate	849	1.507501	1.145518	0.1703233	8.225
placement_rate	690	3.202855	1.868814	0.1643755	11.562
placement_percent	690	8.617752	6.396722	0.4088571	42.19733
Independent Variables—Set I: Outrage Measures					
fatal_rate	867	0.0184599	0.018789	0	0.3154622
sexoffender_law	867	0.7658593	0.423705	0	1
current_courtcase	867	0.5236448	0.4997289	0	1
CPS_courtorder	867	0.3956171	0.4892651	0	1
positive_equil_chg	867	0.0392157	0.1942198	0	1
negative_equil_chg	867	0.0703576	0.2558963	0	1
Independent Variables—Set II: Hazard Measures					
p_chil_pov	867	17.61994	6.103774	4.068622	50.01
p_blk_chpop	867	13.75959	14.16208	0.3315179	78.85101
p_hisp_chpop	867	10.52494	11.26386	0.5915503	55.20549
p_age03_chpop	867	21.88458	1.502015	18.13157	28.90728
p_age47_chpop	867	21.95779	0.9608975	19.93652	27.05309
p_age811_chpop	867	22.30622	0.855735	19.10482	25.48332
p_age1215_chpop	867	22.77717	1.279211	17.19422	26.48153
p_male_chpop	867	51.40804	0.6545087	48.51834	55.07737
p_chil_singparhh	867	28.98962	6.781726	14	68
p_chil_noparentemp	867	29.74856	6.567397	13	56
Independent Variables—Set III: CPS Task Environment Measures					
wkrs_1000caseload	830	22.37469	21.69794	0.0134735	168.3492
fedex_caseload	864	6992555	5737219	128732.8	5.14e + 07
statex_caseload|	864	6753357	7017574	29516.74	4.95e + 07
p_capta	867	68.16577	25.19694	0	100
rep_chlevel_data	867	0.5847751	0.4930452	0	1
p_union_cov	867	38.49135	16.90402	7.4	76

(continued)

Table 6.2 *(Continued)*

Variable	Obs	Mean	Std. Dev.	Min	Max
Independent Variables—Set IV: Public Welfare Measures					
famcap	867	0.3517878	0.4778038	0	1
work_req	867	0.4405998	0.4967456	0	1
time_limit	867	0.3529412	0.4781604	0	1
severe_sanction	867	0.5778547	0.4941865	0	1
ln_caseload	867	−3.952918	0.8540147	−7.571559	−2.039551
real_maxben	867	500.7665	215.3487	0	1396.964
Independent Variables—Set V: Economy					
unemp	867	5.210957	1.625819	2.3	12.5
fem_lfp	867	60.84371	4.313552	43.7	71.20205

We present our regression results in Tables 6.3–6.11. In all of the models, the state fixed effects are jointly significant, indicating that models without such effects will yield biased estimates of our measured variables.

In Table 6.3 we report the impact of the (lagged) child fatality rate on CPS decision outcomes. In three out of eight analyses—maltreatment substantiation rate, neglect rate, and child placement rate—we find a statistically significant effect of child fatality, controlling for a series of hazard, CPS task environment, public welfare policy, and economic climate factors. Each additional fatality (marginal effect) increases the substantiation rate by 40 children per 1000 in the population, the classified neglect rate by over 34 children per 1000 population, and the child placement rate by 11.5 children

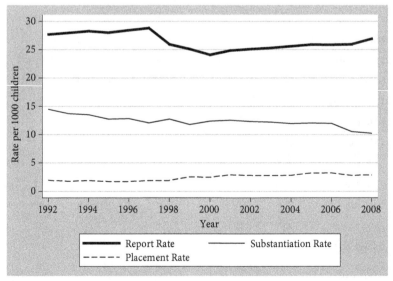

FIG 6.1 Report, Substantiation, and Placement Rates: 1992–2008.

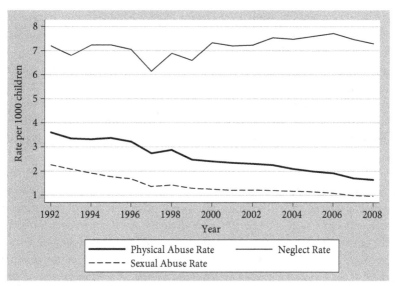

FIG 6.2 Rates of Various Types of Maltreatment: 1992–2008.

per 1000 child population. Fatalities also exert a positive influence on screened-in case reports, substantiation percentages, and placement percentages; however, these effects are not significant. The predictions are all consistent with the notion that fatalities are the trigger events for social outrage.

All eight models show reasonably good fit, with a significant overall F-statistic and R^2 statistic ranging from 18% [*neglect_rate*] to about 39% [*substan_percent*]. It is worth noting that one hazard variable, percentage of Hispanic children in the state's population (*p_hisp_chpop*), and an indicator of state CPS quality control, percentage of required CAPTA items reported (*p_capta*), exert patterns of consistently significant

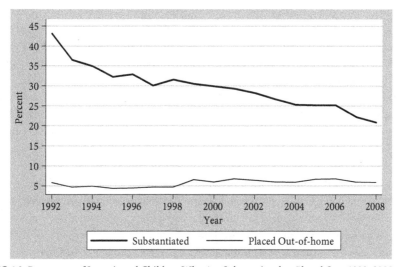

FIG 6.3 Percentage of Investigated Children Who Are Substantiated or Placed Out: 1992–2008.

effects across outcome measures. In the case of the former, the impact is consistently negative whereas for the latter it is positive. These effects are small when compared to the magnitude of the fatality coefficients, however.

Although the results in Table 6.3 provide some compelling evidence that child fatalities influence CPS operations, they shed less light on how the outrage these archetypical cases generate becomes routinized into agency workflows and decision processes. In our subsequent regression analyses (Tables 6.4 to 6.11) we replace fatalities with our measures of legislative, judicial, and workforce punctuations that we believe are responsible for suffusing CPS decisions with the specter of the dead child.

In Table 6.4 we present our results from the regression analyses of these outrage mechanisms on the CPS screened-in report rate. The two workforce punctuation measures exert strong effects on the screening process with dramatic workforce expansion decreasing the rate by about 5 per 1000 and dramatic workforce contraction increasing the rate by about 3 per 1000. It would appear that positive mobilization results in an organization slowing down demand and taking stock while orienting substantial numbers of new workers. Negative mobilization, on the other hand, appears to generate a doubling down of effort even as the organization copes with dramatic workforce attrition.

The analysis of screened-in reports indicates that percent population Hispanic systematically lowers this rate, as do number of CPS workers (*wkrs_1000caseload*) and amount of federal expenditures. The state's child population, ages 4 to 7 years and especially 8 to 11 years, increases the screened-in report rate as does the state's unemployment rate.

The regression analyses of substantiation rate (Table 6.5) indicate that, once again, two measures of outrage have significant impacts. Dramatic workforce contraction increases the substantiation rate by 2 per 1000 whereas active litigation (*current_courtcase*) increases substantiations by nearly 2 per 1000. Other consistently significant independent variables in these substantiation models are percentage of children living below poverty, percentages of black and Hispanic children, level of federal expenditures, welfare reform time limits (*time_limit*)—all with negative impacts—and percentage of children with no employed parent (*p_chil_noparentemp*), logged per capita public welfare caseload (*ln_caseload*), unemployment rate (*unemp*), and female labor force participation rate (*fem_lfp*), all of which increase the substantiation rate.

When we examine substantiations not as a rate per 1000 child population but as a percentage of maltreatment investigations (Table 6.6), only one outrage variable, an abrupt increase in workforce, influences this percentage. A positive workforce mobilization increases the substantiations by over 4%. Table 6.6 also indicates that the risk factors of children in poverty, percentage of black and Hispanic children, and children aged 0–3 reduce this substantiation percentage whereas the percentage of children with no employed parents and logged per capita public welfare caseload increase the rate.

In Table 6.7 we show our results from the regression of physical abuse rate on the five social outrage measures; here we find no effect for these mechanisms. Factors that do have a consistently significant effect are percentage of children in poverty and

Table 6.3 Model 1: Fixed Effects Regression of (Lagged) Fatality Rate

	report_rate	substan_rate	substan_percent	phyabuse_rate	neglect_rate	sexabuse_rate	placement_rate	placement_percent
	b/se	b/se	b/se	b/se	b/se	b/se	b/se	b/se
fatal_rate (lagged)	20.438	40.441*	13.983	6.957	34.660**	-0.781	11.510**	27.456
	(24.40)	(23.49)	(32.15)	(5.57)	(14.28)	(2.81)	(5.71)	(19.71)
p_chil_pov	-0.007	-0.136*	-0.260	-0.048*	-0.061	-0.027**	-0.015	0.017
	(0.09)	(0.07)	(0.18)	(0.03)	(0.05)	(0.01)	(0.03)	(0.12)
p_blk_chpop	-0.627	-1.196**	-1.526*	-0.167	0.345	-0.086	0.007	-0.171
	(0.49)	(0.45)	(0.80)	(0.12)	(0.26)	(0.07)	(0.08)	(0.32)
p_hisp_chpop	-0.833***	-0.515**	-1.458**	-0.165**	-0.319***	-0.052*	0.017	-0.738**
	(0.26)	(0.24)	(0.68)	(0.08)	(0.11)	(0.03)	(0.10)	(0.35)
p_age03_chpop	1.703	-0.467	-4.013**	-0.150	-0.500	-0.136	-0.333	-1.227*
	(1.17)	(0.88)	(1.63)	(0.28)	(0.54)	(0.15)	(0.23)	(0.68)
p_age47_chpop	2.690*	-0.249	-1.910	0.043	1.268	-0.076	0.062	1.160
	(1.51)	(0.92)	(1.94)	(0.36)	(1.04)	(0.15)	(0.29)	(0.84)
p_age811_chpop	3.133***	1.057	0.647	0.198	0.071	0.103	0.125	1.315*
	(1.08)	(0.95)	(1.92)	(0.33)	(0.58)	(0.15)	(0.26)	(0.73)
p_age1215_chpop	3.080*	-0.819	-4.287*	0.203	0.632	-0.029	-0.204	0.086
	(1.73)	(1.15)	(2.30)	(0.36)	(0.68)	(0.16)	(0.29)	(0.79)
p_male_chpop	-3.393	0.473	4.548	0.029	-0.985	0.165	0.137	-0.625
	(2.24)	(1.54)	(3.19)	(0.54)	(1.02)	(0.23)	(0.42)	(1.05)
p_chil_singparhh	-0.278	0.005	-0.122	0.030	-0.005	0.008	0.063	0.020
	(0.21)	(0.12)	(0.23)	(0.04)	(0.08)	(0.02)	(0.04)	(0.13)

(continued)

Table 6.3 (Continued)

	report_rate	substan_rate	substan_percent	phyabuse_rate	neglect_rate	sexabuse_rate	placement_rate	placement_percent
	b/se	b/se	b/se	b/se	b/se	b/se	b/se	b/se
p_chil_noparentemp	0.038	0.218**	0.450*	-0.015	0.059	0.012	0.029	0.113
	(0.11)	(0.10)	(0.24)	(0.02)	(0.07)	(0.01)	(0.03)	(0.10)
wkrs_1000caseload	-0.157***	-0.028	0.077	-0.011	-0.012	-0.003	0.006	0.104***
	(0.04)	(0.02)	(0.08)	(0.01)	(0.02)	(0.00)	(0.01)	(0.02)
fedex_caseload (lagged)	-0.000***	-0.000**	-0.000	-0.000	-0.000**	-0.000**	-0.000	0.000
	(0.00)	(0.00)	(0.00)	(0.00)	(0.00)	(0.00)	(0.00)	(0.00)
statex_caseload (lagged)	0.000	-0.000	0.000	-0.000	-0.000	0.000	0.000	0.000**
	(0.00)	(0.00)	(0.00)	(0.00)	(0.00)	(0.00)	(0.00)	(0.00)
p_capta	-0.002	0.019	0.029	0.013***	0.020**	0.006***	0.010**	0.014
	(0.02)	(0.01)	(0.02)	(0.00)	(0.01)	(0.00)	(0.00)	(0.01)
rep_chlevel_data	-1.450	-1.556*	-0.401	-0.244	-0.234	-0.124	0.182	1.141
	(1.22)	(0.91)	(1.80)	(0.30)	(0.61)	(0.14)	(0.24)	(0.70)
p_union_cov	-0.019	-0.089	0.013	-0.053**	-0.045	-0.024*	-0.024	0.002
	(0.08)	(0.08)	(0.19)	(0.03)	(0.04)	(0.01)	(0.02)	(0.06)
ln_caseload	0.945	1.908*	2.881*	0.204	0.267	0.238	0.149	-0.512
	(1.17)	(0.96)	(1.57)	(0.31)	(0.41)	(0.19)	(0.24)	(0.76)
famcap	0.265	-0.277	-0.670	-0.196	0.110	-0.249	-0.214	-0.082
	(1.54)	(1.15)	(2.62)	(0.43)	(0.65)	(0.23)	(0.37)	(1.42)
work_req	1.109	0.554	1.792	-0.492	-0.397	-0.165	-0.426	-0.645
	(1.51)	(0.92)	(2.28)	(0.35)	(0.65)	(0.17)	(0.38)	(1.09)

	(1)	(2)	(3)	(4)	(5)	(6)	(7)	(8)
time_limit	-0.148	-2.986**	-3.890	-0.224	-1.421*	-0.077	-0.516	-2.002*
	(1.57)	(1.22)	(2.72)	(0.34)	(0.77)	(0.16)	(0.34)	(1.11)
severe_sanction	-1.864	-1.172	1.683	0.210	-1.283*	0.049	0.092	1.499
	(1.35)	(1.16)	(2.08)	(0.37)	(0.75)	(0.18)	(0.34)	(1.01)
real_maxben	-0.008	-0.007	0.033	0.007**	0.005	0.003	0.001	0.004
	(0.01)	(0.01)	(0.02)	(0.00)	(0.01)	(0.00)	(0.00)	(0.01)
unemp	0.255**	0.276**	0.214	0.001	-0.060	-0.022	0.077	0.258
	(0.12)	(0.13)	(0.29)	(0.03)	(0.08)	(0.01)	(0.05)	(0.16)
fem_lfp	0.134	0.165*	0.253*	0.014	0.007	0.003	0.011	0.130**
	(0.11)	(0.08)	(0.15)	(0.02)	(0.06)	(0.01)	(0.02)	(0.05)
time	-0.252	0.208	-1.586	-0.057	0.490	-0.120*	0.205	-0.303
	(0.72)	(0.53)	(0.98)	(0.17)	(0.37)	(0.07)	(0.14)	(0.45)
timesq	0.058*	0.011	0.102*	0.007	-0.006	0.008**	-0.005	0.038
	(0.03)	(0.02)	(0.05)	(0.01)	(0.02)	(0.00)	(0.01)	(0.02)
constant	-8.293	19.460	18.904	-2.913	20.365	-1.777	-1.063	-4.281
	(20.42)	(22.13)	(42.29)	(4.27)	(16.90)	(2.37)	(7.71)	(21.61)
N	779	779	754	779	779	779	643	643
R^2	0.2690	0.2551	0.3851	0.3246	0.1893	0.3408	0.2064	0.2831
p-value for F-statistic	0.0001	0.0033	0.0000	0.0000	0.0000	0.0000	0.0000	0.0000

$*p < 0.1$, $**p < 0.05$, $***p < 0.01$.

b is the regression coefficient.

SE is the robust standard error adjusted for heteroskedasticity and serial correlation.

Table 6.4 Fixed Effects Regression of Outrage Mechanisms on Report Rate

	Model 2	Model 3	Model 4	Model 5	Model 6
	b/se	b/se	b/se	b/se	b/se
sexoffender_law (lagged)	1.005				
	(1.31)				
current_courtcase		0.897			
		(1.76)			
CPS_courtorder			0.698		
			(1.57)		
positive_equil_chg				−5.174***	
				(1.61)	
negative_equil_chg					3.413**
					(1.48)
p_chil_pov	−0.034	−0.045	−0.032	−0.044	−0.048
	(0.09)	(0.10)	(0.10)	(0.09)	(0.08)
p_blk_chpop	−0.478	−0.549	−0.553	−0.585	−0.494
	(0.46)	(0.44)	(0.44)	(0.46)	(0.45)
p_hisp_chpop	−0.835***	−0.841***	−0.837***	−0.815***	−0.848***
	(0.26)	(0.26)	(0.26)	(0.25)	(0.25)
p_age03_chpop	1.897	1.853	1.841	1.685	1.640
	(1.15)	(1.19)	(1.20)	(1.15)	(1.14)
p_age47_chpop	2.971*	2.772*	2.785*	2.545*	2.533*
	(1.54)	(1.53)	(1.53)	(1.50)	(1.47)
p_age811_chpop	3.123***	3.117***	3.108***	2.830***	2.843**
	(1.07)	(1.09)	(1.09)	(1.04)	(1.08)
p_age1215_chpop	3.421*	3.207*	3.245*	2.949*	3.039*
	(1.76)	(1.73)	(1.74)	(1.70)	(1.67)
p_male_chpop	−3.798*	−3.567	−3.553	−3.163	−3.183
	(2.26)	(2.27)	(2.27)	(2.21)	(2.18)
p_chil_singparhh	−0.287	−0.272	−0.272	−0.288	−0.248
	(0.21)	(0.21)	(0.21)	(0.21)	(0.20)
p_chil_noparentemp	0.041	0.048	0.046	0.008	0.033
	(0.11)	(0.11)	(0.11)	(0.11)	(0.11)
wkrs_1000caseload	−0.158***	−0.157***	−0.159***	−0.125***	−0.162***
	(0.04)	(0.04)	(0.04)	(0.04)	(0.04)
fedex_caseload (lagged)	−0.000***	−0.000***	−0.000***	−0.000***	−0.000***
	(0.00)	(0.00)	(0.00)	(0.00)	(0.00)
statex_caseload (lagged)	−0.000	0.000	0.000	−0.000	−0.000
	(0.00)	(0.00)	(0.00)	(0.00)	(0.00)

(continued)

Table 6.4 (*Continued*)

	Model 2	Model 3	Model 4	Model 5	Model 6
	b/se	b/se	b/se	b/se	b/se
p_capta	−0.004	−0.005	−0.005	−0.003	−0.001
	(0.02)	(0.02)	(0.02)	(0.02)	(0.02)
rep_chlevel_data	−1.474	−1.397	−1.441	−1.187	−1.315
	(1.19)	(1.22)	(1.20)	(1.17)	(1.24)
p_union_cov	−0.011	−0.008	−0.008	−0.002	0.002
	(0.07)	(0.07)	(0.07)	(0.07)	(0.08)
ln_caseload	0.885	0.883	0.899	0.766	0.855
	(1.15)	(1.18)	(1.17)	(1.10)	(1.12)
famcap	0.161	0.164	0.125	0.254	0.357
	(1.53)	(1.53)	(1.48)	(1.51)	(1.49)
work_req	1.131	1.255	1.231	0.911	0.655
	(1.47)	(1.53)	(1.52)	(1.45)	(1.48)
time_limit	−0.094	−0.162	−0.139	−0.242	−0.067
	(1.58)	(1.59)	(1.61)	(1.52)	(1.60)
severe_sanction	−1.829	−1.742	−1.789	−1.753	−1.785
	(1.35)	(1.31)	(1.33)	(1.30)	(1.36)
real_maxben	−0.007	−0.007	−0.007	−0.008	−0.006
	(0.01)	(0.01)	(0.01)	(0.01)	(0.01)
unemp	0.254**	0.243**	0.239**	0.239**	0.229*
	(0.11)	(0.11)	(0.12)	(0.12)	(0.12)
fem_lfp	0.125	0.127	0.125	0.107	0.125
	(0.11)	(0.11)	(0.11)	(0.11)	(0.11)
time	−0.455	−0.296	−0.289	−0.047	−0.247
	(0.77)	(0.72)	(0.71)	(0.69)	(0.69)
timesq	0.065*	0.059*	0.059*	0.045	0.057*
	(0.03)	(0.03)	(0.03)	(0.03)	(0.03)
constant	−6.351	−7.815	−8.943	−5.382	−8.987
	(20.56)	(20.62)	(21.44)	(20.14)	(20.62)
N	779	779	779	779	779
R^2	0.2688	0.2688	0.2684	0.2901	0.2829
p-value for F-statistic	0.0000	0.0001	0.0000	0.0000	0.0000

$*p < 0.1$, $**p < 0.05$, $***p < 0.01$.

b is the regression coefficient.

SE is the robust standard error adjusted for heteroskedasticity and serial correlation.

Table 6.5 Fixed Effects Regression of Outrage Mechanisms on Substantiation Rate

	Model 2	Model 3	Model 4	Model 5	Model 6
	b/se	b/se	b/se	b/se	b/se
sexoffender_law (lagged)	0.573				
	(1.19)				
current_courtcase		1.775*			
		(1.00)			
CPS_courtorder			0.373		
			(1.10)		
positive_equil_chg				−0.593	
				(0.98)	
negative_equil_chg					2.133**
					(0.92)
p_chil_pov	−0.195**	−0.212**	−0.194**	−0.198**	−0.203**
	(0.09)	(0.09)	(0.09)	(0.09)	(0.08)
p_blk_chpop	−0.955**	−1.041**	−0.997**	−0.985**	−0.963**
	(0.42)	(0.43)	(0.43)	(0.42)	(0.42)
p_hisp_chpop	−0.507**	−0.531**	−0.508**	−0.501**	−0.516**
	(0.24)	(0.24)	(0.24)	(0.24)	(0.24)
p_age03_chpop	−0.233	−0.171	−0.267	−0.306	−0.388
	(0.89)	(0.93)	(0.95)	(0.92)	(0.91)
p_age47_chpop	0.039	−0.086	−0.067	−0.096	−0.224
	(0.98)	(0.96)	(0.95)	(0.96)	(0.94)
p_age811_chpop	1.004	1.026	0.996	0.960	0.831
	(0.96)	(0.96)	(0.97)	(0.95)	(0.99)
p_age1215_chpop	−0.432	−0.567	−0.534	−0.580	−0.660
	(1.22)	(1.17)	(1.19)	(1.17)	(1.17)
p_male_chpop	0.024	0.128	0.164	0.211	0.395
	(1.59)	(1.58)	(1.60)	(1.58)	(1.60)
p_chil_singparhh	0.002	0.018	0.010	0.006	0.025
	(0.12)	(0.12)	(0.13)	(0.12)	(0.12)
p_chil_noparentemp	0.233**	0.239**	0.235**	0.231**	0.227**
	(0.11)	(0.10)	(0.11)	(0.11)	(0.11)
wkrs_1000caseload	−0.030	−0.028	−0.030	−0.026	−0.032
	(0.03)	(0.02)	(0.03)	(0.03)	(0.03)
fedex_caseload (lagged)	−0.000**	−0.000**	−0.000**	−0.000**	−0.000**
	(0.00)	(0.00)	(0.00)	(0.00)	(0.00)
statex_caseload (lagged)	−0.000	−0.000	−0.000	−0.000	−0.000
	(0.00)	(0.00)	(0.00)	(0.00)	(0.00)

(continued)

Table 6.5 *(Continued)*

	Model 2	*Model 3*	*Model 4*	*Model 5*	*Model 6*
	b/se	b/se	b/se	b/se	b/se
p_capta	0.014	0.014	0.014	0.014	0.016
	(0.01)	(0.01)	(0.01)	(0.01)	(0.01)
rep_chlevel_data	−1.521*	−1.452	−1.502	−1.462	−1.425
	(0.91)	(0.93)	(0.92)	(0.91)	(0.93)
p_union_cov	−0.075	−0.067	−0.073	−0.074	−0.066
	(0.08)	(0.08)	(0.07)	(0.08)	(0.07)
ln_caseload	1.825*	1.786*	1.834*	1.823*	1.805*
	(0.97)	(0.99)	(0.98)	(0.98)	(0.95)
famcap	−0.399	−0.476	−0.417	−0.362	−0.280
	(1.22)	(1.20)	(1.17)	(1.20)	(1.20)
work_req	0.660	0.842	0.715	0.654	0.359
	(0.93)	(0.97)	(0.96)	(0.91)	(0.92)
time_limit	−2.983**	−3.013**	−3.010**	−3.034**	−2.963**
	(1.26)	(1.23)	(1.26)	(1.25)	(1.23)
severe_sanction	−1.118	−0.930	−1.098	−1.115	−1.090
	(1.17)	(1.15)	(1.18)	(1.16)	(1.18)
real_maxben	−0.005	−0.006	−0.005	−0.005	−0.004
	(0.01)	(0.01)	(0.01)	(0.01)	(0.01)
unemp	0.263**	0.254**	0.254**	0.257*	0.248*
	(0.12)	(0.13)	(0.13)	(0.13)	(0.13)
fem_lfp	0.148*	0.151*	0.149*	0.147*	0.148*
	(0.08)	(0.08)	(0.08)	(0.08)	(0.08)
time	0.037	0.122	0.131	0.158	0.158
	(0.63)	(0.52)	(0.53)	(0.53)	(0.52)
timesq	0.017	0.012	0.013	0.012	0.012
	(0.03)	(0.02)	(0.02)	(0.02)	(0.02)
constant	21.800	20.407	20.377	21.426	20.212
	(22.43)	(21.66)	(22.15)	(22.52)	(22.67)
N	779	779	779	779	779
R^2	0.2459	0.2538	0.2456	0.2456	0.2552
p-value for F-statistic	0.0102	0.0002	0.0094	0.0115	0.0032

*p<0.1 **p<0.05 ***p<0.01

b is the regression coefficient

SE is the robust standard error adjusted for heteroskedasticity and serial correlation

Table 6.6 Fixed effects regression of outrage mechanisms on substantiations as a percent of investigations

	Model 2	Model 3	Model 4	Model 5	Model 6
	b/se	b/se	b/se	b/se	b/se
sexoffender_law (lagged)	2.552				
	(2.32)				
current_courtcase		1.114			
		(2.08)			
CPS_courtorder			−1.211		
			(1.95)		
positive_equil_chg				4.314*	
				(2.40)	
negative_equil_chg					0.272
					(1.70)
p_chil_pov	−0.283	−0.301	−0.306*	−0.303	−0.290
	(0.18)	(0.18)	(0.18)	(0.19)	(0.18)
p_blk_chpop	−1.348*	−1.490**	−1.374*	−1.392*	−1.447*
	(0.70)	(0.74)	(0.73)	(0.72)	(0.72)
p_hisp_chpop	−1.486**	−1.469**	−1.433**	−1.474**	−1.457**
	(0.68)	(0.68)	(0.66)	(0.68)	(0.68)
p_age03_chpop	−3.737**	−3.894**	−4.080**	−3.913**	−3.983**
	(1.66)	(1.64)	(1.63)	(1.60)	(1.64)
p_age47_chpop	−1.385	−1.880	−1.862	−1.678	−1.876
	(2.06)	(1.96)	(1.96)	(1.95)	(1.98)
p_age811_chpop	0.649	0.623	0.593	0.830	0.591
	(1.93)	(1.92)	(1.90)	(1.88)	(1.96)
p_age1215_chpop	−3.710	−4.238*	−4.251*	−4.009*	−4.224*
	(2.43)	(2.33)	(2.31)	(2.28)	(2.33)
p_male_chpop	3.868	4.461	4.481	4.188	4.497
	(3.32)	(3.19)	(3.21)	(3.13)	(3.24)
p_chil_singparhh	−0.141	−0.109	−0.129	−0.103	−0.116
	(0.22)	(0.23)	(0.23)	(0.23)	(0.23)
p_chil_noparentemp	0.445*	0.458*	0.458*	0.492**	0.456*
	(0.24)	(0.24)	(0.24)	(0.24)	(0.24)
wkrs_1000caseload	0.077	0.076	0.076	0.046	0.075
	(0.08)	(0.08)	(0.08)	(0.08)	(0.08)
fedex_caseload (lagged)	−0.000	−0.000	−0.000	−0.000	−0.000
	(0.00)	(0.00)	(0.00)	(0.00)	(0.00)

(continued)

Table 6.6 *(Continued)*

	Model 2	Model 3	Model 4	Model 5	Model 6
	b/se	b/se	b/se	b/se	b/se
statex_caseload (lagged)	0.000	0.000	0.000	0.000	0.000
	(0.00)	(0.00)	(0.00)	(0.00)	(0.00)
p_capta	0.030	0.028	0.027	0.025	0.028
	(0.02)	(0.02)	(0.02)	(0.02)	(0.02)
rep_chlevel_data	−0.505	−0.362	−0.343	−0.542	−0.371
	(1.75)	(1.83)	(1.77)	(1.78)	(1.82)
p_union_cov	0.022	0.022	0.011	0.013	0.019
	(0.19)	(0.19)	(0.19)	(0.19)	(0.19)
ln_caseload	2.800*	2.855*	2.907*	3.033*	2.872*
	(1.59)	(1.57)	(1.56)	(1.52)	(1.57)
famcap	−0.830	−0.765	−0.470	−0.603	−0.671
	(2.63)	(2.61)	(2.62)	(2.63)	(2.64)
work_req	1.736	1.919	1.666	1.930	1.774
	(2.24)	(2.26)	(2.25)	(2.23)	(2.32)
time_limit	−3.642	−3.856	−3.926	−3.776	−3.875
	(2.75)	(2.71)	(2.72)	(2.70)	(2.71)
severe_sanction	1.768	1.801	1.625	1.596	1.701
	(2.08)	(2.09)	(2.09)	(2.09)	(2.09)
real_maxben	0.034	0.033	0.035	0.035	0.034
	(0.02)	(0.02)	(0.02)	(0.02)	(0.02)
unemp	0.234	0.208	0.216	0.204	0.207
	(0.29)	(0.29)	(0.29)	(0.29)	(0.29)
fem_lfp	0.244	0.248	0.247*	0.262*	0.247
	(0.15)	(0.15)	(0.14)	(0.15)	(0.15)
time	−2.043*	−1.613	−1.634*	−1.842*	−1.612
	(1.06)	(0.98)	(0.97)	(0.98)	(0.98)
timesq	0.119**	0.102*	0.105*	0.116**	0.103*
	(0.05)	(0.05)	(0.05)	(0.05)	(0.05)
constant	21.995	19.157	22.315	17.820	19.423
	(42.02)	(42.56)	(41.37)	(42.60)	(42.65)
N	754	754	754	754	754
R^2	0.3879	0.3856	0.3859	0.3904	0.3849
p-value for F-statistic	0.0000	0.0000	0.0000	0.0000	0.0000

$*p < 0.1, **p < 0.05, ***p < 0.01.$

b is the regression coefficient.

SE is the robust standard error adjusted for heteroskedasticity and serial correlation.

Table 6.7 Fixed Effects Regression of Outrage Mechanisms on Physical Abuse Rate

	Model 2	Model 3	Model 4	Model 5	Model 6
	b/se	b/se	b/se	b/se	b/se
sexoffender_law (lagged)	0.372				
	(0.45)				
current_courtcase		−0.079			
		(0.40)			
CPS_courtorder			−0.470		
			(0.28)		
positive_equil_chg				−0.381	
				(0.38)	
negative_equil_chg					0.208
					(0.29)
p_chil_pov	−0.057**	−0.057**	−0.061**	−0.058**	−0.059**
	(0.03)	(0.03)	(0.03)	(0.03)	(0.03)
p_blk_chpop	−0.115	−0.126	−0.104	−0.134	−0.128
	(0.11)	(0.11)	(0.11)	(0.11)	(0.11)
p_hisp_chpop	−0.165**	−0.161**	−0.156**	−0.161**	−0.164**
	(0.07)	(0.07)	(0.07)	(0.07)	(0.07)
p_age03_chpop	−0.081	−0.126	−0.154	−0.128	−0.129
	(0.26)	(0.29)	(0.28)	(0.28)	(0.28)
p_age47_chpop	0.144	0.074	0.071	0.056	0.058
	(0.35)	(0.36)	(0.36)	(0.36)	(0.36)
p_age811_chpop	0.195	0.185	0.180	0.166	0.171
	(0.32)	(0.33)	(0.32)	(0.32)	(0.34)
p_age1215_chpop	0.325	0.250	0.230	0.229	0.238
	(0.35)	(0.36)	(0.36)	(0.36)	(0.36)
p_male_chpop	−0.117	−0.022	−0.021	0.004	−0.002
	(0.52)	(0.55)	(0.54)	(0.54)	(0.55)
p_chil_singparhh	0.027	0.030	0.026	0.029	0.032
	(0.04)	(0.04)	(0.04)	(0.04)	(0.04)
p_chil_noparentemp	−0.014	−0.012	−0.012	−0.015	−0.013
	(0.02)	(0.02)	(0.02)	(0.02)	(0.02)
wkrs_1000caseload	−0.011	−0.011	−0.011	−0.009	−0.012
	(0.01)	(0.01)	(0.01)	(0.01)	(0.01)
fedex_caseload (lagged)	−0.000	−0.000	−0.000	−0.000	−0.000
	(0.00)	(0.00)	(0.00)	(0.00)	(0.00)
statex_caseload (lagged)	−0.000	−0.000	−0.000	−0.000	−0.000
	(0.00)	(0.00)	(0.00)	(0.00)	(0.00)

(continued)

Table 6.7 (*Continued*)

	Model 2	Model 3	Model 4	Model 5	Model 6
	b/se	b/se	b/se	b/se	b/se
p_capta	0.012***	0.012***	0.012***	0.012***	0.012***
	(0.00)	(0.00)	(0.00)	(0.00)	(0.00)
rep_chlevel_data	−0.254	−0.234	−0.215	−0.216	−0.227
	(0.30)	(0.30)	(0.29)	(0.29)	(0.30)
p_union_cov	−0.050*	−0.051*	−0.054**	−0.050*	−0.050*
	(0.03)	(0.03)	(0.03)	(0.03)	(0.03)
ln_caseload	0.183	0.195	0.200	0.182	0.189
	(0.30)	(0.31)	(0.31)	(0.30)	(0.30)
famcap	−0.233	−0.207	−0.148	−0.209	−0.203
	(0.43)	(0.43)	(0.40)	(0.43)	(0.42)
work_req	−0.486	−0.477	−0.508	−0.489	−0.501
	(0.35)	(0.36)	(0.34)	(0.34)	(0.35)
time_limit	−0.203	−0.231	−0.251	−0.236	−0.225
	(0.36)	(0.35)	(0.34)	(0.35)	(0.35)
severe_sanction	0.223	0.210	0.184	0.225	0.222
	(0.37)	(0.36)	(0.36)	(0.36)	(0.37)
real_maxben	0.007**	0.008**	0.008**	0.007**	0.007**
	(0.00)	(0.00)	(0.00)	(0.00)	(0.00)
unemp	0.001	−0.002	0.002	−0.002	−0.003
	(0.03)	(0.03)	(0.03)	(0.03)	(0.03)
fem_lfp	0.011	0.011	0.011	0.010	0.011
	(0.02)	(0.02)	(0.02)	(0.02)	(0.02)
time	−0.131	−0.071	−0.073	−0.053	−0.068
	(0.20)	(0.17)	(0.16)	(0.17)	(0.17)
timesq	0.009	0.007	0.007	0.006	0.007
	(0.01)	(0.01)	(0.01)	(0.01)	(0.01)
constant	−2.220	−2.580	−1.587	−2.465	−2.710
	(4.23)	(4.32)	(4.06)	(4.31)	(4.27)
N	779	779	779	779	779
R^2	0.3247	0.3219	0.3284	0.3237	0.3226
p-value for F-statistic	0.0000	0.0000	0.0000	0.0000	0.0000

*$p < 0.1$, **$p < 0.05$, ***$p < 0.01$.

b is the regression coefficient.

SE is the robust standard error adjusted for heteroskedasticity and serial correlation.

percentage of Hispanic children in the population—both of which serve to reduce the physical abuse rate. More thorough reporting of CAPTA items and generosity level of welfare benefits show positive influences on the rate.

Our analyses of neglect rate (Table 6.8) find that dramatic declines in workforce (*negative_equil_chg*) increase the rate of children classified as neglected by 1 per 1000. This apparent doubling down impact also occurred in our analyses of screened-in reports and substantiations and hence is consistent with decisions to minimize false-negative cases. Four additional variables in the model have strong, consistently negative effects on neglect rate, e.g., percentages of Hispanic children, children living in poverty, (lagged) federal expenditures in the state, and public welfare term limits, whereas the percentage of black children exerts a consistently significant and positive effect on neglect findings.

Table 6.9 reveals that states with active court orders have lower sexual abuse rates. This is the first instance in which this measure of social outrage is significant, reducing the sexual abuse rate by 0.35 per 1000 children. The percentage of children living in poverty, percentage of Hispanic children, federal CPS expenditures in a state, and proportion of workers who are unionized (*p_union_cov*) are also responsible for lowering the rate. The only measure that shows a significant positive relationship to the outcome is thorough reporting by a state of required CAPTA items.

In Tables 6.10 and 6.11 we examine the impact of outrage mechanisms on placement decisions. Table 6.10 indicates that states with active court cases experience higher out-of-home placement rates—about 0.6 children per 1000. When placements as a percentage of investigations are analyzed, as we show in Table 6.11, it is states that are under court order that demonstrate a significant relationship; in this instance approximately 1.8 more child placements occur for every 100 cases investigated.

Although there are few significant variables in the regression of child placement rates, the regression of placements as a percentage of investigations shows that CPS workers per 1000 cases, state child welfare expenditures, and female population in the labor force all increase child placement decisions. The percentage of Hispanic children in the state population and welfare time limit exhibit a strong negative effect on placements.

Tables 6.4 to 6.11 also demonstrate reasonably good fit as indicated by a significant overall *F*-statistic, and R^2 statistic ranging from 18% [*neglect_rate*] to nearly 40% [*substan_percent*].

Summary of Results

We realize that the sheer volume of results produced by this series of econometric analyses can be a bit daunting, and have summarized the principal impacts of our outrage measures in Table 6.12. This table shows that outrage affects a wide range of CPS decision outcomes including (1) acceptance of a referral for investigation, (2) substantiating a report as child maltreatment, and (3) placing children in foster care or institutions. Some mechanisms of outrage also affect sexual abuse and child neglect classification decisions.

Table 6.8 Fixed Effects Regression of Outrage Mechanisms on Neglect Rate

	Model 2	*Model 3*	*Model 4*	*Model 5*	*Model 6*
	b/se	*b/se*	*b/se*	*b/se*	*b/se*
sexoffender_law (lagged)	−0.205 (0.84)				
current_courtcase		0.100 (0.70)			
CPS_courtorder			−0.199 (0.51)		
positive_equil_chg				−0.854 (0.80)	
negative_equil_chg					1.158** (0.44)
p_chil_pov	−0.113* (0.06)	−0.113* (0.06)	−0.114* (0.06)	−0.113** (0.06)	−0.116** (0.05)
p_blk_chpop	0.525** (0.24)	0.529** (0.24)	0.543** (0.24)	0.521** (0.24)	0.540** (0.24)
p_hisp_chpop	−0.306*** (0.11)	−0.310*** (0.10)	−0.305*** (0.10)	−0.306*** (0.11)	−0.315*** (0.11)
p_age03_chpop	−0.374 (0.53)	−0.345 (0.55)	−0.366 (0.54)	−0.369 (0.54)	−0.403 (0.54)
p_age47_chpop	1.384 (0.98)	1.422 (1.01)	1.422 (1.01)	1.384 (1.01)	1.339 (1.00)
p_age811_chpop	0.009 (0.60)	0.016 (0.61)	0.012 (0.61)	−0.030 (0.60)	−0.073 (0.61)
p_age1215_chpop	0.822 (0.69)	0.862 (0.70)	0.855 (0.71)	0.819 (0.70)	0.803 (0.69)
p_male_chpop	−1.196 (1.01)	−1.249 (1.04)	−1.246 (1.04)	−1.183 (1.04)	−1.123 (1.03)
p_chil_singparhh	−0.001 (0.08)	−0.002 (0.08)	−0.004 (0.08)	−0.005 (0.08)	0.007 (0.08)
p_chil_noparentemp	0.075 (0.08)	0.074 (0.08)	0.075 (0.08)	0.068 (0.08)	0.070 (0.08)
wkrs_1000caseload	−0.014 (0.02)	−0.014 (0.02)	−0.014 (0.02)	−0.008 (0.02)	−0.015 (0.02)
fedex_caseload (lagged)	−0.000** (0.00)	−0.000** (0.00)	−0.000** (0.00)	−0.000** (0.00)	−0.000** (0.00)
statex_caseload (lagged)	−0.000 (0.00)	−0.000 (0.00)	−0.000 (0.00)	−0.000 (0.00)	−0.000 (0.00)

(continued)

Table 6.8 *(Continued)*

	Model 2	Model 3	Model 4	Model 5	Model 6
	b/se	b/se	b/se	b/se	b/se
p_capta	0.015*	0.015*	0.015*	0.016*	0.017*
	(0.01)	(0.01)	(0.01)	(0.01)	(0.01)
rep_chlevel_data	−0.164	−0.174	−0.168	−0.138	−0.142
	(0.62)	(0.62)	(0.62)	(0.60)	(0.62)
p_union_cov	−0.034	−0.033	−0.035	−0.032	−0.029
	(0.04)	(0.04)	(0.04)	(0.04)	(0.04)
ln_caseload	0.213	0.205	0.211	0.184	0.189
	(0.42)	(0.42)	(0.42)	(0.40)	(0.40)
famcap	0.045	0.027	0.060	0.039	0.080
	(0.66)	(0.67)	(0.65)	(0.65)	(0.65)
work_req	−0.276	−0.276	−0.301	−0.328	−0.461
	(0.69)	(0.70)	(0.68)	(0.66)	(0.67)
time_limit	−1.469*	−1.454*	−1.463*	−1.466*	−1.420*
	(0.79)	(0.77)	(0.76)	(0.76)	(0.76)
severe_sanction	−1.245	−1.232	−1.257	−1.228	−1.224
	(0.76)	(0.75)	(0.75)	(0.74)	(0.76)
real_maxben	0.006	0.006	0.007	0.006	0.007
	(0.01)	(0.01)	(0.01)	(0.01)	(0.01)
unemp	−0.078	−0.076	−0.074	−0.077	−0.081
	(0.08)	(0.08)	(0.08)	(0.08)	(0.08)
fem_lfp	−0.007	−0.007	−0.007	−0.010	−0.007
	(0.05)	(0.05)	(0.05)	(0.05)	(0.05)
time	0.456	0.422	0.422	0.463	0.438
	(0.44)	(0.36)	(0.36)	(0.36)	(0.36)
timesq	−0.006	−0.005	−0.004	−0.007	−0.005
	(0.02)	(0.02)	(0.02)	(0.02)	(0.02)
constant	21.631	21.805	22.283	22.185	21.317
	(16.81)	(17.04)	(16.82)	(16.88)	(16.81)
N	779	779	779	779	779
R^2	0.1715	0.1713	0.1716	0.1738	0.1786
p-value for F-statistic	0.0020	0.0003	0.0016	0.0019	0.0002

*$p < 0.1$, **$p < 0.05$, ***$p < 0.01$.

b is the regression coefficient.

SE is the robust standard error adjusted for heteroskedasticity and serial correlation.

Table 6.9 Fixed Effects Regression of Outrage Mechanisms on Sexual Abuse Rate

	Model 2	Model 3	Model 4	Model 5	Model 6
	b/se	b/se	b/se	b/se	b/se
sexoffender_law (lagged)	0.327				
	(0.25)				
current_courtcase		−0.183			
		(0.20)			
CPS_courtorder			−0.358**		
			(0.16)		
positive_equil_chg				−0.229	
				(0.18)	
negative_equil_chg					0.116
					(0.15)
p_chil_pov	−0.024*	−0.024*	−0.028**	−0.026*	−0.026*
	(0.01)	(0.01)	(0.01)	(0.01)	(0.01)
p_blk_chpop	−0.078	−0.084	−0.071	−0.094	−0.090
	(0.06)	(0.06)	(0.06)	(0.06)	(0.06)
p_hisp_chpop	−0.055*	−0.049*	−0.047*	−0.051*	−0.053*
	(0.03)	(0.03)	(0.03)	(0.03)	(0.03)
p_age03_chpop	−0.105	−0.152	−0.165	−0.144	−0.144
	(0.13)	(0.15)	(0.14)	(0.15)	(0.15)
p_age47_chpop	−0.018	−0.078	−0.081	−0.090	−0.088
	(0.14)	(0.15)	(0.14)	(0.15)	(0.15)
p_age811_chpop	0.112	0.100	0.100	0.092	0.095
	(0.15)	(0.15)	(0.14)	(0.15)	(0.16)
p_age1215_chpop	0.033	−0.032	−0.049	−0.046	−0.040
	(0.14)	(0.15)	(0.15)	(0.15)	(0.15)
p_male_chpop	0.090	0.175	0.174	0.188	0.184
	(0.20)	(0.22)	(0.21)	(0.22)	(0.22)
p_chil_singparhh	0.004	0.006	0.005	0.007	0.009
	(0.02)	(0.02)	(0.02)	(0.02)	(0.02)
p_chil_noparentemp	0.010	0.011	0.012	0.010	0.011
	(0.01)	(0.01)	(0.01)	(0.01)	(0.01)
wkrs_1000caseload	−0.003	−0.003	−0.003	−0.002	−0.003
	(0.00)	(0.00)	(0.00)	(0.00)	(0.00)
fedex_caseload (lagged)	−0.000*	−0.000*	−0.000**	−0.000**	−0.000**
	(0.00)	(0.00)	(0.00)	(0.00)	(0.00)
statex_caseload (lagged)	0.000	0.000	0.000	0.000	0.000
	(0.00)	(0.00)	(0.00)	(0.00)	(0.00)

(continued)

Table 6.9 *(Continued)*

	Model 2	Model 3	Model 4	Model 5	Model 6
	b/se	b/se	b/se	b/se	b/se
p_capta	0.006***	0.006***	0.006***	0.006***	0.006***
	(0.00)	(0.00)	(0.00)	(0.00)	(0.00)
rep_chlevel_data	−0.145	−0.129	−0.112	−0.116	−0.122
	(0.14)	(0.14)	(0.13)	(0.14)	(0.14)
p_union_cov	−0.024*	−0.025*	−0.027*	−0.024*	−0.024*
	(0.01)	(0.01)	(0.01)	(0.01)	(0.01)
ln_caseload	0.231	0.245	0.245	0.233	0.238
	(0.18)	(0.19)	(0.19)	(0.18)	(0.18)
famcap	−0.266	−0.235	−0.198	−0.245	−0.242
	(0.23)	(0.22)	(0.21)	(0.23)	(0.23)
work_req	−0.182	−0.184	−0.196	−0.179	−0.185
	(0.17)	(0.17)	(0.17)	(0.17)	(0.18)
time_limit	−0.052	−0.077	−0.091	−0.079	−0.073
	(0.16)	(0.16)	(0.16)	(0.16)	(0.16)
severe_sanction	0.051	0.028	0.022	0.051	0.049
	(0.17)	(0.17)	(0.17)	(0.17)	(0.18)
real_maxben	0.003	0.003	0.003	0.003	0.003
	(0.00)	(0.00)	(0.00)	(0.00)	(0.00)
unemp	−0.019	−0.021	−0.018	−0.022	−0.022
	(0.01)	(0.01)	(0.01)	(0.01)	(0.01)
fem_lfp	0.003	0.003	0.004	0.003	0.004
	(0.01)	(0.01)	(0.01)	(0.01)	(0.01)
time	−0.172**	−0.118*	−0.120*	−0.108*	−0.117*
	(0.08)	(0.06)	(0.06)	(0.06)	(0.06)
timesq	0.010**	0.008**	0.008**	0.007**	0.008**
	(0.00)	(0.00)	(0.00)	(0.00)	(0.00)
constant	−1.464	−1.730	−1.029	−1.721	−1.864
	(2.45)	(2.43)	(2.35)	(2.38)	(2.40)
N	779	779	779	779	779
R^2	0.3505	0.3444	0.3572	0.3437	0.3419
p-value for F-statistic	0.0000	0.0000	0.0000	0.0000	0.0000

*$p < 0.1$, **$p < 0.05$, ***$p < 0.01$.

b is the regression coefficient.

SE is the robust standard error adjusted for heteroskedasticity and serial correlation.

Table 6.10 Fixed Effects Regression of Outrage Mechanisms on Placement Rate

	Model 2	Model 3	Model 4	Model 5	Model 6
	b/se	b/se	b/se	b/se	b/se
sexoffender_law (lagged)	−0.260				
	(0.28)				
current_courtcase		0.633*			
		(0.32)			
CPS_courtorder			0.638		
			(0.39)		
positive_equil_chg				−0.117	
				(0.35)	
negative_equil_chg					0.170
					(0.29)
p_chil_pov	−0.020	−0.032	−0.016	−0.018	−0.018
	(0.03)	(0.03)	(0.03)	(0.03)	(0.03)
p_blk_chpop	0.022	0.025	0.008	0.033	0.034
	(0.08)	(0.09)	(0.09)	(0.08)	(0.08)
p_hisp_chpop	0.023	−0.003	0.007	0.021	0.016
	(0.10)	(0.10)	(0.10)	(0.10)	(0.10)
p_age03_chpop	−0.347	−0.282	−0.262	−0.325	−0.323
	(0.23)	(0.23)	(0.21)	(0.23)	(0.23)
p_age47_chpop	0.050	0.099	0.128	0.094	0.097
	(0.29)	(0.29)	(0.28)	(0.29)	(0.29)
p_age811_chpop	0.133	0.152	0.150	0.130	0.133
	(0.26)	(0.26)	(0.25)	(0.26)	(0.26)
p_age1215_chpop	−0.204	−0.154	−0.105	−0.157	−0.150
	(0.29)	(0.28)	(0.29)	(0.29)	(0.29)
p_male_chpop	0.164	0.088	0.069	0.106	0.102
	(0.43)	(0.42)	(0.42)	(0.42)	(0.43)
p_chil_singparhh	0.066	0.070	0.071	0.064	0.066
	(0.04)	(0.04)	(0.04)	(0.04)	(0.04)
p_chil_noparentemp	0.031	0.034	0.031	0.029	0.029
	(0.03)	(0.02)	(0.03)	(0.03)	(0.03)
wkrs_1000caseload	0.005	0.006	0.005	0.006	0.005
	(0.01)	(0.01)	(0.01)	(0.01)	(0.01)
fedex_caseload (lagged)	−0.000*	−0.000*	−0.000*	−0.000	−0.000*
	(0.00)	(0.00)	(0.00)	(0.00)	(0.00)
statex_caseload (lagged)	0.000	0.000*	0.000*	0.000	0.000
	(0.00)	(0.00)	(0.00)	(0.00)	(0.00)

(continued)

Table 6.10 *(Continued)*

	Model 2	Model 3	Model 4	Model 5	Model 6
	b/se	b/se	b/se	b/se	b/se
p_capta	0.009**	0.009**	0.009**	0.009**	0.010**
	(0.00)	(0.00)	(0.00)	(0.00)	(0.00)
rep_chlevel_data	0.203	0.205	0.175	0.189	0.188
	(0.24)	(0.24)	(0.24)	(0.25)	(0.25)
p_union_cov	−0.020	−0.018	−0.014	−0.020	−0.019
	(0.02)	(0.02)	(0.02)	(0.02)	(0.02)
ln_caseload	0.161	0.158	0.167	0.150	0.152
	(0.24)	(0.23)	(0.24)	(0.24)	(0.25)
famcap	−0.227	−0.284	−0.325	−0.243	−0.238
	(0.38)	(0.35)	(0.36)	(0.37)	(0.37)
work_req	−0.396	−0.315	−0.323	−0.406	−0.406
	(0.37)	(0.37)	(0.38)	(0.38)	(0.38)
time_limit	−0.578*	−0.534	−0.497	−0.547	−0.543
	(0.34)	(0.34)	(0.33)	(0.34)	(0.34)
severe_sanction	0.098	0.165	0.130	0.102	0.107
	(0.34)	(0.34)	(0.34)	(0.34)	(0.34)
real_maxben	0.002	0.001	0.001	0.002	0.002
	(0.00)	(0.00)	(0.00)	(0.00)	(0.00)
unemp	0.075	0.078	0.070	0.077	0.076
	(0.05)	(0.05)	(0.05)	(0.05)	(0.05)
fem_lfp	0.006	0.006	0.004	0.006	0.007
	(0.02)	(0.02)	(0.02)	(0.02)	(0.02)
time	0.251	0.186	0.195	0.212	0.208
	(0.16)	(0.14)	(0.15)	(0.14)	(0.14)
timesq	−0.006	−0.004	−0.004	−0.005	−0.005
	(0.01)	(0.01)	(0.01)	(0.01)	(0.01)
constant	−2.164	−2.302	−3.226	−1.707	−1.951
	(7.38)	(7.42)	(6.90)	(7.47)	(7.48)
N	643	643	643	643	643
R^2	0.2024	0.2147	0.2157	0.2006	0.2012
p-value for F-statistic	0.0000	0.0000	0.0000	0.0000	0.0000

*$p < 0.1$, **$p < 0.05$, ***$p < 0.01$.

b is the regression coefficient.

SE is the robust standard error adjusted for heteroskedasticity and serial correlation.

Table 6.11 Fixed Effects Regression of Outrage Mechanisms on Placements as a Percentage of Investigations

	Model 2	Model 3	Model 4	Model 5	Model 6
	b/se	b/se	b/se	b/se	b/se
sexoffender_law (lagged)	0.823				
	(1.16)				
current_courtcase		0.675			
		(0.79)			
CPS_courtorder			1.846**		
			(0.88)		
positive_equil_chg				1.285	
				(1.17)	
negative_equil_chg					−0.539
					(0.90)
p_chil_pov	0.009	−0.007	0.016	0.000	0.004
	(0.13)	(0.12)	(0.12)	(0.12)	(0.12)
p_blk_chpop	−0.073	−0.117	−0.181	−0.102	−0.110
	(0.31)	(0.32)	(0.34)	(0.32)	(0.32)
p_hisp_chpop	−0.744**	−0.757**	−0.768**	−0.748**	−0.722**
	(0.36)	(0.36)	(0.35)	(0.36)	(0.36)
p_age03_chpop	−1.113*	−1.157*	−1.029	−1.145*	−1.188*
	(0.65)	(0.68)	(0.62)	(0.66)	(0.66)
p_age47_chpop	1.411	1.252	1.332	1.321	1.265
	(0.93)	(0.83)	(0.80)	(0.85)	(0.83)
p_age811_chpop	1.374*	1.365*	1.382*	1.456*	1.373*
	(0.75)	(0.73)	(0.69)	(0.74)	(0.74)
p_age1215_chpop	0.387	0.210	0.343	0.299	0.217
	(0.86)	(0.75)	(0.75)	(0.77)	(0.75)
p_male_chpop	−0.943	−0.732	−0.799	−0.850	−0.747
	(1.16)	(1.03)	(1.00)	(1.05)	(1.05)
p_chil_singparhh	0.015	0.028	0.043	0.023	0.017
	(0.13)	(0.13)	(0.12)	(0.12)	(0.13)
p_chil_noparentemp	0.110	0.119	0.116	0.124	0.116
	(0.10)	(0.10)	(0.10)	(0.10)	(0.10)
wkrs_1000caseload	0.102***	0.103***	0.102***	0.092***	0.102***
	(0.02)	(0.02)	(0.02)	(0.02)	(0.02)
fedex_caseload (lagged)	0.000	0.000	0.000	0.000	0.000
	(0.00)	(0.00)	(0.00)	(0.00)	(0.00)
statex_caseload (lagged)	0.000**	0.000**	0.000**	0.000**	0.000**
	(0.00)	(0.00)	(0.00)	(0.00)	(0.00)

(continued)

Table 6.11 *(Continued)*

	Model 2	Model 3	Model 4	Model 5	Model 6
	b/se	b/se	b/se	b/se	b/se
p_capta	0.014	0.013	0.013	0.013	0.013
	(0.01)	(0.01)	(0.01)	(0.01)	(0.01)
rep_chlevel_data	1.083	1.168	1.119	1.094	1.133
	(0.71)	(0.71)	(0.68)	(0.73)	(0.71)
p_union_cov	0.009	0.013	0.027	0.009	0.006
	(0.06)	(0.06)	(0.06)	(0.06)	(0.06)
ln_caseload	−0.500	−0.490	−0.463	−0.400	−0.473
	(0.79)	(0.75)	(0.74)	(0.74)	(0.75)
famcap	−0.215	−0.197	−0.387	−0.189	−0.179
	(1.43)	(1.42)	(1.40)	(1.42)	(1.42)
work_req	−0.558	−0.483	−0.365	−0.424	−0.526
	(1.12)	(1.10)	(1.14)	(1.13)	(1.11)
time_limit	−1.972*	−2.061*	−1.933*	−2.055*	−2.083*
	(1.07)	(1.13)	(1.10)	(1.10)	(1.11)
severe_sanction	1.524	1.588	1.606	1.492	1.496
	(1.02)	(1.02)	(0.99)	(1.02)	(1.03)
real_maxben	0.005	0.004	0.003	0.005	0.005
	(0.01)	(0.01)	(0.01)	(0.01)	(0.01)
unemp	0.265	0.259	0.237	0.259	0.263
	(0.17)	(0.16)	(0.17)	(0.16)	(0.17)
fem_lfp	0.118**	0.118**	0.112*	0.122**	0.115**
	(0.05)	(0.05)	(0.06)	(0.05)	(0.05)
time	−0.435	−0.320	−0.332	−0.352	−0.300
	(0.53)	(0.46)	(0.47)	(0.45)	(0.46)
timesq	0.043	0.039	0.039	0.042	0.038
	(0.03)	(0.02)	(0.03)	(0.03)	(0.03)
constant	−4.537	−6.492	−10.196	−6.216	−5.211
	(21.49)	(21.14)	(19.71)	(21.50)	(21.22)
N	643	643	643	643	643
R^2	0.2819	0.2815	0.2918	0.2828	0.2808
p-value for F-statistic	0.0000	0.0000	0.0000	0.0000	0.0000

The juxtaposition of results from our child fatality and mechanism regressions in Table 6.12 points up the large disparity in outrage effect sizes between Model 1 and Models 2–6. We have conceptualized child fatalities as an instrumental variable that creates social outrage but that impacts CPS decision outcomes primarily through a set of channeling mechanisms. It is clear from these analyses that although the outrage

Table 6.12 Summary of Significant Outrage Impacts

I. Regression of child fatalities (lagged) on eight CPS decision outcomes
- An increase of one fatality per 1000 child population
  - Increases the child neglect classification rate by 34.6 children per 1000 child population
  - Increases the child placement rate by 11.5 children per 1000 child population
  - Increases the case substantiation rate by 40 cases per 1000 child population

II. Regression of outrage mechanisms on eight CPS decision outcomes
- Sex offender notification laws (Model 2)
  - No impact on outcomes
- Current court case (Model 3)
  - Increases the case substantiation rate by 1.8 children per 1000 child population
  - Increases the child placement rate by 0.63 children per 1000 child population
- State CPS under court order (Model 4)
  - Decreases the sexual abuse classification rate by 0.36 children per 1000 child population
  - Increases the child placements to case investigation ratio by 1.8 placements per 100 cases investigated
- Positive workforce punctuation (Model 5)
  - Decreases the rate of screened-in reports by 5.2 per 1000 child population
  - Decreases the case substantiation-investigation ratio by 4.3 cases per 100 cases investigated
- Negative workforce punctuation (Model 6)
  - Increases the rate of screened-in reports by 3.4 per 1000 child population
  - Increases the case substantiation rate by 2.1 cases per 1000 child population
  - Increases the child neglect classification rate by 1.2 children per 1000 child population

mechanisms we have proposed account for some of the variance in screened-in reports, substantiations, and placements explained by fatalities, they are by no means responsible for the total effect. Any routinization of outrage that occurs—at least through these mechanisms—does not approach the direct influence of child deaths on CPS decision outcomes.

With respect to the other sets of independent variables employed in our regression analyses, we offer these observations:

The measures of hazard that consistently exert some influence on CPS decisions are children's race/ethnicity, child age, and residence in nonworking households. Contrary to the predictions of Pelton, Roberts, and some others, we find that the percentage of minority children in a state's population is negatively related to most CPS decision outcomes. This finding corroborates work by Paxson and Waldfogel (2002). We also find that child poverty, although significant in a number of analyses, is also negatively related to substantiations and sexual abuse, physical abuse, and child neglect classification rates. This is not to be expected if poverty is a cause of child maltreatment. Our finding that the percentage of children who live in households in which neither parent works increases substantiation rates also mirrors results reported by Paxson and Waldfogel (2002).

Several CPS organizational inputs also produced consistent effects on decisions. A larger caseload-adjusted CPS workforce is related to screening-in fewer referrals while increasing placement decisions. Resources in the form of state and/or federal dollars consistently lead to fewer reports, less substantiation of reports, fewer findings of neglect and sexual abuse, and fewer placements. States' information systems capability (captured by their reporting of items required by CAPTA to a central national database) is significantly related to increases in classification of abuse and neglect and to out-of-home placement decisions.

Our analyses uncover some effects of welfare reform. State policies governing time-limited welfare payments lower both substantiation and placement decisions, whereas work requirement and sanction rules lower findings of physical abuse and neglect. The negative effect of work requirement on physical abuse cases that we report is corroborated by the only other national study that has examined this relationship (Paxson & Waldfogel, 2002, 2003). Although this finding is somewhat surprising since work requirements might be expected to increase the mother's stress levels and therefore her proneness to be less patient with her child, it can occur for several reasons. As Paxson and Waldfogel (2002) point out, it is possible that such work requirements (1) may have coincided with the states' adoption of other measures such as better treatment services or more diligent case management services that led to a decrease in physical abuse rates; or (2) may have made it less likely that such cases will be reported in the first place because of fewer contacts with welfare workers or other reporting professionals. As these researchers point out, the use of state-level data cannot distinguish among the various explanations. Our findings on welfare time limits and sanctions, however, do not agree with Paxson and Waldfogel (2003), who find that these two provisions *increase* substantiations, physical abuse, and neglect. Although the Paxson and Waldfogel studies (2002, 2003) come closest to the data and analytic methods we use here, there are also many differences—our data form a much longer time series than theirs (17 years vs. 7 or 9 years), the timing of the analysis (we use 5 years of pre-PRWORA data and 12 years of postwelfare reform data, whereas their analyses use only 2 years of post-PRWORA when welfare reform was still in its nascent stages), and the differences in the functional form of the dependent variables.

SENSITIVITY ANALYSES

One major criticism of econometric modeling is that it can easily fall prey to the problem of specification bias. The problem can occur if important variables are omitted from analyses, extraneous variables are included, or incorrect functional forms are estimated. A protection from specification bias is found in modeling that ema-nates from strong, a priori, conceptualization and consistency with existing theory. We believe our reliance on the general framework of outrage motivated punctuated equilibrium helps ensure that our estimates are driven by conceptualization and not by the econometrics. Our selection of hazard, organizational environment, welfare reform, and economic environment variables was also conducted with the guidance of existing research. We have also sought to contrast and reconcile our findings with empirical results of other researchers, and this too is a way of addressing possible specification bias.

Still another method for dealing with possible specification bias is the use of specification checks to examine the robustness of our regression results to additions or omissions of variables, changes in time period, and modifications of functional form. One specification check we conducted was to determine if the independent effects of our outreach mechanisms could be sensitive to the inclusion of all mecha-nisms simultaneously in a regression analysis. The results of these models are shown in Appendix V. In only two instances do these regressions demonstrate outrage impacts that differ from the one-mechanism-at-a-time estimates. The impact of an existing court order on physical abuse rate changes from a nonsignificant –0.47 per 1000 (Model 4, Table 6.7) to a significant –0.58 per 1000. In the second case, a sig-nificant impact of court orders on out-of-home placements (Model 3, Table 6.10) changes from 0.623 per 1000 to 0.456 per 1000 and falls out of significance.

We undertake another set of analyses limiting the analysis to the years 1997–2008, years for which we have more systematically collected data for two key CPS task environment measures, the number of CPS workers and federal/state dollars spent on child welfare. [Recall that we have had to impute data for these variables for the earlier years (see Table 6.1).] These results, summarized in Appendix VI, should indi-cate whether our main findings are affected by the imputation. We see that significant effects reported as our main results are again confirmed, with the exception of two outrage mechanisms, the positive and negative equilibrium change. In these instances the signs of the effects remain consistent, however. Perhaps the shortening of the time series could have reduced the variability in these change variables, which could have affected their predictive ability.

Finally, we change the functional form of the dependent variables and use their logged form, as is done in other research (Paxson & Waldfogel, 2002, 2003). Instead of using rates per 1000 child population, here we estimate models using the natural log-arithm of the number of reports, substantiations, physical abuse, neglect and sexual abuse, and placements. We also log the percentage of substantiations and placements. All models here control for the state's total population and its child population. These results are summarized in Appendix VII, and indicate again that the main results we have reported are robust to changing the functional form of the dependent variables. The effects of child fatality and three outrage mechanisms (CPS court order, positive equilibrium change, and negative equilibrium change) are particularly robust, quali-tatively speaking. Quantitatively, however, because the dependent variables are logged here, the coefficients obviously vary in size compared to our base specification.

CONCLUSIONS

In this chapter we provide econometric support for our argument that social outrage as measured by child fatalities, class action litigation, and workforce punctuations influences CPS decisions. We do not find any evidence that state sex offender laws influence any of the eight decision outcomes we examined. This is consistent with the research reported by Zgoba et al. (2010). Our findings also indicate that outrage generally outperforms hazards, CPS organizational inputs, welfare reform, poverty, and economic conditions in explaining variance in CPS outcomes.

Of course, our analyses have limitations, some of which stem from state-level data we employ, others that arise from problems of missing data in a number of states. We recognize, for example, that even on such a critical measure as fatalities reported to NCANDS there is the possibility of incomplete counts (Riehl, 2012; U.S. Government Accountability Office, 2011). And there is the issue of missing outrage mechanisms that our analyses appear to have uncovered.

7

AN OUTRAGE MANAGEMENT STRATEGY FOR CHILD PROTECTIVE SERVICES

To be or not to be: that is the question: Whether 'tis nobler in the mind to suffer the slings and arrows of outrageous fortune, Or to take arms against a sea of troubles....
Shakespeare (1601)
Hamlet

In the econometric and case study analyses presented in this book, we have sought to establish the pivotal role that social outrage has played in the Child Protective Services (CPS) decision-making process. Outrage precipitated by a child fatality or other horrific case of child abuse unleashes a torrent of public guilt and, along with it, cries for redemption by governmental officials and especially by CPS. Outrage is also responsible, however, for the punctuated change and the temporary equilibria in CPS that make true redemption exceedingly difficult if not impossible.

Our analyses have shown that two mechanisms of outrage, litigation and workforce punctuation, alter how child risk is assessed by CPS workers and supervisors and exert a significant influence on the rates of screened-in reports, substantiations, out-of-home placements, and even the types of maltreatment identified. These effects, however, are mere shadows of the impact demonstrated by the archetypical cases themselves.

The punctuated equilibrium wrought by social outrage requires that CPS evolve case management and governing strategies that ensure high levels of competence in an environment of more or less continuous paroxysm. These punctuations also indicate to us that any amelioration strategy premised solely on shoring up staff quality, removing a few "bad apples," or improving agency quality control processes is likely to fall short. When attempting to function in a generally disapproving and unsupportive environment CPS must effectively communicate its vision and accomplishments with the goal of regaining community support for its mission. Hence, a recognition of the very public contribution that outrage makes to risk assessment and management can equip CPS for a new kind of public dialogue, one in which the public's impetus for change gives vent to both constructive and deleterious pressures.

THE SEARCH FOR SOLUTIONS

Concomitant with pressures for major institutional reform in CPS has been the development of management approaches, borrowed in most cases from public health or business, that attempt to comprehensively address the worker-level, organizational, and community factors responsible for poor agency performance. The call by some child welfare scholars for the replacement of a risk assessment orientation in CPS with a system of risk management is one prominent example (Gambrill, 2008; Gambrill & Shlonsky, 2001; Rzepnicki & Johnson, 2005). The distinction between assessment and management according to Gambrill and Shlonsky (2001) stems from how hazard is conceptualized:

> Ideally, risk management should minimize risks from all sources that contribute to unwanted outcomes (e.g., harm to children), not only risks posed by parents to their children, but risks posed by child welfare staff and service providers to clients and all procedures put in place to decrease both. Elements also include safeguarding the assets of the organization (financial, reputational and staff morale) under aims of risk management as well as responding effectively to client concerns....(p. 89)

Although this movement to risk management is movement in the right direction, its roll-out in CPS reveals two principal shortcomings. The first is the issue of guidance; risk management in this literature has typically taken the form of long lists of prescriptions and prohibitions that can range from case review strategies and hiring practices to service coordination and service "gap" reporting (Gambrill, 2008; Gambrill & Shlonsky, 2001). One list of components from Gambrill and Shlonsky is provided in Figure 7.1.

Such lists are as overwhelming as they are exhaustive. Most CPS managers would likely agree that many or even all of the components in Figure 7.1 are critical for real CPS reform; however, without clear principles for prioritization it is easy to see how efforts could be swallowed up in Alvin Schorr's aptly named "palate of gray" (Schorr, 2000, p. 130).

A second issue with these risk management lists is the scant attention paid to risk communication, i.e., "an interactive process of exchange of information and opinion among individuals, groups, and institutions that involves multiple messages about the nature of risk and other messages, not strictly about risk, that express concerns, opinions or reactions to risk messages or to legal and institutional arrangements for risk management" (Covello, Peters, Wojtecki, & Hyde, 2001, p. 3). In essence, risk management without risk communication amounts to a Risk = f(Hazard) formulation of the problem. Sandman (2003), for example, has identified four types of risk communications: (1) public education—when hazard is high but outrage is low, (2) stakeholder relations—when both hazard and outrage are at moderate levels, (3) outrage management for situations of low hazard and high outrage, and (4) crisis communication for circumstances of high hazard and high outrage. A principal task in risk management, from the risk communication perspective, is to reduce social outrage by listening,

FIG 7.1 Components of Risk Management Systems in Child Welfare

1. Clear description of practice and policy components likely to maximize attainment of hoped-for outcomes.
2. Effective implementation of a risk assessment instrument that contributes to sound decisions.
3. Clear performance standards for all staff and selection of standards based on what has been found, via rigorous appraisal, to maximize hoped-out outcomes (e.g., increase safety for children).
4. Monthly random audit of a sample of cases of each staff member and provision of individualized feedback and training based on this review.
5. Hiring supervisors with the values, knowledge and skills required to help staff maintain desired staff performance levels and random audit of a random sample of related supervisory behaviors/ products.
6. Hiring staff who possess values, knowledge and skills required to fulfill expected tasks at minimal levels of competence as demonstrated by their performance on related asks.
7. Hiring administrators who encourage evidence-based practices and policies (see text) and who are expert in arranging positive contingencies to support related staff behaviors; routine review of their policies and practices in relation to key indicators.
8. the evidentiary base of each service offered.
9. Description of variations in services provided and related outcomes that are provided to staff, clients, and funding sources.
10. Clear description of what is needed to achieve hoped-for outcomes and what is provided on each case.
11. Access to computer databases that facilitate sound decision-making.
12. A whistle blowing policy that contributes to constructive criticism of current agency policies and practices.
13. A nonpunitive (anonymous?) system for identifying errors and mistakes and use of these data to improve service quality.
14. An accountable, accessible, user-friendly client feedback system and regular review of complaints and compliments to enhance quality of services. Complaint forms should be readily accessible in every office.
15. Selection of evidence-based training programs for staff (i.e., programs that include instructional formats that maximize learning and that incorporate content found via rigorous appraisal to help clients achieve certain outcomes) and evaluation of training via review of on-the-job practices and outcomes.

acknowledging, apologizing, and sharing control and credit as a means of paving the way for a discussion of actual hazard.

In her expanded list of components of a systematic risk management system in child welfare, Gambrill (2008) does make mention of needed attention to community engagement and advocacy. It is not obvious from this inclusion, however, if this input is part of a conscious risk communication effort or mainly a needs assessment tool. Conceptualizations of risk management systems outside of CPS have called for the close coordination of risk assessment and risk communication endeavors. One of these models, adapted by the European Commission, Health and Consumer Protection Directorate General (2004), is depicted in Figure 7.2.

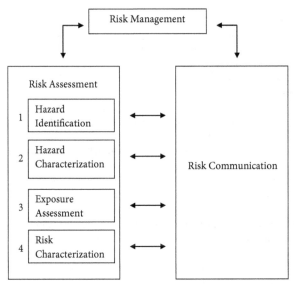

FIG 7.2 The Interconnected Components of Risk Analysis–Risk Assessment, Risk Communication, and Risk Management

Here a full-throated risk communication strategy interacts sequentially with hazard identification communications, hazard characterization levels, exposure data, and overall risk level characterization. Although outrage management is not explicitly referenced in this model, it is not difficult to imagine how these multiple messages can be fashioned to address emotional as well as technical/analytic content.

Another management approach that has gained some popularity in discussions of CPS reform has been the utilization of "balanced scorecards." Developed in 1992 for business and industry by Robert Kaplan and David Norton, balanced scorecards have been characterized as follows:

> A good balanced scorecard should have a mix of outcome (status) measures and (system) performance drivers. Outcome measures without performance drivers do not communicate how the outcomes are to be achieved. They also do not provide an early indication about whether the strategy is being implemented successfully. Conversely, performance drivers—such as cycle time or part-per-million defect rates—without outcome measures may enable the business to achieve short term operational improvements but fail to reveal whether the operational improvements have been translated into enhanced financial performance. (Kaplan & Norton, 1996, p. 150)

Within this framework a company's business strategy is evaluated from the four linked perspectives shown in Figure 7.3.

Financial performance is measured as profitability and growth and this, in turn, is seen as dependent on customer valuation and internal business practices that help

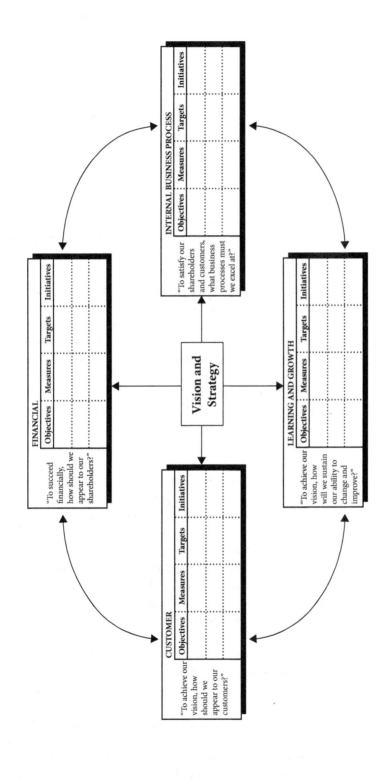

FIG 7.3 The Four Perspectives of a Balanced Scorecard: Business and Industry Application

ensure cost control, quality, and reliability. Measures of employee learning and growth are viewed as enablers of the other three perspectives, capturing employee commitment and productivity (Kaplan & Norton, 1992). Effective balanced scorecards are characterized by a relatively few measures that can be ranked numerically on simple scales across six criteria: (1) linkage to strategy, (2) ability to quantify, (3) accessibility, (4) understandability, (5) balance, and (6) common definition (Kaplan & Norton, 1996). These measures are linked in cause–effect sequences that describe the strategic story of the company and provide the outline of the specific path(s) the organization should follow to achieve success when employing that strategy. As Figure 7.3 indicates, specific objectives and performance measures are accompanied by targets, benchmarks, and timeframes for initiatives designed to accomplish those objectives. To be successful, this management approach requires that an organization's senior managers possess a strategic vision and that these managers be comfortable with accepting employee-initiated objectives, measures, and initiatives.

Balanced scorecards have made their way into CPS through several consent decrees (see, for example, Center for the Study of Social Policy, 2010; Golden, 2009; Noonan, Sabel, & Simon, 2009) and provide the ostensive structure for Child and Family Services Reviews (CFSR). The adoption of what is essentially a business model into a public child welfare environment has not been straightforward, nor has it been easy. In addition to the suspicions that many in the social work profession have about any "bottom line" accountability models, balanced scorecards have three additional issues that have impeded more widespread implementation, viz: complexity, lack of a management component, and leadership from central management.

Managed healthcare is the human services setting with the most exposure to the balanced scorecards (Inamdar & Kaplan, 2002; Yeager, 2004). Yeager notes, however, that despite the scorecard's "simplistic" approach (p. 891), healthcare organizations have experienced difficulty in applying this tool to centralized systems that frequently are driven by multiple missions, have multiple practice services, and have competing political and programmatic goals. Multiple missions typically have multiple objectives and measures that lead inexorably to laundry lists and metrics overload. Mark Brown (2007) maintains that scorecards with too many metrics usually contain too few multiple measures for individual objectives and high ratios of lagging-to-leading performance indicators. A paucity of leading metrics makes establishing cause–effect linkages almost impossible.

In his recent writings on the evolution of the balanced scorecard, Kaplan (2010) has discussed the necessity of augmenting his twin pillars of financial performance, i.e., growth and profitability, with a third pillar, risk management. He notes that there is now an intense focus in companies around the world on the measurement and management of risk and many companies lack the strategic guidance and empirical data to create a business model that is structured to optimally counterbalance risk, growth, and profitability. A balanced scorecard without a risk management component would appear to make little sense for an organization such as CPS, whose raison d' tre is the assessment and management of risk.

Kaplan and Norton (1992; Kaplan, 1996, 2010) emphasize that the most important variable in explaining the success or failure of balanced scorecards is real executive leadership. Leadership is necessary to translate vision into the linked strategic objectives and to use performance measures interactively. Absent leadership, maintaining this management tool will devolve into just another ad hoc reporting system (Kaplan, 2010).

STRATEGIC BALANCING IN CPS

Incorporating a risk management system, a scorecard that balances outcome measures and performance drivers, or, for that matter, any management approach that attempts to improve mission clarity and tangible forms of accomplishment in CPS would appear to have few detractors. Successful adoption of systems that rely on quantifiable metrics and analytics occurs frequently in settings such as managed care or market-based business; success stories in the public sector, however, are much more difficult to find. We propose a management model that, if implemented, we believe could dramatically reform the way CPS conducts its daily operations. When evaluating the feasibility of our approach, the reader needs to ask if what we are suggesting can take place in any government-run human services agency.

The core structure of the framework is presented in Figure 7.4. The model integrates risk management into a balanced scorecard, making outrage management and hazard assessment the pair of reciprocal linkages that binds overall reform vision to system performance and child outcomes. The staff learning and growth perspective in Figure 7.4 addresses the issues of human capital readiness and capability to engage in the organization's strategic vision and achieve CPS performance goals.

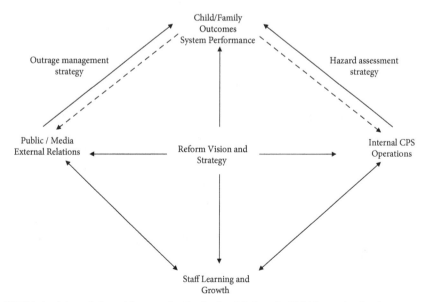

FIG 7.4 Applying a Balanced Scorecard to Institutional Reform in Child Protective Services.

Planning and implementation of the framework would require an up-front commitment of the organization's strategic apex (top administration and middle managers) and the commitment of the technostructure, operating core, and support staffs to participate and help generate an organizational climate immersed in metrics and analytics (Mintzberg, 1979).

Federal legislation and regulations, especially CAPTA (1974), the Adoption and Safe Families Act (1997), and the Child and Family Services Improvement Act (2006), provide a very general adumbration and a broad mission of child protection with which states must comply if they are to receive federal funding. It is states, however, that make the programmatic and fiscal decisions that shape specific strategies in CPS organizations. In New Jersey, the mission of the Department of Children and Families is to ensure the safety, permanency, and well-being of children and to support families (New Jersey Department of Children and Families, 2007). States retain the right to have blurry, nonspecific, or even ambiguous visions; states also have the prerogative to create visions that in Niven's (2004) words can clarify direction, motivate action, and coordinate effort. One thing, however, is hardly debatable—it is unlikely that an organization, public or private, can formulate a coherent strategy for effective operations without a vision containing an organization's core values and cause–effect principles. The pivotal importance of clear organization vision can be found at many of America's most successful businesses. Johnson & Johnson (2010), one of America's A-list corporations, guides strategic decision making with its famous Credo built around responsibilities to multiple constituencies:

> We believe our first responsibility is to the doctors, nurses and patients,
> to mothers and fathers and all others who use our products and services...
> We are responsible to our employees,
> the men and women who work with us throughout the world...
> We are responsible to the communities in which we live and work
> and to the world community as well...
>
> Johnson & Johnson (2010)

Johnson & Johnson describes the Credo as not only a moral compass but its recipe for business success. It is noteworthy that this statement of vision shares several attributes that can be found in most well thought through mission statements, viz. it balances the interests of the various stakeholders in describing how the organization will reach performance goals and create future value. At minimum, therefore, it would appear eminently practical for state CPS agencies to formulate a strategic vision that addresses the needs of staff, the public, media, the legal system, and politicians as well as child and family victims.

What would a CPS vision statement look like that is capable of clarifying direction, motivating action, and coordinating effort? At the risk of appearing presumptuous we offer this starting point:

> We are an organization that must protect children from child maltreatment by making decisions about risk that are trusted in the community, that are based on

a thorough scientific knowledge of hazards, and that are the product of employees with the commitment, capabilities, and readiness to achieve excellence.

The statement serves to focus the operational objectives and metrics that are necessary for CPS to realize its vision. It also focuses the specific communication, internal operations, and staff development tasks that need to be undertaken. For those who believe that the CPS vision we have offered is worthy of pursuit, or who are simply willing to indulge our overactive imaginations, we now provide some concrete suggestions for how it could be implemented.

IMPLEMENTING A COMPREHENSIVE RISK ASSESSMENT STRATEGY

What must CPS excel at in order for children to be protected and for the public, including judges, court appointed masters, politicians, and law enforcement, to express its satisfaction with the level of protection being rendered? According to the vision we have laid out, this would have to be a service characterized by rapid response, on-time delivery, and, most importantly, few errors. Stated differently, CPS internal operations must be premised on a vital, organization-encompassing quality control system.

As we have discussed in earlier chapters, some institutional reform litigation has required states to initiate or revamp quality assurance efforts with the goal of forcing explicit and standardized explanations and measurement of system and child outcomes. The Quality System Review (QSR) adopted in Alabama, Utah, and nearly a dozen other states has proven to be the central measure of compliance in decisions to terminate court supervision (Golden, 2009; Noonan et al., 2009). At the core of QSR is an extensive and intensive case review of random, proportionate-to-size, samples of cases from all county offices. Reviews are conducted by teams of caseworkers and supervisors who begin with a file analysis and then proceed to interviews with the child(ren), family members, nonfamily caregivers, professional consultants, and teachers. Case results are scored numerically on a series of indicators that measure system performance and child/family status. In essence, the two sets of indicators provide the inchoate form of the balanced scorecard we have introduced in Figures 7.3 and 7.4.

In Utah, QSR indicators are scored on a six-point scale, with six being optimal and one being totally unacceptable; four is considered minimally acceptable. An example of an individual case summary is provided in Figure 7.5. Subsequent to case scoring reviewers meet with caseworkers and supervisors to discuss their findings.

Cases are aggregated and summaries are produced that show the number of cases scored as acceptable and nonacceptable. As Noonan et al. (2009) observe, in addition to functioning as a performance measure, the QSR data serve as a form of clinical training for workers and as a means of values elaboration for the entire organization.

From the high perch we have constructed, the QSR provides CPS with a good starting point for implementing a data-based, hazard assessment strategy. In two respects, however, the current iterations of QSR do not go far enough in establishing metrics for codable decision-making processes and including analytics that permit worker, work

Child Status	Rating		System Performance	Rating
1a. Safety of the Child	5		1. Child and Family Participation	5
1b. Safety Risk to Others	5		2. Child and Family Team/ Coordination	4
1. Overall Safety	5		3. Child and Family Assessment	4
2. Stability	5		4. Long-Term View	5
3. Appropriateness of Placement	6		5. Child and Family Planning Process	5
4. Prospect of Permanence	4		6. Plan Implementation	6
5. Health/Physical Well-Being	6		7. Formal & Informal Supports &	
6. Emotional/Behavioral Well-Being	4		Services	5
7. Learning Progress (5 and older)	3		8. Successful Transitions	5
8. Developing/Learning Progress			9. Effective Results	4
(under 5)	n/a		10. Tracking and Adaptation	5
9. Caregiver Functioning	5		11. Caregiver Support	5
10. Family Functioning and			12. OVERALL PERFORMANCE	5
Resourcefulness	n/a			
11a. Child Satisfaction	5			
11b. Parent/Guardian Satisfaction	5			
11c. Substitute Caregiver Satisfaction	6			
11. Overall Satisfaction	5			
12. OVERALL STATUS	5			

FIG 7.5 Child Status and System Performance Ratings for a Sample Case Evaluated by the Utah QSR

unit, and office profiling. Borrowing from the early work of the quality assessment pioneer, Avedis Donabedian (1980), Camasso and Jagannathan (1992) developed and implemented a 61-page case record audit protocol that tracks the following 12 fundamental components of decision-making style, which when taken together map a CPS worker's or supervisor's hazard assessment strategy:

1. Amount, type, and source of information collected
2. Speed of information seeking and collection
3. Value of information items sought (a) according to office norms and (b) professional standards
4. Sequence in which items are collected
5. Information reevaluation (in light of contemporaneous or subsequent information collection)

6. Degree of redundancy
7. Stereotyping
8. Search patterns with respect to the problems known/believed to be central
9. Tendencies to act prior to amassing sufficient information
10. Tendencies to seek information beyond the point of reasonable assurance about the solution
11. Error tolerance
12. Degree of success sought in achieving a solution.

By incorporating these measures into a quality control system the organization can significantly enhance its clinical diagnosis and teaching capacity.

QSR comparisons of simple rankings on child status or system performance indicators have a great deal of utility but like any point estimates they tell only a partial story. The simple method of control charting (Crocker, 1990; Knapp & Miller, 1983) offers a way of tracking a performance indicator over time and across individuals to determine if scores are above or below acceptable limits, usually set at 95% or 99% confidence intervals. Receiver operating curve (ROC) analysis, which we discussed at some length in Chapter 3, allows CPS to venture beyond the simple juxtaposition and side-by-side comparison of outcome and process scores to a formal analysis of judgment patterns and clinical errors. Control charting and ROC analysis are natural, analytic extensions of QSR; both are widely used in business and industry; and both are readily available in popular statistical packages.

If the analysis and arguments we have presented in this book are compelling, however, a real balance between CPS penultimate and ultimate outcomes, on the one hand, and risk management processes, on the other, can be achieved only with the inclusion of an aggressive outrage management strategy (see Figure 7.4). Just as business must take into consideration a customer perspective (i.e., consumer satisfaction, cost to customer, market share) to ensure a successful financial outcome, so must CPS develop and implement a risk communication process that can change the public perception about agency effectiveness. By aggressive management here we are not talking about a public relations campaign. Image repackaging and impression management are not likely to be successful for an organization struggling to explain a child's death or starvation. Public relations strategies assume a high-hazard, low-outrage circumstance in which monologues issued through the media are employed to grab attention (Sandman, 2003). Inattentiveness to CPS actions, especially in archetypical cases, is clearly not the problem.

Outrage management is not likely to be successful, moreover, if the organization interprets the problem as a matter of public education. As dreadful as child fatalities and torture are, they are not pervasive hazards experienced by American children or encountered by CPS workers. Relative rarity tends to exacerbate the difficulty of educating individuals about the nature of risk for reasons described by Covello and Sandman (2001):

Largely because of gaps in knowledge, risk assessment seldom provides exact answers. In this sense, it suffers from the same weaknesses as many other fields of scientific inquiry. A variety of confounding factors often make it difficult, if not impossible, to reach definitive conclusions about cause and effect. This is especially the case for health risk assessments where usually direct testing on humans is ethically prohibited. As a result, outcome of most risk assessments are best seen as estimates, with varying degrees of uncertainties about the actual nature of risk. These uncertainties can justify conflicting interpretations of the data, typically grounded as much in value judgments as in scientific judgments. (p. 166)

Public education programs, like public relations, assume a high-hazard, low-outrage set of circumstances. Archetypical cases of child maltreatment, conversely, place CPS agencies in low-hazard but high-outrage situations that are not likely to be emended by technical discussions laden with probabilistic caveats. More likely than enlightenment is the prospect of even higher levels of outrage.

Low-hazard, high-outrage circumstances call for risk communications that address the emotion and worry experienced by the general public. These situations need to contain content that risk perception research has found to play a major role in determining an audience's anxiety, fear, hostility, and outrage. Covello and his colleagues (Covello et al., 2001; Covello, Sandman, & Slovic, 1988), for example, have isolated 15 "perception factors" that significantly influence attitudes and behavior at times of high outrage (see Figure 7.6).

Outrage has been found most often when risk is perceived to be involuntary, uncontrollable, unfamiliar, unfair, poorly understood, uncertain, dreadful, ethically objectionable, and associated with untrustworthy institutions. From a purely Risk = f(Hazard) definition, these perception factors can be viewed as distortions, "hype," or misconceptions; from a balanced risk management perspective, disdain for the outrage potential of these perceptions should be viewed as a serious organizational dereliction.

A close examination of Figure 7.6 reveals that underpinning many of these outrage factors is the element of trust. In point of fact, only when institutions and their employees engender trust in their customers and/or client base and the broader public can that institution hope to begin the task of public education and consensus building (Covello et al., 1988, 2001). The core of any CPS outrage management strategy must contain a recipe for regaining the public trust. One ingredient in that recipe must be the close affiliation of CPS with trusted state and national institutions, inside and outside the child welfare field. Perfunctory affiliations will not suffice; successful trading-in on the reputations of others will require tangible interactions that produce tangible accomplishments, viz. accreditations, continuing education credits, certificates, awards, degrees, and testimonials. The expert panels or special masters appointed in institutional reform litigation can serve as a springboard for subsequent trust-building associations when consent decrees are terminated—assuming these entities are trusted.

Insight into the trust levels of CPS may be educed from the authors' experience on a research project they conducted with the New Jersey Division of Youth and Family Services (DYFS) some years ago. One aspect of this research was the administration of a questionnaire to the parents of children who had been referred to DYFS for suspected

1) **Voluntariness.** Risks perceived to be involuntary or imposed are less readily accepted and perceived to be greater than risks perceived to be voluntary.

2) **Controllability.** Risks perceived to be under the control of others are less readily accepted and perceived to be greater than risks perceived to be under the control of the individual.

3) **Familiarity.** Risks perceived to be unfamiliar are less readily accepted and perceived to be greater than risks perceived to be familiar.

4) **Equity.** Risks perceived as unevenly and inequitably distributed are less readily 5) accepted than risks perceived as equitably shared.

5) **Benefits.** Risks perceived to have unclear or questionable benefits are less readily accepted and perceived to be greater than risks perceived to have clear benefits.

6) **Understanding.** Risks perceived to be poorly understood are less readily accepted and perceived to be greater than risks from activities perceived to be well understood or self-explanatory.

7) **Uncertainty.** Risks perceived as relatively unknown or that have highly uncertain dimensions are less readily accepted than risks that are relatively known to science.

8) **Dread.** Risks that evoke fear, terror, or anxiety are less readily accepted and perceived to be greater than risks that do not arouse such feelings or emotions.

9) **Trust in institutions.** Risks associated with institutions or organizations lacking in trust and credibility are less readily accepted and perceived to be greater than risks associated with trustworthy and credible institutions and organizations.

10) **Reversibility.** Risks perceived to have potentially irreversible adverse effects are less readily accepted and perceived to be greater than risks perceived to have reversible adverse effects.

11) **Personal stake.** Risks perceived by people to place them personally and directly at risk are less readily accepted and perceived to be greater than risks that pose no direct or personal threat.

12) **Ethical/moral nature.** Risks perceived to be ethically objectionable or morally wrong are less readily accepted and perceived to be greater than risks perceived not be ethically objectionable or morally wrong.

13) **Human vs. natural origin.** Risks perceived to be generated by human action are less readily accepted and perceived to be greater than risks perceived to be caused by nature or "Acts of God."

14) **Victim identity.** Risks that produce identifiable victims are less readily accepted and perceived to be greater than risks that produce statistical victims.

15) **Catastrophic Potential.** Risks that produce fatalities, injuries, and illness grouped spatially and temporally are less readily accepted and perceived to be greater than risks that have random, scattered effects.

FIG 7.6 Risk Perception Factors Influence the Level of Public Outrage

abuse or neglect. After many hours of discussion and a pretest we acquiesced to DYFS appeals that we *not* use their stationary, *not* have DYFS officials sign any introductory letters, and *not* refer to DYFS as an agency that helps families in New Jersey! Our response rate was just short of 85%.

A second ingredient for successful outrage management strategy (and this over the long run is more important than the first) requires a fully functioning and productive hazard assessment strategy. It is incumbent upon CPS to provide services of impeccable quality. Some first steps in this direction include the creation of a QSR system that reviews, analyzes, and reports sufficiently large numbers of cases, and achieving compliance with CFSR process standards. These actions are unlikely by themselves, however, to build sufficient levels of public trust. Case and systems audits will need, at least initially, to be conducted by independent agencies external to child protective services—Quality Improvement Organization (QIO) Programs and/or The Joint Commission (TJC) Programs are the types of agencies that come to mind. If these types of agencies do not exist, then they need to be created.

A balance of outrage and hazard strategies can go a long way in preparing CPS to deal more effectively with news media, often a fount of oversimplified, distorted, or inaccurate information. A substantial amount of research has shown that journalists report risk in a selective fashion and are inclined to report stories that are unusual, emotional, or sensational, in effect playing to the set of outrage factors that the public already uses to evaluate risks (Covello & Sandman, 2001; Sandman, Sachsman, & Greenberg, 1987). We saw in Chapter 2 how the New Jersey Department of Children and Families (DCF), under the direction of Commissioner Kevin Ryan, sought to blunt sensational media coverage of child fatalities through the formulation of a new policy limiting individual case details to the press/public. Will limited access to gory details help reduce lurid reporting and citizen outrage? Without a reputation for high-quality service and public trust the answer is probably "not for long." While CPS builds its risk management capacity to address both outrage and hazard issues, the organization will have to learn how to function with more professionalism and grace in an environment of punctuations and mistrust.

IMPROVING WORKFORCE READINESS AND STABILITY

It is quite noteworthy that Robert Kaplan, a co-founder of the balanced scorecard, refers to the "learning and growth perspective" (see Figure 7.3) as the "black hole" of the model (Kaplan, 2010, p. 22). He goes on to discuss why measures such as turnover, absenteeism, training hours, education level, and employee production have proven to be inadequate metrics for connecting worker capabilities to overall decision strategy. The development by Kaplan and Norton (2004) of the notion of a strategic human capital readiness appears to have provided a bridging conceptualization that fills the hole.

When viewed through the prism of employee readiness it is not enough that CPS workers and supervisors share some brave new vision. Workers need to be ready to implement rigorous quality control processes and must be ready to exhibit a professionalism that garners the praise and trust of citizens, politicians, law enforcement, and the legal profession. The general respect given to fireman and emergency medical technicians (EMTs) would be a level worthy of aspiration.

Praise, however, is not enough. High levels of performance, as measured by productivity and low levels of false positives and negatives, need to be compensated financially through a merit-pay system. Just as many of the academics who research child welfare receive added compensation for the books and articles they write on the topic, so too should the CPS workers who serve as the exemplars of professional child welfare practice. Issues of BSW vs. BA, MSWs vs. BSWs, and Title IV-E vs. traditional pathways into CPS need to be revisited as the organization utilizes hard audit data and competence assessments from outside organizations such as, for example, the International Critical Incident Stress Foundation (ICISF), to rate a worker's investigation prowess, evidence-gathering skills, and crisis intervention performance. Unlike the Child Welfare League of America and the National Association of Social Workers, ICISF and similar organizations have substantial credibility outside the social work profession, and because of these linkages, engender more public trust. In child welfare, the human capital assessments we have are largely impressionistic; nothing approaching the rigorous evaluations done in the 1970s and 1980s of nurse practitioners, and physician assistants capabilities to deliver quality healthcare exists. Absent comparative performance data it is best to regard CPS worker education and training as merely signaling mechanisms for efficacy and nothing more.

A natural experiment undertaken by the state of Florida legislature in 1998 suggests that the road to creating work readiness for reform may require an entirely different organizational aegis. As reported by Cohen, Kinnevy, and Dichter (2007), several counties in the state had the responsibility for CPS investigations transferred from the public child welfare agency to the sheriff's office. When CPS workers at the sheriff's office were compared with CPS workers operating out of traditional child welfare agencies, the former group exhibited significantly higher levels of concern for child health and safety, had more active participation in team decisions, saw greater opportunity for advancement, and had better communication flows. Of course, dramatic reorganization of CPS, as we have seen, has been a remedy sought by many child welfare scholars, among them Lindsey, Waldfogel, and Pelton. Would any of the modifications sought by these experts create a climate that facilitates more comprehensive risk management, strategic balancing, and worker readiness? If a change in organizational scenery is an answer, why not broaden the landscape to include public–private partnerships or even for-profit investigation agencies? In these settings intractable obstacles to readiness such as civil service "bumping" and union seniority are obviated, though new barriers might be encountered (Collins-Camargo et al., 2011). Guided by the vision statement and strategic map (Figure 7.4) presented earlier, we should all be open to any structuring of human capital that results in optimal child safety and well-being.

The remedies we have proposed, viz. balanced scorecards, a coherent risk communication strategy, case-based quality control and performance measurement, linkage to publicly respected professional groups outside social work, and merit pay, presuppose that public CPS can be saved and, indeed, can prosper. Our research suggests, however, that if the dynamic of extreme workforce punctuation associated with child fatalities cannot be controlled, CPS can never develop into the professional investigation and intervention agency the official boilerplate promulgates. CPS appears to be following the script from "Groundhog Day," but unlike the movie, each reprise unfolds either with a great many missing actors or a host of new ones.

GETTING REAL ABOUT CPS OUTCOMES

Successful implementation of true risk management in business and industry has been characterized by performance objectives constructed around two principles: viz. objectives are related as cause–effect sequences between perspectives and they contain both leading and lagging indicators of accomplishment within a perspective (Niven, 2004; Kaplan & Norton, 2004). Kaplan (2010) illustrates a simple causal chain of strategic objectives as

> employees better trained in quality management tools reduce process cycle times and process defects; the improved processes lead to shorter customer lead times, improved on-time delivery and fewer defects experienced by customers; the quality improvements experienced by customers lead to higher satisfaction, retention and spending, which drives, ultimately higher revenues and margins. (p. 21)

Within the financial perspective, revenue growth is a lagging indicator, and therefore is a consequence of leading indicators such as inventory turnover, profits as a percentage of sales, and rate of investment return. Exemplary companies have strong causal chains and tight lead-to-lag performance regimens.

The decision flow at CPS provides an example of an organization with weak causal linkages between perspectives and, at best, opaque relationships between lagging and leading indicators. Evidence for this contention can be found in the utter imbalance reported in CFSR audits of agency child outcome and system measures and in the ostensibly enigmatic findings of the National Incidence Studies (NIS) surveys. There is no doubt that a portion of this attenuation is a function of poor hazard identification resulting in misinformed investigations, substantiations, placements, and services. A larger portion, however, can be traced to negligent outrage management and the cascade of events in which horrific cases of maltreatment encourage (1) worker defensiveness and passivity, which, in turn, (2) generate high levels of false positives leading to (3) inefficient allocation of CPS resources, which are manifest in (4) case recidivism and lower response times, all of which (5) activate more opprobrium and oversight.

As we have seen, in no instance do the weak-linked causal chains fashioned by and for CPS create more trepidation for the agency than child fatalities. Deaths from maltreatment have always comprised cases that (1) were under agency supervision, (2) had prior supervision, and (3) were never under agency supervision. Yet in recent years the distinction has been blurred by politicians, the media, and CPS itself. Most assuredly some closed cases should have not been closed and other cases should have been identified, but the aggregation of (1), (2), and (3) most likely confounds and ultimately attenuates CPS system performance.

Holding CPS responsible for all child safety and well-being ensures that CPS will probably never measure up; instead, it is more likely to perpetuate the principles of "infinite jeopardy" and "panoptic accountability." The child outcome measures listed in Figure 7.5 offer a case in point. The child status scale included several satisfaction measures, permanency assessments, and family functioning indicators along with a series of child safety, health, educational, and physical well-being measures. Wouldn't we expect some of these measures to lead and others to lag? Would we expect satisfaction to have a strong causal linkage with system performance as well as child safety? Does adding such measures together cover up areas of effectiveness? If we are ever to replace the principle of infinite jeopardy with one of "reasonable expectation" we first must identify and, if necessary, create within CPS the strong cause–effect relationships that are the signature of balanced scorecards in business.

HOW CAN RESEARCH HELP CPS?

Michael Wiseman (2007) has made the sly observation that much of the research conducted in the era of public welfare reform served simply as salve for conscience or ammunition for debate, never as the foundation for reform. Yet even public welfare had its Manpower Development Research Corporation (MDRC) and significant advances in research design and analysis techniques (Camasso, 2007; Cook, 2010; Duflo, 2004). The state of child welfare research, by comparison, is in considerably poorer shape, summed up quite well by Patrick McCarthy's (2007) aphorism "we do not know enough about child abuse and neglect, and much of what we think we know is questionable" (p. 7). Calls by Gambrill, Littell, and others for evidence-based practices go largely unheeded; Campbell or Cochrane-like collaborations in child welfare remain fanciful daydreams.

In the tradition of the Campbell and Cochrane Collaborations, CPS needs to accumulate evidence of efficacy and effectiveness through strong quantitative research designs and state-of-the-art statistical/econometric techniques. Donald Cook (2010) observes that causal questions "should be addressed using whatever blend of experimental design and statistical manipulation permits capturing all the cause and effect constructs, as well as all the populations, settings and times that surfaced when formulating the policy problem" (p. 29). Resistance to Cook's advice in social work remains strong, steeped as the profession is in the traditions of qualitative case analyses and postpositivist research perspectives.

Illustrative of the long journey ahead of CPS and child welfare as the profession attempts to develop its evidence base is reaction to studies conducted by Donald Baumann and his associates (Baumann, Law, Sheets, Reid, & Graham, 2005) on the effectiveness of actuarial risk assessment models. As we noted in Chapter 3, these studies utilized true and natural experiments and failed to find any substantial impact of structured risk assessment. In his commentary on the study of Baumann et al., Will Johnson (2006) alleges many flaws with these studies and to be sure, these studies do have flaws. Here, however, we focus only on Johnson's critique of experimental design.

Johnson begins his remarks with calculations that estimate "massive attrition from the experimental condition"—rates of 78.5%, 90.6%, and 53% from the various treatment and control groups. Our first thought when reading these rates was pure astonishment—how could a prestigious journal such as *Children and Youth Services Review* agree to publish the work of Baumann et al. with such egregious numbers? Careful examination of Baumann et al., however, reveals that what Johnson is labeling attrition is "right censoring" of observations, and this in and of itself does not produce biased experimental estimators. Johnson goes on to critique the experiment for biases stemming from improper random assignment and reactivity of research participants to experimental conditions. These biases are not empirically established by Johnson, we should note; they are simply alleged. From his review Johnson concludes without presenting any actual empirical evidence that Baumann et al. have not been able to establish any causal relationship between type of treatment and likelihood of substantiation or rereport.

Although Johnson displays a good deal of knowledge regarding the possible shortcomings of experiments, he is extremely modest about delineating their possible strengths, even in the experiment he critiques. Experiments, for example, solve the fundamental evaluation problem that arises from the impossibility of observing what would happen to a person in both the treatment and nontreatment states. In other words, unlike the myriad of ex post facto, pre-post, and cross-sectional studies in child welfare that Johnson apparently uses as his frame of reference, experiments establish the counterfactual condition better than any other. Experiments are also superior among research designs in controlling unobserved sources of variation, minimizing selection bias, establishing cause–effect relationships, minimizing researcher manipulation of results, and following the time path of effects (Camasso, 2007; Cook & Payne, 2002; Duflo, 2004). What is more, issues such as nonresponse bias, sample representativeness, limited duration bias, Hawthorne effects, ethical considerations, and costs are not limited to experiments and affect weaker designs as well.

In spite of the clamor for evidence-based practice and reform in CPS, experiments are exceedingly rare. Their utilization needs to be encouraged as it was during public welfare reform over a decade ago. Critiques of these applications need to advance beyond the recitation of textbook compilations of flaws to actual reanalyses, comparison of estimates with nonexperimental results, and computations of alternative estimates from the same experiment—e.g., intention to treat, treatment on the treated, average treatment effects, and local average treatment effects (Bloom, Michalopoulos, & Hill, 2005).

There are times, settings, and situations when experiments will be impractical and in these situations researchers need to consider strong quasiexperimental alternatives. To answer public welfare policy reform questions natural experiments, regression discontinuity designs, propensity scores, and Heckman selection models have proven to be the most popular of these strong design substitutes. Like experiments, the use of quasiexperimental designs and econometric modeling research in CPS to study employee readiness, hazard assessment, outrage management, system performance, or child outcomes is much too infrequent. This must change if academic research hopes to contribute to evidence-based CPS reform.

GAUGING CPS FUTURE SUCCESS

In this book we have sought to provide current and future child welfare reformers with a different perspective from which to observe and evaluate CPS decisions to protect children. Our case study and econometric analyses illustrate the critical role played by social outrage, particularly the outrage accompanying child fatalities, in altering agency decision-making flows and modulating operational practices. We have pointed up the limitations of viewing risk as simply hazard from both research and management perspectives and have cataloged the personnel, technology, internal control, and training deficits that have plagued CPS reform efforts for decades.

This final chapter attempts to transform our empirical findings into a strategic blueprint for agency improvement. It takes a promising management model that has been trumpeted in the CPS institutional reform litigation and recasts it with a Risk $= f($Outrage $+$ Hazard$)$ management orientation. Whether or not states are willing to adopt the management strategy we propose is likely to depend on equal measures of managerial courage and desperation. Title IV-B or IV-E waivers could provide the necessary resources and demonstration status that would allow agencies to experiment with many of the remedies we have discussed. Counterfactuals in the form of CPS agencies doing what they usually do would also be in plentiful supply.

What can the public and child protective services professional expect to happen if CPS agencies are successful in implementing the comprehensive risk assessment strategy we have presented? Correct and reliable identification of maltreatment cases performed by a well-qualified and trained workforce will certainly go a long way in engendering trust among major CPS stakeholders. A preponderance of correct decisions will eliminate or reduce the unnecessary resource expenditures accruing from false positives and curb the potential danger to children resulting from false negatives and from the delivery of inappropriate services.

Success in CPS will likely not come quickly—and reputation, when damaged, is never easy to repair. One indicator of real accomplishment will emerge from CFSRs documenting substantial levels of state compliance with both system and child outcome measures. Another form of evidence will be found in much higher levels of congruency between maltreatment cases reported to the Child Protective Studies-National Child Abuse and Neglect Data System (CPS-NCANDS) and in the NIS. As CPS gains credibility as the primary sentinel for child maltreatment identification, so will the public gain trust in the agency as the source of true maltreatment prevalence rates. Decisions by CPS to protect children should become less and less reactive; punctuations to operations should be less frequent.

If the critics are correct and child protective services needs to be reformed now, new approaches to CPS service delivery must be implemented sooner rather than later. The longer we wait to do so, the more we have to risk.

APPENDIX I

Registration and Implementation Years for Sex Offender Laws

State	"Registry Begins" (Agan, 2007)	"Registration and Notification Implementation" (Walker et al., 2005)
Alabama	1996	1998
Alaska	1994	1994
Arizona	1996	1996
Arkansas	1997	1997
California	1955	1996
Colorado	1996	1998
Connecticut	1998	1998
Delaware	1994	1994
Washington, DC	2000	1999
Florida	1993	1997
Georgia	1996	1996
Hawaii	1997	1998
Idaho	1993	1993
Illinois	1996	1996
Indiana	1994	1998
Iowa	1995	1995
Kansas	1993	1994
Kentucky	1994	1994
Louisiana	1992	1992
Maine	1996	1995
Maryland	1995	1995
Massachusetts	1996	1999
Michigan	1995	1995
Minnesota	1991	1998
Mississippi	1994	1995
Missouri	1979	1995
Montana	1989	1995
Nebraska	1997	1997
Nevada	1998	1998

(continued)

(Continued)

State	"Registry Begins" (Agan, 2007)	"Registration and Notification Implementation" (Walker et al., 2005)
New Hampshire	1993	1996
New Jersey	1994	1993
New Mexico	1995	1995
New York	1996	1995
North Carolina	1996	1996
Ohio	1997	1997
Oklahoma	1989	1998
North Dakota	1991	1995
Oregon	1989	1993
Pennsylvania	1996	1996
Rhode Island	1992	1996
South Carolina	1994	1999
South Dakota	1994	1995
Tennessee	1995	1997
Texas	1991	1999
Utah	1984	1996
Vermont	1996	1996
Virginia	1994	1997
Washington	1990	1990
West Virginia	1993	1993
Wisconsin	1997	1997
Wyoming	1994	1999

Source: Agan (2007); Walker et al. (2005).

APPENDIX II

Litigation and Child Protective Services

State	History of Litigation before 1992?	Cases
Alabama	Yes	*R.C. v. Walley* filed in 1988; court ordered 1991–2007.
Alaska	No	
Arizona	Yes	*J.K. v. Eden* filed in 1991 against Medicaid and certified as class action in 1993; Legislature made $20 million appropriation for children's behavioral health programs in 2001. *Bogutz v. State of Arizona* filed in 1993; court denied class certification for Class A in 1997; plaintiffs filed petition in 2002 asking court to grant certiorari of class action; court denied petition in 2004. Individual cases were subsequently tried by various lawyers with varying results.
Arkansas	Yes	*Angela R. v. Clinton* filed in 1991; court ordered in 1992; settlement expired in 2001; DCFS still makes quarterly presentations to executive/legislative branches and advisory groups still meet.
California	No	*Rene M. v. Anderson* filed in 1996; stipulated agreement reached in 1997. *Jones-Mason v. Anderson* filed in 1996; stipulated agreement reached in 1997. *Bohler v. Anderson* filed in 1997; later that year court ordered Department to develop/implement system for assessing children by 1998; current status unknown. *Mark A. v. Wilson* filed in 1998; court ordered in 1999; plaintiffs continue to monitor compliance with settlement terms. *Katie A. v. Bontá* filed in 2002; court ordered 2003 to present. *Higgins v. Saenz* filed in 2002; court ordered 2002 to present. *Belcher-Dixon v. Saenz* filed in 2003; dismissed in 2003. *Booraem v. Orange County* filed in 1998; consent decree in 2000; dismissed in 2002. *Laurie Q. v. Contra Costa County* filed in 1996; individual plaintiffs' claims resolved for significant damages, attorneys' fees, and prospective relief in 2005. *Leonard v. Wagner* filed in 2007; state court judge ordered State to develop plan to address disparity in 2009; oral argument held in 2010; case ongoing. *Rosales v. Thompson* filed in 1999; court ordered 2004–2006. *Warren v. Saenz* filed in 2000; court ordered in 2001; stipulated agreement reached in 2002. *Wheeler v. Sanders* filed in 2003; settlement agreement reached in 2005.

(continued)

(Continued)

State	History of Litigation before 1992?	Cases
Colorado	No	In 1992, Colorado Lawyers Committee (CLC) found DCWS had "serious deficiencies"; found justification for class action suit; state, counties, and CLC agreed to settlement in 1994 to avoid litigation.
Connecticut	Yes	*Juan F. v. Rell* filed in 1989; court ordered from 1991 to 2005 and again in 2008. *Emily J. v. Weicker* filed in 1993; court ordered 1997 to present. *W.R. v. Connecticut Department of Children and Families* filed in 2002; settlement agreement from 2005 to 2010.
Delaware	No	
District of Columbia	Yes	*LaShawn A. v. Fenty* filed in 1989; court ordered from 1993 to 2000 and 2008 to present.
Florida	Yes	*M.E. v. Bush* filed in 1990; court ordered 2001–2003; settlement agreement dismissed in 2003. *Ward v. Kearney* filed in 1998; court ordered 2000–2001; case ended in 2001. *Bonnie L. v. Bush* filed in 2000; district court dismissed many of plaintiffs' claims in 2001; settlement agreement on remaining claims reached in 2002; plaintiffs appealed dismissal of claims to circuit court in 2002; circuit court upheld district court's decision in 2003. *Brown v. Kearney* filed in 1991; amended to include class action allegations in 1993; trial court denied plaintiffs' motion in 1997. *Doe v. Kearney* filed in 2000; district court dismissed case in 2000; plaintiffs appealed to circuit court, which upheld district court's decision in 2003. *Lofton v. Kearney* filed in 1999; district court granted defendants' summary judgment motion in 2000; plaintiffs appealed to circuit court, which upheld district court's decision in 2004; Supreme Court declined to hear case in 2005. *Two Forgotten Children v. The State of Florida* filed in 1995; jury trial in 1999; settled in 2003.
Georgia	Yes	*Kenny A. v. Perdue* filed in 2002; court ordered 2008 to present. *J.J. v. Ledbetter* filed in 1980; court ordered in 1984; plaintiffs still monitoring state compliance with court orders as of January 2000; current status unknown. *Harris v. Martin* filed in 2003; defendants filed to dismiss but court denied the motion and reversed ALJ's decision to deny plaintiff's claim for adoption assistance benefits in 2004.
Hawaii	No	*Jennifer Felix v. Cayetano* filed in 1994; court ordered 2000–2005.
Idaho	No	*Oglala Sioux Tribe v. Harris* filed in 1994; court ordered in 2005; settlement agreement expired.

State	History of Litigation before 1992?	Cases
Illinois	Yes	*B.H. v. McDonald* filed in 1988; court ordered 1991 to present. *Aristotle P. v. McDonald* filed in 1988; court ordered 1994 to present. *Bates v. McDonald* filed in 1984; court ordered 1986 to present; no recent activity on class action. *Norman v. Suter* filed in 1990, court ordered 1991 to present. *Burgos v. Suter* filed in 1975; court ordered 1977 to present. *Katie I. v. Kimbrough* filed in 1989; court ordered to present. *Hill v. Erickson* filed in 1988; court ordered 1994 to present. *In re Lee/Wesley* filed in 1971; court ordered 1981 to present. *Aisha W. v. Aunt Martha's Youth Services Center* filed in 2000; six-figure settlement reached in 2005. *Apostol v. Aunt Martha's Youth Services Center* filed in 2000; six-figure settlement reached in 2003. *Artist M. v. Suter* filed in 1988; district court granted preliminary injunction in 1990 and circuit court upheld it; Supreme Court reversed it in 1992. *Dupuy v. Samuels* filed in 1997; preliminary injunction directing DCFS to revise its system of conducting investigations 2003 to 2006. *Letisha v. Morgan* filed in 1993; settlement reached in 1994. *Mabel A. v. Woodard* filed in 1997; settlement reached in 2001. *Willingham v. McDonald* filed in 1996; settlement reached in 2000. *Youakim v. McDonald* filed in 1995; court made final judgment requiring compensatory payments to plaintiffs.
Indiana	Yes	*B.M. v. Richardson* filed in 1989; court ordered 1992 to present.
Iowa	No	
Kansas	Yes	*Sheila A. v. Finney* filed in 1990; court ordered 1993–2002; state exited from agreement in June 2002 and Department of Social and Rehabilitation Services (SRS) agreed to replace settlement agreement with internal monitoring.
Kentucky	Yes	*Timmy S. v. Stumbo* filed in 1980; case dismissed and attorneys' fees awarded in 1994.
Louisiana	Yes	*Del A. v. Edwards* filed in 1986; dates of court order unknown.
Maine	No	
Maryland	Yes	*L.J. v. Massinga* filed in 1984; court ordered 1988 to present.

(continued)

(Continued)

State	History of Litigation before 1992?	Cases
Massachusetts	Yes	*MacFarland v. Dukakis* filed in 1978; preliminary injunction ordered; case dismissed in 1993. *Connor B. v. Patrick* filed in 2010.
Michigan	Yes	*Committee to End Racism in Michigan's Child Care System v. Mansour* filed in 1985; stipulated agreement reached in 1986. *Dwayne B. v. Granholm* filed in 2006; court ordered 2008 to present.
Minnesota	No	*Budreau v. Hennepin County Welfare Board* filed in 1994; stipulated agreement reached in 1996.
Mississippi	Yes	*Olivia Y. v. Barbour* filed in 2004; court ordered 2008 to present. *E.F. v. Scafidi* filed in 1991; certified class action in 1993; district court dismissed case in 1996; circuit court and Supreme Court denied certiorari in 1997.
Missouri	Yes	*G.L. v. Sherman* filed in 1977; court ordered 1983–1992 and 1994–2006. *E.C. v. Sherman* filed in 2005; court ordered 2006 to present. *S.S. v. McMullen* filed in 1983; district court dismissed case but plaintiff appealed; circuit court reversed in 1999; judgment vacated and rehearing en banc granted in 1999; after en banc reversal, plaintiff applied and was denied certiorari by Supreme Court.
Montana	No	
Nebraska	No	*Carson P. v. Heineman* filed in 2005; court denied plaintiffs' petition for class certification in 2007; dismissed case on basis of abstention under *Younger v. Harris*; plaintiffs did not appeal ruling.
Nevada	No	*Clark K. v. Willden* filed in 2006; district court ruled that plaintiffs could proceed with the majority of their claims in 2007; class certification denied in 2008; named plaintiffs' claims became moot and plaintiffs voluntarily dismissed their complaint. Subsequently, a new group of 13 plaintiffs filed *Henry A. v. Willden* in 2010.
New Hampshire	Yes	*Eric L. v. Bird* filed in 1991; court ordered 1997–2004; agreement expired in 2004 but plaintiffs sought continued enforcement, and determination of extending the decree is still pending. *James O. v. Marston* filed in 1986; court ordered in 1991; court approved continuation of consent decree in 2000.

State	History of Litigation before 1992?	Cases
New Jersey	No	*Baby Sparrow v. Waldman* filed in 1996; court ordered 1996–2001; settled in 2001. *Charlie and Nadine H. v. Corzine* filed in 1999; court ordered 2003 to present. *K.J. v. Division of Youth and Family Services* filed in 2004; settlement reached in 2005; one of the largest damages awards ever paid by New Jersey.
New Mexico	Yes	*Joseph A. v. Bolson* filed in 1980; court ordered 1983–2005. *K.L. v. State of New Mexico* filed in 1993; class certification denied in 1996; court dismissed claims of all children who had experienced state abuse/neglect in 1999 on the grounds that the court could not hear the case because of *Younger v. Harris*; plaintiffs appealed dismissal/denial of class certification but were denied by circuit court; plaintiffs decided not to seek certiorari to Supreme Court.
New York	Yes	*Marisol A. v. Giuliani* filed in 1995; court ordered 1999 to present. *Freeman v. Scoppetta* filed in 1998; court ordered 1999 to present. *Jesse E. v. NYCDSS* filed against Department of Social Services in 1990; court ordered 1993–1999. *Wilder v. Bernstein* filed in 1973; court ordered 1985–1998; in 1998 city still remained out of compliance in certain areas but terms of Wilder consent decree were incorporated into *Marisol v. Giuliani* agreement. *Nicholson v. Williams* filed in 2002; court ordered 2004–2005. *Cosentino v. Perales* (consolidated with *Martin A. v. Giuliani*) filed in 1985; plaintiffs began systemic enforcement proceedings in 1994; parties reached settlement agreement in 2008. *Martin A. v. Giuliani* (consolidated with *Cosentino v. Perales*) filed in 1985; class certification denied, individual plaintiffs all reached settlement agreements in 2000. *Grant v. Cuomo* filed in 1985; trial court issued preliminary injunction in 1986; appellate court modified lower court's order in 1987; Court of Appeals upheld appellate court's decision in 1988. *People United for Children, Inc. v. City of New York* filed in 1999; settlement agreement reached in 2007.
North Carolina	Yes	*Willie M. et al. v. Hunt* filed in 1979; court ordered 1980–1998.
North Dakota	No	
Ohio	Yes	*Roe v. Staples* filed in 1983; court ordered 1986 to present. *Ward v. Neal* filed in 1987; plaintiffs' individual damages settled in 1994.
Oklahoma	No	*D.G. v. Henry* filed in 2008; appeals court allowed it to proceed as class-action suit in 2010; no court order yet
Oregon	No	*A.S.W. v. Mink* filed in 2003; settlement agreement reached in 2008.

(continued)

(Continued)

State	History of Litigation before 1992?	Cases
Pennsylvania	Yes	*Anderson v. Houston* filed in 2000; court ordered 2005 to present. *Baby Neal v. Ridge* filed in 1990; court ordered 1999–2001. *T.M. v. City of Philadelphia* filed in 1989; court ordered 1990–1998.
Rhode Island	Yes	*Office of the Child Advocate v. Lindgren* filed in 1988; court ordered 1989 to present. *Sam and Tony M. v. Carcieri* filed in 2007 and dismissed by federal court in 2009; no court order.
South Carolina	No	
South Dakota	No	
Tennessee	No	*Brian A. v. Bredesen* filed in 2000; court ordered 2001 to present.
Texas	No	
Utah	No	*David C. v. Leavitt* filed in 1993; court ordered 1994 to present.
Vermont	No	
Virginia	No	
Washington	Yes	*Braam v. DSHS* filed in 1998; court ordered 2004 to present. *Guardianship Estate of Keffeler v. Washington State* filed in 1996; Supreme Court of Okanogan County ruled in favor of plaintiffs; Washington Supreme Court affirmed decision in 2001; U.S. Supreme Court reversed and remanded decision in 2003; Washington Supreme Court finally held that children were not denied equal protection in 2004. *Washington State Coalition for the Homeless v. Dept. of Social & Health Services* filed in 1991; class certified in 1992; court ruled that agency's plan was inadequate to address needs of homeless children in 1994; Washington Supreme Court upheld trial court's decision in 1997; Washington's legislature put out legislation that codified the ruling/substantial increases in funding; plaintiffs joined defendants in seeking dismissal of lawsuit in 2000.

State	History of Litigation before 1992?	Cases
West Virginia	Yes	*Gibson v. Ginsberg* filed in late 1970s; court ordered 1981 to present. *Sanders v. Weston* filed in 1992; court ordered in 1993; *K.H. v. Dorsey* filed in 2004; after 3-week trial, jury returned positive verdict of $1,250,000 in emotional distress damages.
Wisconsin	No	*Jeanine B. v. Doyle* filed in 1993; court ordered 2002 to present.
Wyoming	No	

Sources: Shay Bilchik and Howard Davidson (2005) (http://www.cwla.org/advocacy/consentde-crees.pdf).

Center for the Study of Social Policy (http://www.cssp.org/).

Children's Rights (http://www.childrensrights.org/reform-campaigns/legal-cases/).

National Center for Youth Law (http://www.youthlaw.org).

APPENDIX III

Risk Matrix

Operational Definitions of Key Variables of Interest

Risk Factor Matrix Reference Sheet

Risk Factor	Family Strengths	Low (1)	Moderate (3)	High (5)
I. Child Characteristics				
a. Age		12–17	6–11	0–5
b. Physical, Mental, or Social Development	No physical, mental, social, or developmental delay	Mild physical, mental, social, or developmental delay	Significant physical, mental, social, or developmental delay	Profound physical, mental, social, or developmental delay
c. Behavioral Issues	Child displays normal, age-appropriate behavior	Child displays minor behavioral problems	Child is behaviorally disturbed	Child is severely behaviorally disturbed
d. Self-Protection	Child is willing and able to protect self	Child displays consistent ability to protect self	Child displays occasional ability to protect self	Child is unable to protect self
e. Fear of Caretaker or Home Environment	Child is comfortable with caretaker and/or home environment	Child evidences mild doubt or concern about caretaker and/or home environment	Child evidences anxiety and/or discomfort about caretaker and/or home environment	Child is extremely fearful about caretaker and/or home environment
II. Severity of Child Abuse and Neglect (CA/N)				
f. Dangerous Acts	Parents exercise care and control to ensure child's safety and not cause injury to child	Acts that place the child at risk of minor pain or injury	Acts that place the child at risk of significant pain or moderate injury	Acts that place the child at risk of impairment or loss of bodily function

(continued)

Operational Definitions of Key Variables of Interest

Risk Factor Matrix Reference Sheet

Risk Factor	Family Strengths	Low (1)	Moderate (3)	High (5)
g. Extent of Physical Injury or Harm	No injury and no medical treatment required	Superficial injury, no medical attention required	Significant injury, unlikely to require medical attention	Major injury requiring medical treatment
h. Extent of Emotional Harm or Damage Exhibited by Child	Child exhibits normal behavior and social functioning	Minor distress or impairment in functioning related to CA/N	Behavior problems related to CA/N that impair social relationships or role functioning	Extensive emotional or behavioral impairment related to CA/N
i. Adequacy of Medical and Dental Care	Routine and crisis care provided consistently	Failure to provide routine medical, dental, or prenatal care	Failure to provide appropriate medical care for injury or illness that usually requires treatment	Failure to provide treatment for a critical or life-threatening condition
j. Provision for Basic Needs	Food, clothing, shelter, and hygiene needs adequately met	Failure to provide for basic needs places child at risk of minor distress/discomfort	Failure to provide for basic needs places child at risk of cumulative harm	Failure to provide for basic needs places child at risk of significant pain, injury, or harm
k. Adequacy of Supervision	Supervision meets normal standards appropriate to child's age	Lack of supervision places child at risk of minor discomfort or distress	Lack of supervision places child at risk of cumulative harm	Lack of supervision places child at risk of imminent harm
l. Physical Hazards or Dangerous Objects in the Home or Living Environment	Living condition are safe	Conditions in the home place the child at risk of minor illness or superficial injury	Conditions in the home place the child at risk of harm that is significant but unlikely to require treatment	Hazards in the home environment place the child at risk of serious harm that would likely require treatment
m. Sexual Abuse and/or Exploitation	Adult has a nonsexualized relationship with child and consistently protects child from sexual abuse or exploitation	Caretaker makes sexually suggestive remarks or flirtations with child without clear overtures or physical contact	Adult makes sexual overtures, or engages child in grooming behavior	Adult engages child in sexual contact or sexually exploits child

n. Exploitation (Nonsexual)	Adult has a nonexploitative relationship with the child and does not use the child in any manner for personal gain	Adult occasionally uses the child to obtain shelter or services that will benefit them both	Adult depends upon the child to sustain the home environment and assist in illegal activities to obtain money	Adult engages the child in dangerous activities to support or benefit the adult

III. Chronicity

o. Frequency of Abuse/ Neglect	Child is treated appropriately and there have been no incidents of child abuse or neglect in the past	Isolated incident of abuse or neglect	Intermittent incidents of abuse or neglect	Repeated or ongoing pattern of abuse or neglect

IV. Caretaker Characteristics

p. Victimization of Other Children by Caretaker	Caretaker is positive and appropriate with children	Evidence of minor abuse or neglect toward other children	Evidence of moderate abuse or neglect toward other children	Evidence of serious abuse or neglect toward other children
q. Mental, Physical, or Emotional Impairment of Caretaker	Caretaker is physically, mentally, and emotionally capable of parenting a child	A physical, mental, or emotional impairment mildly interferes with the capacity to parent	A physical, mental, or emotional impairment interferes significantly with the capacity to parent	Due to a physical, mental, or emotional impairment, the capacity to parent is severely inadequate
r. Deviant Arousal	Adult is not sexually aroused by children	Adult is sexually aroused by children and is motivated to have sexual contact with children (all risk levels)		
s. Substance Abuse	Parent does not abuse alcohol or drugs; parent does not sell drugs	History of substance abuse but no current problem	Reduced effectiveness due to substance abuse or addiction	Substantial incapacity due to substance abuse or addiction
t. History of Domestic Violence and Assaultive Behavior	Caretakers resolve conflicts in nonaggressive manner	Isolated incident of assaultive behavior not resulting in injury	Sporadic incidents of assaultive behavior that results in, or could result in, minor injury	Single incident or repeated incidents of assaultive behavior that results in, or could result in, major injury

(continued)

Operational Definitions of Key Variables of Interest

Risk Factor Matrix Reference Sheet

Risk Factor	Family Strengths	Low (1)	Moderate (3)	High (5)
u. History of Abuse or Neglect as a Child	Caretaker was raised in a healthy, nonabusive environment	Occasional incidents of abuse or neglect as a child	Repeated incidents of abuse or neglect as a child	History of chronic and/or severe incidents of abuse or neglect as a child
v. Parenting Skills and Knowledge	Caretaker provides environment that is child-friendly	Caretaker has some unrealistic expectations of the child and/or gaps in parenting skills	Significant gaps in knowledge or skills that interfere with effective parenting	Gross deficits in parenting knowledge and skills or inappropriate demands and expectations of child
w. Nurturance	Caretaker is openly accepting of child, interacts with child, and provides appropriate and adequate stimulation	Caretaker provides inconsistent expression of acceptance and inconsistent stimulation and interaction	Caretaker withholds affection and acceptance, but is not openly rejecting or hostile to child	Caretaker severely rejects child, providing no affection, attention, or stimulation
x. Recognition of Problem	Caretaker openly acknowledges the problem and its severity and is willing to accept responsibility	Caretaker recognizes a problem exists and is willing to take some responsibility	Caretaker has a superficial understanding of the problem, but fails to accept responsibility for own behavior	Caretaker has no understanding or is in complete denial of the problem, and refuses to accept any responsibility
y. Protection of Child by Non-Abusive Caretaker	Caretaker is willing and able to protect child from persons and dangerous situations	Caretaker is willing, but occasionally unable, to protect the child	Caretaker's protection of the child is inconsistent or unreliable	Caretaker refuses or is unable to protect the child

	Caretaker is receptive to social worker intervention	Caretaker accepts intervention and is intermittently cooperative	Caretaker accepts intervention but is noncooperative	Caretaker is extremely hostile to agency contact or involvement with family
z. Cooperation with Agency				
V. Caretaker Relationship				
aa. Response to Child's Behavior or Misconduct	Caretaker responds appropriately to child's behavior	Caretaker responds inappropriately to child's behavior	Caretaker responds to child's behavior with anger, frustration, or helplessness	Caretaker consistently responds abusively to child's behavior
bb. Attachment and Bonding	Secure parent–child attachment	Mild discrepancies or inconsistencies are evident in the parent–child relationship	Parent–child relationship evidences an anxious or disturbed attachment (or lack of attachment)	Obvious lack of bonding between child and parent
cc. Child's Role in the Family	Roles and responsibilities in the family are assigned appropriately	Child is given inappropriate role with no immediately apparent detrimental effects	Child's role in family has detrimental effect on normal development	Child's role in family severely limits or prevents normal development
dd. Child Is Pressured to Recant or Deny	Caretaker supports and insulates child from any pressure to recant or deny the abuse	Caretaker supports and insulates child from outside pressure to recant or deny the abuse	Caretaker indirectly puts pressure on the child to recant or deny the abuse and allows others to directly pressure the child	Caretaker directly pressures child to recant or deny the abuse and solicits or encourages others to do so
ee. Personal Boundary Issues	Personal boundaries are clear and respected	Personal boundaries are usually clear and respected; violations occur occasionally	Personal boundaries are usually clear but nonabusive violations occur occasionally	Even though personal boundaries are usually clear, violations occur regularly, including physical violations
ff. Parental Response to Abuse	Caretaker believes disclosure, shows concern and support for the child, and wants to protect	Caretaker will consider the possibility that abuse occurred, shows support and concern for the child, and expresses desire to protect	Caretaker does not believe disclosure, but shows concern for the child and is willing to protect	Caretaker does not believe disclosure, shows anger toward the child and supports offender

(continued)

(Continued)

Operational Definitions of Key Variables of Interest

Risk Factor Matrix Reference Sheet

Risk Factor	Family Strengths	Low (1)	Moderate (3)	High (5)
VI. Social and Economic Factors				
gg. Stress of Caretaker	Caretaker has no significant life stresses	Caretaker is experiencing mild stress	Caretaker is experiencing significant stresses or life changes	Caretaker is experiencing multiple and/or severe stress or life changes
hh. Employment Status of Caretaker	Caretaker is employed at a level that is consistent with training and personal expectations or unemployed by choice	Caretaker is underemployed or unemployed with immediate prospects for employment	Caretaker is unemployed but with marketable skills and potential for employment	Caretaker is unemployed with no prospects for employment
ii. Social Support for Caretaker	Frequent supportive contact with friends or relatives and appropriate use of community resources	Occasional contact with supportive persons; some use of available community resources	Sporadic supportive contact; underuse of resources	Caretaker is geographically or emotionally isolated and community resources are not available or not used
jj. Economic Resources of Caretaker	Family has resources to meet basic needs	Family's resources usually adequate to meet basic needs	Family's resources inadequate to meet basic needs	Family's resources grossly inadequate to meet basic needs
VII. Perpetrator Access				
kk. Perpetrator Access (Abuse)	Perpetrator's access to the child is limited, planned, and structured to ensure child's safety and well-being	Perpetrator access is supervised and usually controlled or limited	Limited supervised access or primary responsibility for care of child	Unlimited access to the child or full responsibility for care of the child

APPENDIX IV

Number of Positive and Negative Equilibrium Changes in CPS Workforce by State

State	Positive Equilibrium Change	Negative Equilibrium Change
Alabama	1	0
Alaska	2	1
Arizona	0	0
Arkansas	0	1
California	1	1
Colorado	0	0
Connecticut	0	0
Delaware	0	5
Washington, DC	1	0
Florida	0	0
Georgia	0	0
Hawaii	1	0
Idaho	2	2
Illinois	0	0
Indiana	1	2
Iowa	0	0
Kansas	2	5
Kentucky	2	0
Louisiana	0	0
Maine	0	0
Maryland	1	1
Massachusetts	0	0
Michigan	0	0
Minnesota	0	0
Mississippi	1	7
Missouri	0	1
Montana	0	1

(continued)

(Continued)

State	Positive Equilibrium Change	Negative Equilibrium Change
Nebraska	1	5
Nevada	0	0
New Hampshire	1	6
New Jersey	1	1
New Mexico	2	1
New York	0	0
North Carolina	2	1
North Dakota	0	0
Ohio	0	0
Oklahoma	0	0
Oregon	0	0
Pennsylvania	3	2
Rhode Island	0	0
South Carolina	0	0
South Dakota	3	3
Tennessee	0	0
Texas	1	2
Utah	0	0
Vermont	1	8
Virginia	1	1
Washington	0	1
West Virginia	0	0
Wisconsin	1	1
Wyoming	2	2
Overall	34	61

APPENDIX V

Fixed Effects Regression of All Outrage Mechanisms Together on Report Rate

	Model 1	Model 2
	b/se	b/se
sexoffender_law (lagged)	1.320	0.765
	(1.30)	(1.27)
current_courtcase	1.017	0.702
	(1.57)	(1.53)
CPS_courtorder	0.143	0.253
	(1.33)	(1.25)
positive_equil_chg	−5.283***	
	(1.56)	
negative_equil_chg		3.286**
		(1.35)
p_chil_pov	−0.047	−0.049
	(0.09)	(0.09)
p_blk_chpop	−0.582	−0.505
	(0.46)	(0.44)
p_hisp_chpop	−0.843***	0.868***
	(0.26)	(0.25)
p_age03_chpop	1.904	1.793
	(1.18)	(1.17)
p_age47_chpop	2.781*	2.681*
	(1.53)	(1.48)
p_age811_chpop	2.877***	2.887**
	(1.05)	(1.08)
p_age1215_chpop	3.207*	3.204*
	(1.75)	(1.71)
p_male_chpop	−3.507	−3.404
	(2.24)	(2.20)

(continued)

	Model 1	Model 2
	b/se	b/se
p_chil_singparhh	−0.294	−0.250
	(0.21)	(0.20)
p_chil_noparentemp	0.002	0.030
	(0.11)	(0.11)
wkrs_1000caseload	−0.123***	0.161***
	(0.04)	(0.04)
fedex_caseload (lagged)	−0.000***	0.000***
	(0.00)	(0.00)
statex_caseload (lagged)	−0.000	−0.000
	(0.00)	(0.00)
p_capta	−0.001	−0.000
	(0.02)	(0.02)
rep_chlevel_data	−1.244	−1.358
	(1.14)	(1.21)
p_union_cov	0.004	0.007
	(0.07)	(0.08)
ln_caseload	0.697	0.812
	(1.08)	(1.11)
famcap	0.096	0.230
	(1.48)	(1.46)
work_req	0.950	0.724
	(1.44)	(1.47)
time_limit	−0.133	0.001
	(1.54)	(1.61)
severe_sanction	−1.614	−1.683
	(1.26)	(1.34)
real_maxben	−0.008	−0.007
	(0.01)	(0.01)
unemp	0.246**	0.232*
	(0.12)	(0.12)
fem_lfp	0.106	0.125
	(0.11)	(0.11)
time	−0.260	−0.374
	(0.76)	(0.73)
timesq	0.051	0.061*
	(0.03)	(0.03)
_cons	−4.700	−8.980
	(20.63)	(21.11)
N	779	779
R^2	0.2941	0.2848

Fixed Effects Regression of All Outrage Mechanisms Together on Substantiation Rate

	Model 1	Model 2
	b/se	b/se
sexoffender_law (lagged)	0.780	0.543
	(1.18)	(1.13)
current_courtcase	2.140**	2.055**
	(0.99)	(0.98)
CPS_courtorder	−0.573	−0.620
	(1.06)	(1.04)
positive_equil_chg	−0.749	
	(0.96)	
negative_equil_chg		2.023**
		(0.83)
p_chil_pov	−0.217**	−0.223**
	(0.09)	(0.09)
p_blk_chpop	−1.005**	−0.985**
	(0.44)	(0.44)
p_hisp_chpop	−0.533**	−0.543**
	(0.24)	(0.24)
p_age03_chpop	−0.120	−0.228
	(0.91)	(0.90)
p_age47_chpop	0.021	−0.136
	(0.99)	(0.97)
p_age811_chpop	1.005	0.884
	(0.95)	(0.98)
p_age1215_chpop	−0.475	−0.591
	(1.23)	(1.22)
p_male_chpop	−0.014	0.207
	(1.57)	(1.58)
p_chil_singparhh	0.006	0.027
	(0.12)	(0.12)
p_chil_noparentemp	0.230**	0.229**
	(0.11)	(0.11)
wkrs_1000caseload	−0.022	−0.029
	(0.02)	(0.02)
fedex_caseload (lagged)	−0.000**	−0.000**
	(0.00)	(0.00)
statex_caseload (lagged)	−0.000	−0.000
	(0.00)	(0.00)

(continued)

(Continued)

	Model 1	Model 2
	b/se	b/se
p_capta	0.016	0.017
	(0.01)	(0.01)
rep_chlevel_data	−1.436	−1.395
	(0.89)	(0.91)
p_union_cov	−0.067	−0.061
	(0.08)	(0.08)
ln_caseload	1.743*	1.741*
	(0.98)	(0.95)
famcap	−0.461	−0.359
	(1.18)	(1.18)
work_req	0.756	0.485
	(0.97)	(0.97)
time_limit	−2.988**	−2.937**
	(1.24)	(1.23)
severe_sanction	−0.911	−0.906
	(1.15)	(1.18)
real_maxben	−0.006	−0.005
	(0.01)	(0.01)
unemp	0.264**	0.254**
	(0.12)	(0.12)
fem_lfp	0.148*	0.151*
	(0.08)	(0.08)
time	0.028	0.058
	(0.62)	(0.60)
timesq	0.015	0.015
	(0.03)	(0.03)
_cons	22.620	21.285
	(20.94)	(21.08)
N	779	779
R^2	0.2565	0.2646

Fixed Effects Regression of All Outrage Mechanisms Together on Substantiations as a Percentage of Investigations

	Model_1	Model_2
	b/se	b/se
sexoffender_law (lagged)	2.500	2.669
	(2.33)	(2.34)
current_courtcase	2.273	2.442
	(1.93)	(1.97)
CPS_courtorder	−2.056	−2.211
	(1.86)	(1.81)
positive_equil_chg	3.965*	
	(2.32)	
negative_equil_chg		0.066
		(1.62)
p_chil_pov	−0.335*	−0.327*
	(0.18)	(0.18)
p_blk_chpop	−1.256*	−1.298*
	(0.71)	(0.71)
p_hisp_chpop	−1.492**	−1.476**
	(0.66)	(0.66)
p_age03_chpop	−3.696**	−3.741**
	(1.65)	(1.67)
p_age47_chpop	−1.276	−1.419
	(2.04)	(2.06)
p_age811_chpop	0.851	0.646
	(1.88)	(1.95)
p_age1215_chpop	−3.641	−3.808
	(2.40)	(2.44)
p_male_chpop	3.601	3.828
	(3.23)	(3.32)
p_chil_singparhh	−0.124	−0.140
	(0.22)	(0.23)
p_chil_noparentemp	0.480*	0.447*
	(0.24)	(0.24)
wkrs_1000caseload	0.053	0.080
	(0.08)	(0.08)
fedex_caseload (lagged)	−0.000	−0.000
	(0.00)	(0.00)
statex_caseload (lagged)	0.000	0.000
	(0.00)	(0.00)

(continued)

(Continued)

	Model_1	Model_2
	b/se	b/se
p_capta	0.028	0.030
	(0.02)	(0.02)
rep_chlevel_data	−0.540	−0.391
	(1.72)	(1.76)
p_union_cov	0.015	0.019
	(0.19)	(0.19)
ln_caseload	2.924*	2.777*
	(1.54)	(1.60)
famcap	−0.581	−0.644
	(2.58)	(2.59)
work_req	1.877	1.747
	(2.17)	(2.25)
time_limit	−3.599	−3.678
	(2.73)	(2.75)
severe_sanction	1.773	1.877
	(2.10)	(2.11)
real_maxben	0.036	0.035
	(0.02)	(0.02)
unemp	0.242	0.248
	(0.29)	(0.29)
fem_lfp	0.260*	0.246*
	(0.14)	(0.14)
time	−2.268**	−2.089*
	(1.10)	(1.08)
timesq	0.131**	0.120**
	(0.06)	(0.06)
_cons	24.058	26.088
	(39.81)	(39.70)
N	754	754
R^2	0.3961	0.3914

Fixed Effects Regression of All Outrage Mechanisms Together on Physical Abuse Rate

	Model 1	Model 2
	b/se	b/se
sexoffender_law (lagged)	0.386	0.346
	(0.42)	(0.42)
current_courtcase	0.255	0.230
	(0.41)	(0.41)
CPS_courtorder	−0.583*	−0.570*
	(0.29)	(0.29)
positive_equil_chg	−0.450	
	(0.38)	
negative_equil_chg		0.202
		(0.27)
p_chil_pov	−0.064**	−0.064**
	(0.03)	(0.03)
p_blk_chpop	−0.099	−0.092
	(0.11)	(0.11)
p_hisp_chpop	−0.160**	−0.162**
	(0.07)	(0.07)
p_age03_chpop	−0.113	−0.118
	(0.26)	(0.26)
p_age47_chpop	0.120	0.119
	(0.35)	(0.34)
p_age811_chpop	0.170	0.177
	(0.31)	(0.32)
p_age1215_chpop	0.278	0.283
	(0.35)	(0.35)
p_male_chpop	−0.088	−0.090
	(0.51)	(0.51)
p_chil_singparhh	0.022	0.025
	(0.04)	(0.04)
p_chil_noparentemp	−0.016	−0.014
	(0.02)	(0.02)
wkrs_1000caseload	−0.008	−0.011
	(0.01)	(0.01)
fedex_caseload (lagged)	−0.000	−0.000
	(0.00)	(0.00)
statex_caseload (lagged)	−0.000	−0.000
	(0.00)	(0.00)

(continued)

(Continued)

	Model 1	Model 2
	b/se	b/se
p_capta	0.013***	0.013***
	(0.00)	(0.00)
rep_chlevel_data	−0.208	−0.221
	(0.28)	(0.29)
p_union_cov	−0.052**	−0.052*
	(0.03)	(0.03)
ln_caseload	0.172	0.183
	(0.29)	(0.30)
famcap	−0.167	−0.160
	(0.40)	(0.40)
work_req	−0.534	−0.541
	(0.35)	(0.36)
time_limit	−0.231	−0.222
	(0.35)	(0.35)
severe_sanction	0.216	0.209
	(0.35)	(0.36)
real_maxben	0.008**	0.008**
	(0.00)	(0.00)
unemp	0.006	0.005
	(0.03)	(0.03)
fem_lfp	0.010	0.011
	(0.02)	(0.02)
time	−0.115	−0.127
	(0.19)	(0.19)
timesq	0.008	0.009
	(0.01)	(0.01)
_cons	−0.867	−1.196
	(3.94)	(3.90)
N	779	779
R^2	0.3349	0.3330

Fixed Effects Regression of All Outrage Mechanisms Together on Neglect Rate

	Model 1	Model 2
	b/se	b/se
sexoffender_law (lagged)	−0.160	−0.319
	(0.81)	(0.81)
current_courtcase	0.282	0.213
	(0.78)	(0.78)
CPS_courtorder	−0.354	−0.363
	(0.59)	(0.55)
positive_equil_chg	−0.876	
	(0.79)	
negative_equil_chg		1.204***
		(0.44)
p_chil_pov	−0.119**	−0.121**
	(0.06)	(0.06)
p_blk_chpop	0.524**	0.540**
	(0.23)	(0.23)
p_hisp_chpop	−0.304***	−0.311***
	(0.11)	(0.10)
p_age03_chpop	−0.393	−0.451
	(0.54)	(0.54)
p_age47_chpop	1.348	1.271
	(1.00)	(0.98)
p_age811_chpop	−0.034	−0.084
	(0.60)	(0.61)
p_age1215_chpop	0.768	0.719
	(0.70)	(0.69)
p_male_chpop	−1.145	−1.041
	(1.00)	(0.99)
p_chil_singparhh	−0.004	0.009
	(0.08)	(0.08)
p_chil_noparentemp	0.069	0.072
	(0.08)	(0.08)
wkrs_1000caseload	−0.008	−0.015
	(0.02)	(0.02)
fedex_caseload (lagged)	−0.000**	−0.000**
	(0.00)	(0.00)
statex_caseload (lagged)	−0.000	−0.000
	(0.00)	(0.00)

(continued)

(Continued)

	Model 1	Model 2
	b/se	b/se
p_capta	0.016*	0.017*
	(0.01)	(0.01)
rep_chlevel_data	−0.109	−0.104
	(0.60)	(0.61)
p_union_cov	−0.033	−0.030
	(0.04)	(0.04)
ln_caseload	0.184	0.195
	(0.41)	(0.41)
famcap	0.079	0.137
	(0.65)	(0.65)
work_req	−0.326	−0.465
	(0.70)	(0.71)
time_limit	−1.491*	−1.456*
	(0.78)	(0.78)
severe_sanction	−1.225	−1.230
	(0.75)	(0.76)
real_maxben	0.006	0.007
	(0.01)	(0.01)
unemp	−0.076	−0.082
	(0.08)	(0.08)
fem_lfp	−0.009	−0.006
	(0.05)	(0.05)
time	0.488	0.488
	(0.43)	(0.44)
timesq	−0.008	−0.007
	(0.02)	(0.02)
_cons	22.673	21.655
	(16.28)	(16.17)
N	779	779
R^2	0.1748	0.1799

Fixed Effects Regression of All Outrage Mechanisms Together on Sexual Abuse Rate

	Model 1	Model 2
	b/se	b/se
sexoffender_law (lagged)	0.323	0.300
	(0.23)	(0.22)
current_courtcase	0.034	0.020
	(0.19)	(0.19)
CPS_courtorder	−0.370**	−0.361**
	(0.17)	(0.16)
positive_equil_chg	−0.273	
	(0.18)	
negative_equil_chg		0.111
		(0.13)
p_chil_pov	−0.028**	−0.028**
	(0.01)	(0.01)
p_blk_chpop	−0.064	−0.060
	(0.06)	(0.06)
p_hisp_chpop	−0.049*	−0.050*
	(0.03)	(0.03)
p_age03_chpop	−0.135	−0.137
	(0.13)	(0.13)
p_age47_chpop	−0.033	−0.033
	(0.14)	(0.14)
p_age811_chpop	0.093	0.099
	(0.14)	(0.15)
p_age1215_chpop	0.002	0.006
	(0.14)	(0.14)
p_male_chpop	0.113	0.110
	(0.20)	(0.20)
p_chil_singparhh	0.001	0.003
	(0.02)	(0.02)
p_chil_noparentemp	0.008	0.010
	(0.01)	(0.01)
wkrs_1000caseload	−0.001	−0.003
	(0.00)	(0.00)
fedex_caseload (lagged)	−0.000**	−0.000**
	(0.00)	(0.00)
statex_caseload (lagged)	0.000	0.000
	(0.00)	(0.00)

(continued)

(Continued)

	Model 1	Model 2
	b/se	b/se
p_capta	0.006***	0.006***
	(0.00)	(0.00)
rep_chlevel_data	−0.118	−0.126
	(0.13)	(0.13)
p_union_cov	−0.026*	−0.026*
	(0.01)	(0.01)
ln_caseload	0.229	0.235
	(0.17)	(0.18)
famcap	−0.216	−0.212
	(0.21)	(0.21)
work_req	−0.222	−0.225
	(0.16)	(0.18)
time_limit	−0.071	−0.066
	(0.16)	(0.16)
severe_sanction	0.033	0.029
	(0.16)	(0.17)
real_maxben	0.003	0.003
	(0.00)	(0.00)
unemp	−0.016	−0.016
	(0.01)	(0.01)
fem_lfp	0.003	0.004
	(0.01)	(0.01)
time	−0.160**	−0.167**
	(0.08)	(0.07)
timesq	0.009**	0.010**
	(0.00)	(0.00)
_cons	−0.568	−0.762
	(2.37)	(2.39)
N	779	779
R^2	0.3704	0.3672

Fixed Effects Regression of All Outrage Mechanisms Together on Placement Rate

	Model 1	Model 2
	b/se	b/se
sexoffender_law (lagged)	−0.155	−0.177
	(0.28)	(0.28)
current_courtcase	0.426	0.420
	(0.35)	(0.35)
CPS_courtorder	0.456	0.456
	(0.43)	(0.43)
positive_equil_chg	−0.140	
	(0.33)	
negative_equil_chg		0.189
		(0.25)
p_chil_pov	−0.025	−0.025
	(0.03)	(0.03)
p_blk_chpop	0.002	0.003
	(0.10)	(0.10)
p_hisp_chpop	−0.001	−0.006
	(0.10)	(0.10)
p_age03_chpop	−0.275	−0.275
	(0.22)	(0.22)
p_age47_chpop	0.082	0.081
	(0.29)	(0.29)
p_age811_chpop	0.140	0.143
	(0.25)	(0.25)
p_age1215_chpop	−0.163	−0.159
	(0.30)	(0.30)
p_male_chpop	0.127	0.127
	(0.43)	(0.43)
p_chil_singparhh	0.074*	0.076*
	(0.04)	(0.04)
p_chil_noparentemp	0.033	0.034
	(0.02)	(0.03)
wkrs_1000caseload	0.007	0.006
	(0.01)	(0.01)
fedex_caseload (lagged)	−0.000*	−0.000*
	(0.00)	(0.00)
statex_caseload (lagged)	0.000*	0.000*
	(0.00)	(0.00)

(continued)

(Continued)

	Model 1	Model 2
	b/se	b/se
p_capta	0.009**	0.009**
	(0.00)	(0.00)
rep_chlevel_data	0.209	0.209
	(0.24)	(0.24)
p_union_cov	−0.014	−0.013
	(0.02)	(0.02)
ln_caseload	0.156	0.161
	(0.23)	(0.23)
famcap	−0.314	−0.307
	(0.36)	(0.36)
work_req	−0.308	−0.308
	(0.38)	(0.38)
time_limit	−0.524	−0.522
	(0.34)	(0.34)
severe_sanction	0.167	0.171
	(0.34)	(0.34)
real_maxben	0.001	0.001
	(0.00)	(0.00)
unemp	0.071	0.069
	(0.05)	(0.05)
fem_lfp	0.004	0.006
	(0.02)	(0.02)
time	0.216	0.215
	(0.16)	(0.16)
timesq	−0.005	−0.005
	(0.01)	(0.01)
_cons	−3.401	−3.707
	(6.86)	(6.88)
N	643	643
R^2	0.2226	0.2233

Fixed Effects Regression of All Outrage Mechanisms Together on Placements as a Percentage of Investigations

	Model 1	Model 2
	b/se	b/se
sexoffender_law (lagged)	0.939	1.042
	(1.10)	(1.10)
current_courtcase	−0.081	−0.019
	(0.84)	(0.83)
CPS_courtorder	1.945*	1.927*
	(0.99)	(0.97)
positive_equil_chg	1.257	
	(1.13)	
negative_equil_chg		−0.648
		(0.85)
p_chil_pov	0.015	0.017
	(0.12)	(0.12)
p_blk_chpop	−0.138	−0.141
	(0.34)	(0.34)
p_hisp_chpop	−0.795**	−0.771**
	(0.35)	(0.35)
p_age03_chpop	−0.879	−0.906
	(0.63)	(0.63)
p_age47_chpop	1.584*	1.551*
	(0.93)	(0.92)
p_age811_chpop	1.509**	1.437*
	(0.72)	(0.72)
p_age1215_chpop	0.628	0.568
	(0.88)	(0.87)
p_male_chpop	−1.174	−1.106
	(1.16)	(1.15)
p_chil_singparhh	0.036	0.029
	(0.12)	(0.13)
p_chil_noparentemp	0.122	0.114
	(0.10)	(0.10)
wkrs_1000caseload	0.092***	0.103***
	(0.02)	(0.02)
fedex_caseload (lagged)	0.000	0.000
	(0.00)	(0.00)
statex_caseload (lagged)	0.000**	0.000**
	(0.00)	(0.00)

(continued)

(Continued)

	Model 1	Model 2
	b/se	b/se
p_capta	0.013	0.013
	(0.01)	(0.01)
rep_chlevel_data	0.994	1.025
	(0.69)	(0.68)
p_union_cov	0.025	0.021
	(0.06)	(0.06)
ln_caseload	−0.385	−0.454
	(0.75)	(0.76)
famcap	−0.493	−0.498
	(1.38)	(1.38)
work_req	−0.215	−0.299
	(1.17)	(1.14)
time_limit	−1.793*	−1.810*
	(1.04)	(1.05)
severe_sanction	1.583	1.588
	(0.96)	(0.97)
real_maxben	0.003	0.003
	(0.01)	(0.01)
unemp	0.244	0.251
	(0.17)	(0.17)
fem_lfp	0.117*	0.110*
	(0.06)	(0.06)
time	−0.542	−0.510
	(0.51)	(0.51)
timesq	0.048*	0.045
	(0.03)	(0.03)
_cons	−9.134	−7.843
	(20.40)	(20.12)
N	643	643
R^2	0.2973	0.2957

*p-values < 0.1.

**p-values < 0.05.

***p-values < 0.01.

Regression Coefficients of Fatality Rate and Outrage Mechanisms on CPS Decision Outcomes [Analyses Restricted to 1997–2008][†]

	CPS Decision Outcomes							
	report_ rate	substan_ rate	substan_ percent	phyabuse_ rate	neglect_ rate	sexabuse_ rate	placement_ rate	placement_ percent
fatal_rate (lagged)	55.2*	**58.5***	6.6	13.5*	**48.6****	3.3	**12.3****	−1.0
sexoffender_ law (lagged)	−2.25	0.19	−0.43	−0.26	−1.5	0.04	−0.38	−0.93
current_ courtcase	2.08	**2.11****	3.4	0.48*	1.17**	0.17	**0.63****	0.39
CPS_ courtorder	1.13	0.21	0.31	0.15	0.29	−0.01	0.51*	0.81
positive_ equil_chg	−1.9	−0.5	−1.02	−0.06	−0.44	−0.08	−0.06	1.02
negative_ equil_chg	0.26	0.5	0.96	−0.26	0.41	−0.08	−0.16	−0.02

*p-values < 0.1.

**p-values < 0.05.

***p-values < 0.01.

[†]All regressions include variables on child hazard, CPS task environment, welfare policies, and economic environment.

APPENDIX VI

APPENDIX VII

Regression Coefficients of Fatality Rate and Outrage Mechanisms on Logged CPS Decision Outcomes[†]

	CPS Decision Outcomes							
	report_ rate	substan_ rate	substan_ percent	phyabuse_ rate	neglect_ rate	sexabuse_ rate	placement_ rate	placement_ percent
fatal_rate (lagged)	0.4	**4.4*****	1.6	2.3*	**4.9*****	−0.3	**3.7***	1.9
sexoffender_ law (lagged)	0.05	0.12	0.10	0.11	0.08	0.25*	−0.1	−0.13
current_ courtcase	0.01	0.15	0.07	0.03	0.13	−0.07	0.18	0.18
CPS_ courtorder	0.01	0.02	−0.05	−0.08	0.02	−0.15	0.17	**0.17***
positive_ equil_chg	**−0.22*****	−0.05	**0.10***	−0.03	−0.06	−0.04	−0.06	0.11
negative_ equil_chg	**0.14****	**0.19****	0.05	0.08	**0.26*****	0.07	0.01	−0.07

*p-values < 0.1.

**p-values < 0.05.

***p-values < 0.01.

[†]All regressions include variables on child hazard, CPS task environment, welfare policies, and economic environment.

REFERENCES

CHAPTER 1

Annie E. Casey Foundation. (2003). *The unsolved challenge of system reform: The condition of the frontline human services workforce*. Baltimore, MD: The Annie E. Casey Foundation.

Associated Press. (2006). To settle suit in boy's death, New Jersey to pay $7.5 million. (November 11). http://www.nytimes.com/2006/11/12/nyregion/12settle.html.

Baumgartner, F. R., & Jones, B. D. (1991). Agenda dynamics and policy subsystems. *The Journal of Politics*, *53*, 1044–1074.

Baumgartner, F. R., & Jones, B. D. (2009). *Agendas and instability in American politics*, 2nd ed. Chicago, IL: University of Chicago Press.

Behn, R. D. (2001). *Rethinking democratic accountability*. Washington, DC: Brookings Institution Press.

Blake, E. R. (1995). Understanding outrage: How scientists can help bridge the risk perception gap. *Environmental Health Perspectives*, *103*, 123–125.

Bradshaw, J., Hoelscher, P., & Richardson, D. (2006). *Comparing child wellbeing in OECD countries. Concepts and Methods*. Innocenti Working Paper (IWP-2006–03). UNICEF, Innocenti Research Centre. Florence, Italy.

Bremner, R. H. (1971). *Children and youth in America: A documentary history*. Volume II. Cambridge, MA: Harvard University Press.

Brittain, C., & Hunt, D. E. (2004). *Helping in child protective services*. New York: Oxford University Press.

Camasso, M. J. (2007). *Family caps, abortion and women of color: Research connection and political rejection*. New York: Oxford University Press.

Charlie and Nadine H. v. Corzine. 83 F. Supp. 2d 476 (D. N. J. 2000); 213 F. R. D. 240 (D. N. J. 2003).

Charlie and Nadine H. v. Corzine. U.S. District Court for the District of New Jersey, 99-3678 (1999).

Child Welfare Information Gateway. (2011). *Major legislation concerned with child protection, child welfare and adoption*. USDHHS, ACF, Children's Bureau/ACYF. Washington, DC: USDHHS.

Covello, V. T., Sandman, P. M., & Slovic, P. (1988). *Risk communication, risk statistics and risk comparisons: A manual for plant managers*. Washington, DC: Chemical Manufacturers Association.

Deal, T. E., & Kennedy, A. A. (1982). *Corporate cultures*. Reading, MA: Addison-Wesley.

DeParle, J. (1997). Welfare to Work: A Sequel. *New York Times*, 28 December.

Eldredge, N., & Gould, S. J. (1997). On punctuated equilibria. *Science*, *276*, 337–341.

Epstein, W. (1999). *Children who could have been*. Madison, WI: University of Wisconsin Press.

Freymond, N., & Cameron, G. (Eds.). (2006). *Toward positive systems of child and family welfare*. Toronto: University of Toronto Press.

Gabel, S. G., & Kamerman, S. B. (2006). Investing in children: Public commitment in twenty-one industrialized countries. *Social Service Review, 80*, 239–263.

Gainsborough, J. F. (2010). *Scandalous politics: Child welfare policy in the States*. Washington, DC: Georgetown University Press.

Geen, R., & Tumlin, K. C. (1999). *State efforts to remake child welfare: Response to new challenges and increased scrutiny*. Occasional Paper No. 29. Washington, DC: The Urban Institute.

Gersick, C. J. G. (1988). Time and transition in work teams: Toward a new model of group development. *Academy of Management Journal, 31*, 9–41.

Gibbs, R. (2006). *Imminent risk: The child welfare state*. Denver, CO: Outskirts Press.

Goffman, E. (1952). On cooling out the mark: Some aspects of adaptation to failure. *Psychiatry, 15*, 451–463.

Golden, O. (2009). *Reforming child welfare*. Washington, DC: The Urban Institute.

Haskins, R., Wulczyn, F., & Webb, M. B. (Eds.). (2007). *Child protection: Using research to improve policy and practice*. Washington, DC: Brookings Institution Press.

Jung, C. G. (1959). The shadow. In *The collected works of C.G. Jung*, Vol. 9/2 (pp. 13–19). Princeton, NJ: Princeton University Press.

Jung, C. G. (1964). After the catastrophe. In *The collected works of C. G. Jung*, Vol. 10 (pp. 400–443). Princeton, NJ: Princeton University Press.

Kamerman, S. B., Neuman, M., Waldfogel, J., & Brooks-Gunn, J. (2003). *Social policies, family types and child outcomes in selected OECD countries*. Social, Employment and Migration Working Papers no. 6. Organization for Economic Cooperation and Development, Paris.

Kasperson, R. E. (1986). Six propositions of public participation and their relevance for risk communication. *Risk Analysis, 6*, 275–281.

Kosanovich, A., & Joseph, R. M. (2005). *Child welfare consent decrees: Analysis of thirty-five court actions from 1995 to 2005*. Washington, DC: Child Welfare League of America and American Bar Association.

Kupchan, C. (2008). America-Europe: A comparison of risk-taking. *The Economist*. http://www.economist.com/node/10766283.

Lindsey, D. (2004). *The welfare of children*, 2nd ed. New York: Oxford University Press.

Lindsey, D., & Shlonsky, A. (Eds.). (2008). *Child welfare research: Advances in practice and policy*. New York: Oxford University Press.

Lowry, M. R. (1998). Commentary: How we can better protect children from abuse and neglect. *The Future of Children, 8*, 123–126.

Marisol A. v. Giuliani, 185F. R. D.152 (S. D. N. Y. 1995).

McDonald, W. R., & Associates, Inc. (2003). *National study of child protective services systems and reform efforts: Review of state CPS policy*. Washington, DC: USDHHS/ACF and OASPE, U.S. Government Printing Office.

Mintzberg, H. (1979). *The structuring of organizations*. Englewood Cliffs, NJ: Prentice-Hall.

Mintzberg, H. (1983). *Structure in fives: Designing effective organizations*. Englewood Cliffs, NJ: Prentice-Hall.

Myers, J. E. B. (2006). *Child protection in America: Past, present and future*. New York: Oxford University Press.

Nelson, B. S. (1984). *Making an issue of child abuse: Political agenda setting for social problems*. Chicago, IL: University of Chicago Press.

Paxson, C., & Haskins, R. (Eds.). (2009). Preventing child maltreatment. *The Future of Children, 19*(2). Princeton, NJ: Princeton University and the Brookings Institution Press.

Price, T. (2005). Child welfare reform: The issues. *CQ Researcher, 15,* 347–364.

Raup, D. M. (1991). *Extinction: Bad genes or bad luck?* New York: W. W. Norton.

Rifkin, J. (2005). *The European dream: How Europe's vision of the future is quietly eclipsing the American dream.* New York: Penguin.

Sandler, R., & Schoenbrod, D. (2003). *Democracy by decree: What happens when courts run the government.* New Haven, CT: Yale University Press.

Sandman, P. (2003). Beyond panic prevention: Addressing emotion in emerging communication. In *Emerging risk communication CDCynergy.* Washington, DC: USDHHS, Centers for Disease Control and Prevention.

Sandman, P. M. (1999). Risk = hazard + outrage: Coping with controversy about utility risks. *Engineering News-Record,* October, A19–A23.

Sandman, P. M., Sachsman, D. B., Greenberg, M. B., & Gochfeld, M. (1987). *Environmental risk and the press.* New Brunswick, NJ: Transaction Books.

Sandman, P. M., Weinstein, N. D., & Hallman, W. K. (1998). Communications to reduce risk underestimation and overestimation. *Risk Decision and Policy, 3,* 93–108.

Schene, P. A. (1998). Past, present and future roles of child protective services. *The Future of Children, 8,* 23–38.

Schorr, A. L. (2000). The bleak prospect for public child welfare. *Social Service Review, 74,* 124–136.

Sedlak, A. J., Meltenberg, J., Basena, M., Petta, I., McPherson, K., Greene, A., & Spencer, L. (2010). *Fourth national incidence study of child abuse and neglect (NIS-4): Report to Congress.* Washington, DC: USDHHS, ACF.

Sjoberg, L. (2000). Factors in risk perception. *Risk Analysis, 20,* 1–11.

Stein, M. (1995). *Jung on evil.* Princeton, NJ: Princeton University Press.

Stoesz, D. (2005). *Quixote's ghost: The right, the liberati and the future of social policy.* New York: Oxford University Press.

U.S. Government Accountability Office. (2006). *Improving social service program, training and technical assistance information would help address long-standing service level and workforce challenges* (GAO-07-75). Washington, DC: GAO.

U.S. House of Representatives, Committee on Ways and Means. (2006). *Hearing before the Subcommittee on Human Resources (Serial No. 109–73).* Washington, DC: U.S. Government Printing Office.

UNICEF, Innocenti Research Centre. (2007). *An overview of child well-being in rich countries.* Report Card 7. Florence, Italy: Innocenti Research Centre.

Waldfogel, J. (1998). *The future of child protection: How to break the cycle of abuse and neglect.* Cambridge, MA: Harvard University Press.

Waldfogel, J. (2010). *Britain's war on poverty.* New York: Russell Sage Foundation.

Walsh, J. (2008). *Tears of rage.* New York: Pocket.

Weber, M. (1947). *The theory of social and economic organization.* A. M. Henderson & T. Parsons (trans.). New York: Free Press.

Welch, M., Price, E. A., & Yankey, N. (2002). Moral panic over youth violence: Wilding and the manufacture of menace in the media. *Youth and Society, 34,* 3–30.

Wiehe, V. R. (1992). *Working with child abuse and neglect.* Itasca, IL: F. E. Peacock.

Will, G. F. (2007). Anger is all the rage. *Washington Post,* March 25, B7.

Wilson, D. (2010). *The decline of child maltreatment.* The Sounding Board. Child Welfare Information Gateway. Washington, DC: Administration for Children & Families, U. S. Department of Health and Human Services.

Winton, M. A., & Mara, B. A. (2001). *Child abuse and neglect.* Boston: Allyn & Bacon.

Wood, P. (2006). *A bee in the mouth: Anger in America now.* New York: Encounter Books.

Zgoba, K. M. (2004). Spin doctors and moral crusaders: The moral panic behind child safety legislation. *Criminal Justice Studies, 17,* 385–404.

CHAPTER 2

Agan, A. (2007). *Sex offender registries: Fear without function?* Unpublished manuscript.

Alaya, A. M. (2003, August 24). Killing a young life often means a lesser sentence: A review finds the average prison time was 11 years for those convicted in child homicide cases. *The Star-Ledger.*

Association for Children of New Jersey. (2003). *DYFS an agency in crisis: Real reform is missing in DYFS' troubled history.* Newark, NJ. Retrieved from http://www.acnj.org/admin.asp?uri =2081&action=15&di=196&ext=pdf&view=yes.

Association for Children of New Jersey. (November 14, 2007). *Child protection data report.* Newark, NJ: Association for Children of New Jersey

Bertelli, A. M. (2004). Strategy and accountability: Structural reform litigation and public management. *Public Administration Review, 64*(1), 28–42.

Center for the Study of Social Policy. (2007). *Progress of the New Jersey Department of Children and Families: Period I Monitoring Report for Charlie and Nadine H. v. Corzine.* July 1–December 31, 2007. Washington, DC.

Center for the Study of Social Policy. (2010). *Progress of the New Jersey Department of Children and Families: Period VII Monitoring Report for Charlie and Nadine H. v. Christie.* July 1–December 31, 2009. Washington, DC.

Charlie and Nadine H. v. Corzine U.S. District Court for the District of New Jersey, 99-3678 (1999).

Charlie and Nadine H. v. Corzine and Ryan Modified Settlement Agreement. Newark, NJ. U.S. District Court for the District of New Jersey (2006).

CNN. (2003). *Starving boys, one child's body, found in basement: Woman sought; homicide charges possible.* Retrieved from http://edition.cnn.com/2003/US/Northeast/01/06/starved. children/.

Davy, J. (2005, December 5). On child welfare, undeniable progress. *The Star-Ledger.*

DePalma, A. (1989, March 31). 7 in abuse case are disciplined by foster unit. *The New York Times.* Retrieved from http://www.nytimes.com/1989/03/31/nyregion/7-in-abuse-case-are-disciplined-by-foster-unit.html.

DYFS/DHS Staffing and Outcome Review Panel/Citizen Review Panel. (2004). *Annual Report for July 1, 2004–June 30, 2005.* Trenton, NJ: New Jersey Department of Human Services

Gainsborough, J. F. (2010). *Scandalous politics: Child welfare policy in the states.* Washington, DC: Georgetown University Press.

Golden, O. A. (2009). *Reforming child welfare.* Washington, DC: Urban Institute Press. Retrieved from http://www.worldcat.org/oclc/311768820.

Harris, G. L. (2003). *Transforming child protective services in New Jersey.* Trenton, NJ: New Jersey Division of Youth and Family Services.

Kleinknecht, W., & Sterling, G. (2003, January 12). Police wonder whether teenager is trying to cover up for his mother: Seeking the truth in child's death. *The Star-Ledger.*

Kleinman, T. G. (2003). DYFS is misdirected and misunderstood: Why DYFS must consider the safety of children, its primary mandate is reunification and preservation of the family. *New Jersey Law Journal, CLXXII*(1), 1–3. Retrieved from http://www.centerforprotection-ofchildreninc.net/Law_Journal_Reprint_of_DYFS_is_Misdirected_and_Mi.pdf.

Kocieniewski, D. (2003, December 6). Top official to step down amid cases of child abuse. *The New York Times.*

Larini, R., & Stewart, A. (November 25, 2004). Codey: Boy's death a sickening tragedy: DYFS failed the toddler, he says. *The Star-Ledger.*

Lezin Jones, R. (2005, September 24). New Jersey's child welfare chief announces his resignation. *The New York Times.*

Lezin Jones, R., & Kaufman, L. (2003, May 4). Foster care secrecy magnifies suffering in New Jersey cases. *The New York Times.* Retrieved from http://www.nytimes.com/2003/05/04/nyregion/foster-care-secrecy-magnifies-suffering-in-new-jersey-cases.html.

Lezin Jones, R., & Kaufman, L. (2003, June 13). Troubled child welfare agency gets a new leader. *The New York Times.* Retrieved from http://www.nytimes.com/2003/06/13/nyregion/troubled-child-welfare-agency-gets-a-new-leader.html.

Lezin Jones, R., & Mansnerus, L. (2004, February 20). In child agency overhaul, mulling cost, not resolve. *The New York Times.*

Lipka, M. (2004, February 15). Long road for N.J. child agency. *The Philadelphia Inquirer.*

Livio, S. K. (2003, June 25). The end of DYFS as we know it. *The Star-Ledger.*

Livio, S. K. (2003, August 6). State flunks fed audit of foster care system: DYFS may have to return millions in aid. *The Star-Ledger.*

Livio, S. K. (2003, August 7). Work soars for child welfare staff. *The Star-Ledger.*

Livio, S. K. (2003, December 8). DYFS reports 37 deaths in 2003: Suspected case from abuse or neglect highest in 13 years. *The Star-Ledger.*

Livio, S. K. (2004, January 11). DYFS reformer quits as plan deadline nears. Governor names top aide to get children's agency overhaul on track. *The Star-Ledger.*

Livio, S. K. (2004, February 5). Report finds DYFS responded slowly to problems: Agency lost foster homes and lagged in hiring staff after settling federal lawsuit. *The Star-Ledger.*

Livio, S. K. (2004, February 29). Clues to fix DYFS lie beyond N.J.: State can learn from troubles encountered at other agencies. *The Star-Ledger.*

Livio, S. K. (2004, March 4). Foster parents balk at DYFS reforms: Speaking at two hearings, some call proposals unworkable but others praise approach. *The Star-Ledger.*

Livio, S. K. (2004, March 31). Panel cuts budget for DYFS plan: Legislators vote down half of $15M request. *The Star-Ledger.*

Livio, S. K. (2004, June 5). DYFS caseload crisis deepens: Problem escalating despite vows of reform. *The Star-Ledger.*

Livio, S. K. (2004, July 20). N.J. agrees to tough list for DYFS overhaul. *The Star-Ledger.* Retrieved from http://loki.stockton.edu/~bcwep/Media/7.htm.

Livio, S. K. (2004, July 22). State balks on list of fixes for DYFS: It calls some mandates unenforceable. *The Star-Ledger.*

Livio, S. K. (2004, August 11). Judge rebuffs meeting on DYFS: State had sought guidance on what changes agency must make. *The Star-Ledger.*

Livio, S. K. (2004, December 3). Legislators doubtful over DYFS reform. *The Star-Ledger.*

Livio, S. K. (2005, March 4). Child welfare overhaul stirs criticism: Draft report praises commitment for change, but says bureaucracy impedes progress. *The Star-Ledger.*

Livio, S. K. (2005, July 10). More trouble for child welfare agency: Human Services official admits failure to make changes on detention centers and shelters on time. *The Star-Ledger.*

Livio, S. K. (2005, July 27). DYFS ordered to take "urgent" action on fixes: Foster care, child supervision woes persist. *The Star-Ledger.*

Livio, S. K. (2005, September 14). Panel faults child-welfare restructuring: Legislators insist "chaos" has resulted, but DYFS officials dispute report's conclusions. *The Star-Ledger.*

Livio, S. K. (2005, October 12). DYFS gets last chance to fend off federal takeover: Fearing state cannot guard the kids in its care, watchdog steps in. *The Star-Ledger.*

Livio, S. K. (2005, October 19). Codey seeking outside expert to measure DYFS reform effort. *The Star-Ledger.*

Livio, S. K. (2005, December 2). Challengers of DYFS look to Corzine: Children's advocates ask judge to give governor reform powers. *The Star-Ledger.*

Livio, S. K. (2005, December 6). Irate Davy defends progress at DYFS: Human services chief says improvements take time. *The Star-Ledger.*

Livio, S. K. (2005, December 20). Probe of 8 deaths finds DYFS mistakes: Report stops short of saying agency could have prevented tragedies. *The Star-Ledger.*

Livio, S. K. (2006, February 28). Watchdog discloses a relapse at DYFS: Angry legislators told reforms falling short. *The Star-Ledger.*

Livio, S. K. (2006, April 5). Costlier programs get less sympathy. *The Star-Ledger.*

Livio, S. K. (2006, July 18). State strikes new deal on child welfare reform. *The Star-Ledger.*

Livio, S. K. (2007, March 5). Children's deaths decline, although tragedy remains. *The Star-Ledger.*

Livio, S. K. (2007, March 13). Progress in child welfare questioned. *The Star-Ledger.*

Livio, S. K. (2007, April 8). A costly wait for a database for DYFS: State officials start to hound contractor. *The Star-Ledger.*

Livio, S. K. (2009, July 27). State limits disclosure on deaths of children: Details of DYFS' actions kept from public in policy change. *The Star-Ledger.*

Livio, S. K., & Donohue, B. (2003, January 10). Governor orders DYFS shakeup. *The Star-Ledger.*

Livio, S. K., & Hepp, R. (2005, June 16). Advocate rips into DYFS on three deaths: Review of Highland Park case finds "nobody was listening" to warnings. *The Star-Ledger.*

Livio, S. K., & Patterson, M. J. (2003, January 7). Newark abuse death gets uglier. *The Star-Ledger.*

Livio, S. K., & Patterson, M. J. (2004, February 13). DYFS let four boys slowly starve: Child advocate's report on Collingswood family case lists years of poor judgement by agency. *The Star-Ledger.*

Livio, S. K., & Schuppe, J. (2004, December 10). Report says state failing at-risk kids: Advocate tells how DYFS, others missed signs and let a dozen die. *The Star-Ledger.*

Mansnerus, L. (2004, August 13). A governor resigns: Overview: McGreevey steps down after disclosing a gay affair. *The New York Times.*

Mezey, S. G. (2000). *Pitiful plaintiffs: Child welfare litigation and the federal courts.* Pittsburgh, PA: University of Pittsburgh Press. Retrieved from http://www.worldcat.org/oclc/42812830.

Moran, T. (2007, February 28). Old ghosts drive Ryan to improve child agency. *The Star-Ledger*.

Moran, T., Whitlow, J., & Jerome-Cohen, D. (2003, February 23). Broken promises: The child welfare system has failed to protect many children from abuse and neglect. What's the best way to fix that system? We asked three experts. *The Star-Ledger*.

Nelson, B. S. (1984). *Making an issue of child abuse: Political agenda setting for social problems*. Chicago, IL: University of Chicago Press.

New Jersey Child Welfare Panel. (2005a). *Period I monitoring report: July 1–December 31, 2004*. Baltimore, MD.

New Jersey Child Welfare Panel. (2005b). *Period II monitoring report: January 1–June 30, 2005*. Baltimore, MD.

New Jersey Child Welfare Panel. (2006). *Briefing on priority issues in child welfare reform*. Baltimore, MD.

New Jersey Department of Children and Families. (2006). *New Jersey child welfare reform: Focusing on the fundamentals*. Trenton, NJ.

New Jersey Department of Children and Families. (2009). *New Jersey federal child and family services review*. Trenton, NJ.

New Jersey Department of Children and Families. (2010). *Child fatalities: Child deaths as a result of abuse or neglect 1998–2009*. Retrieved from http://www.state.nj.us/dcf/abuse/fatalities/.

New Jersey Department of Human Services. (2003). *Commissioner Harris receives 2003 public policy leadership award from Rutgers helps governor unveil cabinet for children*. Trenton, NJ.

New Jersey Department of Human Services. (2004). *A new beginning: The future of child welfare in New Jersey*. Trenton, NJ.

Noonan, K. G., Sabel, C. F., & Simon, W. H. (2009). Legal accountability in the service-based welfare state: Lessons from child welfare reform. *Law & Social Inquiry, 34*(3), 523–568.

Patterson, M. J. (2003, January 19). Fallen guardian angels: How DYFS failed a child: Hearing descends to partisan bickering as legislators place blame. *The Star-Ledger*.

Patterson, M. J. (2003, August 12). DYFS failed to pay heed to signs of child abuse. *The Star-Ledger*.

Prescott, J., & Rockoff, J. (2008). *Do sex offender registration and notification laws affect criminal behavior?* (No. Working Paper # 08–006). Ann Arbor, MI: University of Michigan Law School.

Schwaneberg, R. (May 22, 2004). In child welfare, DYFS gets a resounding F. *The Star-Ledger*.

Spoto, M.A., & Livio, S. K. (November 24, 2004). Mother held in toddler's fatal starving: 14-month-old weighed 10 pounds but DYFS was told he was "small." *The Star-Ledger*.

State of New Jersey Governor's Office. (2003). *McGreevey announces bold new initiatives to reform DYFS: Cabinet for children will make recommendations for improvement and evaluate implementation*. Trenton, NJ.

The New York Times. (1985, December 6). Day-care worker held in assaults on children. P. A-8.

The Philadelphia Inquirer. (2004, February 22). Fixing DYFS: Legislators say the darndest things. *The Philadelphia Inquirer*.

The Star-Ledger. (2004, February 22). Still reason to worry about DYFS reform. *The Star-Ledger*.

The Star-Ledger. (2005, September 19). Don't relent on DYFS: Editorial. *The Star-Ledger*.

The Star-Ledger. (2005, October 13). DYFS' back is to the wall: Editorial. *The Star-Ledger*.

The Star-Ledger. (2006, March 7). Redirect DYFS reform: Editorial. *The Star-Ledger*.

The Star-Ledger. (2007, March 1). Don't relent on child welfare: Editorial. *The Star-Ledger*.

U.S. Department of Health and Human Services, Children's Bureau, Administration for Children and Families. (2004). *Child maltreatment 2002*. Washington, DC.

Waldman, W. & Balasco-Barr, P. (1995). *Children at risk 1993 and 1994*. Trenton, NJ: New Jersey Department of Human Services.

Walker, J. T., Maddan, S., Vasquez, B. E., Vanhouten, A. C., & Ervin-McLarty, G. (2005). The influence of sex offender legislation and notification laws in the United States. Arkansas Crime Information Center. Working Paper.

Zgoba, K., Veysey, B., & Dalessandro, M. (2010). An analysis of the effectiveness of community notification and registration: Do the best intentions predict the best practices? *Justice Quarterly, 27*(5), 667–691. doi:10.1080/07418820903357673.

CHAPTER 3

American Humane Association. (2005). Differential response in child welfare. *Protecting Children, 20*, 1–100.

American Professional Society on the Abuse of Children. (2002). *The APSAC handbook on child maltreatment*. Thousand Oaks, CA: Sage Publications.

Andrews, F., Morgan, J. N., & Sonquist, J. A. (1967). *Multiple classification analysis*. Ann Arbor, MI: University of Michigan, Survey Research Center.

Anechiarico, F., & Jacobs, J. B. (1996). *The pursuit of absolute integrity: How corruption control makes government ineffective. Studies in crime and justice*. Chicago, IL: University of Chicago Press.

Bae, H.-O., Solomon, P. L., & Gelles, R. J. (2007). Abuse type and substantiation status varying by recurrence. *Children and Youth Services Review, 29*, 856–869.

Baird, C., & Wagner, D. (2000). The relative validity of actuarial- and consensus-based risk assessment systems. *Children and Youth Services Review, 22*(11–12), 839–871. doi:10.1016/S0190-7409(00)00122-5.

Baird, C., Wagner, D., Healy, T., & Johnson, K. (1999). Risk assessment in child protective services: Consensus and actuarial model reliability. *Child welfare, 78*(6), 723–748.

Baird, C., Wagner, D., & Neuenfeldt, D. (1991). *Actuarial risk assessment and case management in child abuse and neglect*. Sixth Annual Roundtable on CPS Risk Assessment. Washington, DC: American Public Welfare Association.

Baron, J. (2000). *Thinking and deciding*, 3rd ed. Cambridge, UK, New York: Cambridge University Press.

Baumann, D. J. (1997). Decision theory and CPS decision-making. In T. Morton & W. Holder (Eds.), *Decision making in children's protective services. Advancing the state of the art* (pp. 12–27). Duluth, GA: The National Resource Center on Child Maltreatment.

Baumann, D. J., Law, J. R., Sheets, J., Reid, G., & Graham, J. (2005). Evaluating the effectiveness of actuarial risk assessment models. *Children and Youth Services Review, 27*(5), 465–490.

Baumann, D. J., Law, J. R., Sheets, J., Reid, G., & Graham, J. (2006). Remarks concerning the importance of evaluating actuarial risk assessment models: A rejoinder to Will Johnson. *Children and Youth Services Review, 28*(6), 715–725.

Behn, R. D. (2001). *Rethinking democratic accountability*. Washington, DC: Brookings Institution Press.

Besharov, D. (1990). *Recognizing child abuse: A guide for the concerned*. New York: The Free Press, A Division of Simon and Schuster, Inc. Retrieved from http://www.worldcat.org/oclc/20671624.

Besharov, D. (2009). Recognizing child abuse trainer's manual and training videos. University of Maryland, Welfare Reform Academy. http://www.welfareacademy.org/childabusetraining/index.shtml.

Boruch, R. (2005). Preface: Better evaluation for evidence-based policy: Place randomized trials in education, criminology, welfare, and health. *The Annals of the American Academy of Political and Social Sciences, 599*, 6–18.

Brintall, M. (1981). Caseloads, performance, and street-level bureaucracy. *Urban Affairs Quarterly, (16)*, 281–298.

Brittain, C., & Hunt, D. E. (Eds.). (2004). *Helping in child protective services: A competency-based casework handbook*, 2nd ed. New York: Oxford University Press.

Camasso, M. J., & Jagannathan, R. (1995). Prediction accuracy of the Washington and Illinois risk assessment instruments: An application of receiver operating characteristic curve analysis. *Social Work Research, 19*, 174–183.

Camasso, M. J., & Jagannathan, R. (2000). Modeling the reliability and predictive validity of risk assessment in child protective services. *Children and Youth Services Review, 22*(11–12), 873–896. doi:10.1016/S0190–7409(00)00121–3.

Camasso, M. J., & Jagannathan, R. (2001). Flying personal planes: Modeling the airport choices of general aviation pilots using stated preference methodology. *Human Factors: The Journal of the Human Factors and Ergonomics Society, 43*(3), 392–404. doi:10.1518/001872001775898232.

Camerer, C., & Weber, M. (1992). Recent developments in modeling preferences: Uncertainty and ambiguity. *Journal of Risk and Uncertainty, 5*, 325–370.

Cameron, G., Vanderwoerd, J., & Peirson, L. (1997). *Protecting children and supporting families: Promising programs and organizational realities. Modern applications of social work.* New York: Aldine de Gruyter.

Carroll, J. S., & Johnson, E. J. (1990). *Decision research: A field guide*. Newbury Park, CA: Sage Publications. Retrieved from http://www.worldcat.org/oclc/644883030.

Czerlinski, J., Gigerenzer, G., & Goldstein, D. G. (1999). How good are simple heuristics? In G. Gigerenzer, P. M. Todd, & A. R. G. Group (Eds.), *Evolution and cognition series. Simple heuristics that make us smart* (pp. 97–118). New York: Oxford University Press.

Davidson-Arad, B., Englechin-Segal, D., Wozner, Y., & Arieli, R. (2006). Social workers' decisions on removal. *Journal of Social Service Research, 31*(4), 1–23. doi:10.1300/J079v31n04_01.

Dawes, R. (1979). The robust beauty of improper linear models in decision making. *American Psychologist, 34*(7), 571–582.

DePanfilis, D., & Girvin, H. (2005). Investigating child maltreatment in out-of-home care: Barriers to effective decision-making. *Children and Youth Services Review, 27*(4), 353–374.

DePanfilis, D., & Salus, M. (2003). *Child protective services: A guide for caseworkers.* Washington, DC: U.S. Department of Health and Human Services.

Dharmapala, D., & Ross, S. L. (2004). Racial bias in motor vehicle searches: Additional theory and evidence. *Contributions to Economic Analysis and Policy, 3*(1), 1–21.

Dubowitz, H., & DePanfilis, D. (Eds.). (2000). *Handbook for child protection practice.* Thousand Oaks, CA: Sage Publications.

Einhorn, H. J., & Hogarth, R. M. (1981). Behavioral decision theory: Processes of judgment and choice. *Annual Review of Psychology, 32*, 53–58.

English, D. J., Marshall, D. B., Brummel, S. C., & Coghlan, L. K. (1998). *Decision-making in child protective services: A study of effectiveness. Final Report: Phase I: Quantitative Analysis.* Olympia, WA: Department of Social and Health Services.

English, D. J., Marshall, D. B., Coghlan, L., Brummel, S., & Orme, M. (2002). Causes and consequences of the substantiation decision in Washington State Child Protective Services. *Children and Youth Services Review, 24*(11), 817–851.

European Commission, Risk Assessment Unit. (2004). Public Health and Risk Assessment Directorate.

Feild, T., & Winterfeld, A. P.. (2003). *Tough problems, tough choices: Guidelines for needs-based service planning in child welfare.* Englewood, CO: American Humane Association.

Fluke, J., & Alsop, R. (1999). *Thirteenth national roundtable on child protective services risk assessment.* Englewood, CO: American Humane Association.

Gambrill, E. (2008a). Decision making in child welfare: Constraints and potentials. In D. Lindsey & A. Shlonsky (Eds.), *Child welfare research. Advances for practice and policy* (pp. 175–194). Oxford, UK: Oxford University Press.

Gambrill, E. (2008b). Providing more effective, ethical services: The philosophy and process of evidence-based (-informed) practice. In D. Lindsey & A. Shlonsky (Eds.), *Child welfare research. Advances for practice and policy* (pp. 51–66), Oxford, UK: Oxford University Press.

Gambrill, E., & Shlonsky, A. (2001). The need for comprehensive risk management systems in child welfare. *Children and Youth Services Review, 23*(1), 79–107. doi:10.1016/S0190–7409(00)00124–9.

Gelles, R. J. (1997). *The book of David: How preserving families can cost children's lives.* New York: Basic Books.

Gibbons, J., Conroy, S., & Bell, C. (1995). *Operating the child protection system: A study of child protection practices in English local authorities. Studies in child protection.* London: HMSO.

Gigerenzer, G. (2004). Fast and frugal heuristics: The tools of bounded rationality. In D. J. Koehler & N. Harvey (Eds.), *Blackwell handbook of judgment and decision making*, 1st ed. (pp. 62–88). Oxford, UK, Malden, MA: Blackwell Publications.

Gigerenzer, G., & Goldstein, D. G. (1996). Reasoning of the fast and frugal way: Models of bounded rationality. *Psychological Review,* (*103*), 650–669. Retrieved from www.apa.org/journals/rev/.

Gigerenzer, G., & Goldstein, D. G. (1999). The recognition heuristic: How ignorance makes us smart. In G. Gigerenzer, P. M. Todd, & A. R. G. Group (Eds.), *Evolution and cognition series. Simple heuristics that make us smart* (pp. 37–58). New York: Oxford University Press.

Goldberg, L. R. (1991). Human mind versus regression equation: Five contrasts. In W. M. Grove & D. Cicchetti (Eds.), *Thinking clearly about psychology: Vol. 1. Matters of public interest* (pp. 173–184). Minneapolis: University of Minnesota Press.

Goldman, J., & Salus, M. K. (2003). *A coordinated response to child abuse and neglect: The foundation for practice.* Washington, DC: U.S. Department of Health and Human Services. Retrieved from http://www.childwelfare.gov/pubs/usermanuals/foundation/foundation.pdf.

Goldstein, W., & Hogarth, R. (1997). Judgment and decision research: Some historical context. In W. M. Goldstein & R. M. Hogarth (Eds.), *Cambridge series on judgment and decision making. Research on judgment and decision making. Currents, connections, and controversies* (pp. 3–65). New York: Cambridge University Press.

Gottfredson, S. D., & Moriarty, L. (2006). Statistical risk assessment: Old problems and new applications. *Crime & Delinquency, 52*(1), 178–200. doi:10.1177/0011128705281748.

Grove, W. M., & Meehl, P. E. (1996). Comparative efficiency of informal (subjective, impressionistic) and formal (mechanical, algorithmic) prediction procedures: The clinical-statistical controversy. *Psychology, Public Policy and Law, 2*, 293–323.

Hanley, J. A., & McNeil, B. J. (1982). The meaning and use of the area under a receiver operating characteristic (ROC) curve. *Radiology, 143*(1), 29–36.

Heneghan, A. M., Horwitz, S. M., & Leventhal, J. M. (1996). Evaluating intensive family preservation services: A methodological review. *Pediatrics, 97*, 535–542.

Hoffman, S. D., & Duncan, G. J. (1988). Multinomial and conditional logit discrete-choice models in demography. *Demography, 25*(3), 415–427.

Hornby, H. (1989). *Risk assessment in child protective services: 3 issues in field implementation.* Portland, ME: University of Southern Maine, Human Services Development Institute.

Howitt, D. (1993). *Child abuse errors: When good intentions go wrong.* New Brunswick, NJ: Rutgers University Press.

Jagannathan, R., & Camasso, M. J. (1996). Risk assessment in child protective services: A canonical analysis of the case management function. *Child Abuse & Neglect, 20*(7), 599–612. doi:10.1016/0145–2134(96)00047–6.

Janchill, M. P. (1981). *Guidelines for decision-making in child welfare: Case assessment, Service planning, and appropriateness in service selection*: Human Services Workshop New York, NY, 12 W.12th Street.

Johnson, M. A., Brown, C. H., & Wells, S. J. (2002). Using classification and regression trees (CART) to support worker decision making. *Social Work Research, 26*(1), 19–29.

Johnson, W. (2006). The risk assessment wars: A commentary: Response to "Evaluating the effectiveness of actuarial risk assessment models." *Children and Youth Services Review, 28*(6), 704–714. doi:10.1016/j.childyouth.2005.07.007.

Kahneman, D., Slovic, P., & Tversky, A. (Eds.). (1982). *Judgment under uncertainty: Heuristics and biases.* Cambridge, UK, New York: Cambridge University Press.

Kahneman, D., & Tversky, A. (1979). Prospect theory: An analysis of decision under risk. *Econometrica, 47*(2), 263–292.

Knowles, J., Persico, N., & Todd, P. (2001). Racial bias in motor vehicle searches: Theory and evidence. *Journal of Political Economy, 109*(1), 203–299.

Lave, C. A., & March, J. G. (1975). *An introduction to models in the social sciences.* New York: Harper & Row.

Leschied, A. W., Chiodo, D., Hurley, D., Marshall, L., & Whitehead, P. (2003). The empirical basis of risk assessment in child welfare: Assessing the concurrent and predictive validity of risk assessment and clinical judgment. *Child welfare, 82*(5), 527–542.

Light, R. J. (1973). Abused and neglected children in America: A study of alternative policies. *Harvard Educational Review, 43*(4), 556–598.

Lilienfeld, D. E., & Stolley, P. D. (Eds.). (1994). *Foundations of epidemiology* (revised by D. E. Lilienfeld & P. D. Stolley). New York: Oxford University Press.

Lindsey, D. (1994). *The welfare of children,* 1st ed. New York: Oxford University Press.

Lindsey, D. (1997). What response to progress? Step up or step down? In T. Morton & W. Holder (Eds.), *Decision making in children's protective services. Advancing the state of the art* (pp. 114–127). Duluth, GA: The National Resource Center on Child Maltreatment.

Lindsey, D. (2004). *The welfare of children,* 2nd ed. New York: Oxford University Press.

Littell, J. H. (2008). How do we know what works?: The quality of published reviews of evidence-based practices. In D. Lindsey & A. Shlonsky (Eds.), *Child welfare research. Advances for practice and policy* (pp. 66–93). Oxford, UK: Oxford University Press.

Lyons, P., Doueck, H. J., & Wodarski, J. S. (1996). Risk assessment for child protective services: A review of the empirical literature on instrument performance. *Social Work Research, 20*(3), 143–155.

Mather, J. H., Lager, P. B., & Harris, N. (2007). *Child welfare: Policies and best practices,* 2nd ed. Belmont, CA: Thomson Brooks/Cole.

McDonald, T. P., Poertner, J., & Harris, G. (2001). Predicting placement in foster care: A comparison of logistic regression and neural network analysis. *Journal of Social Service Research, 28*(2), 1–20.

McKenzie, R. B. (2009). *Home away from home: The forgotten history of orphanages,* 1st ed. New York: Encounter Books.

Meehl, P. E. (1954). *Clinical vs. statistical prediction: A theoretical analysis and a review of the evidence.* Minneapolis: University of Minnesota Press.

Meehl, P. E. (1986). Causes and effects of my disturbing little book. *Journal of Personality Assessment, 50*(3), 370–375.

Morton, T. D, (2003). *The risk wars. Commentary.* Columbus, OH: Child Welfare Institute.

Morton, T. D., & Holder, W. (1997). *Decision making in children's protective services: Advancing the state of the art.* Duluth, GA: National Resource Center on Child Maltreatment.

Munro, E. (2004). A simpler way to understand the results of risk assessment instruments. *Children and Youth Services Review, 26*(9), 873–883. doi:10.1016/j.childyouth.2004.02.026.

Munro, E. (2008). Lessons from research on decision making. In D. Lindsey & A. Shlonsky (Eds.), *Child welfare research. Advances for practice and policy* (pp. 194–201). Oxford, UK: Oxford University Press.

Murphy, J. M., Berwick, D. M., Weinstein, M. C., Borus, J. F., Budman, S. H., & Klerman, G. L. (1987). Performance of screening and diagnostic tests: Application of receiver operating characteristic analysis. *Archives of General Psychiatry, 44*(6), 550–555.

Myers, J. E. B. (2006). *Child protection in America: Past, present, and future.* Oxford, UK, New York: Oxford University Press.

National Center for the Prosecution of Child Abuse. (2004). *Investigation and prosecution of child abuse,* 3rd ed. Thousand Oaks, CA: Sage Publications.

National Center on Child Abuse and Neglect (Ed.). (1991). *Symposium on risk assessment in child protective services: Vol. 1,2,3,4.* Washington, DC: National Center on Child Abuse and Neglect (DHHS).

National Child Welfare Resource Center for Management and Administration. (1989). *Risk assessment in child protective services.* Portland, ME: University of Southern Maine.

National Clearinghouse on Child Abuse and Neglect Information. (2008). Retrieved from National Coalition for Child Protection Reform. *The NCCPR quick read: Child welfare in America—an overview.* Alexandria, VA. Retrieved from http://nccpr.info/.

Nezu, A. M., & Nezu, C. M. (1989). *Clinical decision making in behavior therapy: A problem-solving perspective.* Champaign Ill: Research Press Co.

Noonan, K. G., Sabel, C. F., & Simon, W. H. (2009). Legal accountability in the service-based welfare state: Lessons from child welfare reform. *Law & Social Inquiry, 34*(3), 523–568.

Nugent, W. R. (2004). The role of prevalence rates, sensitivity, and specificity in assessment accuracy: Rolling the dice in social work process. *Journal of Social Service Research, 31*(2), 51–75.

O'Reilly, C. A. (1983). The use of information in organizational decision making: A model and some propositions. *Research in Organizational Behavior, 5,* 103–139.

Over, D. (2004). Rationality and the normative/descriptive distinction. In D. J. Koehler & N. Harvey (Eds.), *Blackwell handbook of judgment and decision making,* 1st ed. (pp. 1–18). Oxford, UK, Malden MA: Blackwell Publications.

Paxson C., & Haskins, R. (2009a). Introducing the issue. *The Future of Children, 19*(2), 3–17. doi:10.1353/foc.0.0034.

Paxson, C., & Haskins, R. (Eds.). (2009b). Preventing child maltreatment. In *The future of children,* Vol. *19(2).* Princeton, NJ: Princeton University and the Brookings Institution Press.

Pecora, P. J., Whittaker, J. K., Maluccio, A. N., & Barth, R. P. (2000). *The child welfare challenge: Policy, practice, and research, 2nd ed. Modern applications of social work.* New York: Aldine de Gruyter.

Pelham, W. B., Sumarta, T. T., & Myaskovsky, L. (1994). The easy path from many to much: The numerosity heuristic. *Cognitive Psychology, 2,* 103–133.

Pelton, L. H. (1989). *For reasons of poverty: A critical analysis of the public child welfare system in the United States.* New York: Praeger.

Petrosino, A., Boruch, R. F., Soydan, H., Duggan, L., & Sanchez-Meca, J. (2001). Meeting the challenges of evidence-based policy: The Campbell collaboration. *The Annals of the American Academy of Political and Social Sciences, 578(1),* 14–34.

Ross, T. (2009). *Child welfare: The challenges of collaboration.* Washington, DC: Urban Institute Press. Retrieved from http://www.worldcat.org/oclc/275150362.

Rossi, P. H., Schuerman, J., & Budde, S. (1999). Understanding decisions about child maltreatment. *Evaluation Review, 23*(6), 579–598. doi:10.1177/0193841X9902300601.

Rycus, J. S., & Hughes, R. C. (2008). Assessing risk throughout the life of a child welfare case. In D. Lindsey & A. Shlonsky (Eds.), *Child welfare research. Advances for practice and policy* (pp. 201–214). Oxford, UK: Oxford University Press.

Rzepnicki, T. L., & Johnson, P. R. (2005). Examining decision errors in child protection: A new application of root cause analysis. *Children and Youth Services Review, 27*(4), 393–407.

Salus, M. K. (2004). *Supervising child protective services caseworkers.* Washington, DC: U.S. Department of Health and Human Services. Retrieved from http://www.childwelfare.gov/pubs/usermanuals/supercps/supercps.pdf.

Scheff, T. (1972). Decision rules and types of error and their consequences in medical diagnosis. In E. Friedson & J. Lorber (Eds.), *Medical men and their work* (pp. 309–323). Chicago: Aldine de Gruyter.

Schene, P. A. (1998). Past, present, and future roles of child protective services. *The future of children/center for the future of children, the David and Lucile Packard Foundation, 8*(1), 23–38.

Schuerman, J. R., Rzepnicki, T. L., & Littell, J. H. (1994). *Putting families first: An experiment in family preservation. Modern applications of social work.* New York: Aldine de Gruyter.

Schwalbe, C. (2004). Re-visioning risk assessment for human service decision making. *Children and Youth Services Review, 26*(6), 561–576.

Schwartz, D., Kaufman, A., & Schwartz, I. (2004). Computational intelligence techniques for risk assessment and decision support. *Children and Youth Services Review, 26*(11), 1081–1095. doi:10.1016/j.childyouth.2004.08.007.

Schwartz, I. M., Jones, P. R., Schwartz, D. R., & Obradovic, Z. (2008). 13. Improving social work practice through the use of technology and advanced research methods. In D. Lindsey &

A. Shlonsky (Eds.), *Child welfare research. Advances for practice and policy* (pp. 214–231). Oxford, UK: Oxford University Press.

Shlonsky, A., & Wagner, D. (2005). The next step: Integrating actuarial risk assessment and clinical judgment into an evidence-based practice framework in CPS case management. *Children and Youth Services Review, 27*(4), 409–427. doi:10.1016/j.childyouth.2004.11.007.

Shook, J., & Sarri, R. (2007). Structured decision making in juvenile justice: Judges' and probation officers' perceptions and use. *Children and Youth Services Review, 29*(10), 1335–1351. doi:10.1016/j.childyouth.2007.05.008.

Simon, H. A. (1955). A behavioral model of rational choice. *Quarterly Journal of Economics, 69*, 99–118.

Simon, H. A. (1979). Rational decision making in business organizations. *The American Economic Review, 69*(4), 493–513.

Sjoberg, L. (2000). Factors in risk perception. *Risk Analysis, 20*(1), 1–11.

Slovic, P. (1987). Perception of risk. *Science, 236*, 280–285.

Slovic, P., Finucane, M. L., Peters, E., & MacGregor, D. G. (2004). Risk as analysis and risk as feelings: Some thoughts about affect, reason, risk, and rationality. *Risk Analysis, 24*(2), 311–322.

Spratt, T. (2000). Decision making by senior social workers at point of first referral. *British Journal of Social Work, 30*(5), 597–618. doi:10.1093/bjsw/30.5.597.

Streufert, S., & Swezey, R. (1985). Simulation and related research methods in environmental psychology. In A. Baum & J. E. Singer (Eds.), *Advances in environmental psychology: Vol. 5. Methods and environmental psychology* (pp. 99–117). Hillsdale NJ: Lawrence Erlbaum Associates.

Taylor-Gooby, P., & Zinn, J. (2006). Current directions in risk research: New developments in psychology and sociology. *Risk Analysis, 26*(2), 397–411.

Turner, D. A. (1978). An intuitive approach to receiver operating characteristic curve analysis. *The Journal of Nuclear Medicine, 19*(2), 213–220.

Tversky, A., & Kahneman, D. (1974). Judgment under uncertainty: Heuristics and biases. *Science, 185*, 1124–1131.

Tversky, A., & Kahneman, D. (1982). Judgements of and by representativeness. In D. Kahneman, P. Slovic, & A. Tversky (Eds.), *Judgment under uncertainty. Heuristics and biases* (pp. 84–98). Cambridge, UK, New York: Cambridge University Press.

Tyson, K. (1995). *New foundations for scientific social and behavioral research: The heuristic paradigm.* Boston: Allyn & Bacon.

U.S. Department of Health and Human Services, Administration for Children and Families, Administration on Children, Youth and Families, Children's Bureau. (2010). *Child maltreatment 2009.* Available from *http://www.acf.hhs.gov/programs/cb/stats_research/index. htm#can.*

Wald, M. S., & Woolverton, M. (1990). Risk assessment: The emperor's new clothes? *Child Welfare, 69*(6), 483–511.

Waldfogel, J. (1998a). Rethinking the paradigm for child protection. *The Future of Children, 8*(1), 104–119.

Waldfogel, J. (1998b). *The future of child protection: How to break the cycle of abuse and neglect.* Cambridge, MA: Harvard University Press.

Wexler, R. (2008). *Civil liberties without exception: NCCPR's due process agenda for children and families.* Alexandria, VA: National Coalition for Child Protection Reform. Retrieved from http://nccpr.info/.

Wilson, D., & Morton, T. D. (1997). Issues in CPS decision-making. In T. Morton & W. Holder (Eds.), *Decision making in children's protective services. Advancing the state of the art* (pp. 1–11). Duluth, GA: The National Resource Center on Child Maltreatment.

Winterfeldt, D. von, & Edwards, W. (1986). *Decision analysis and behavioral research.* Cambridge, UK, New York: Cambridge University Press.

Wright, G. (1984). *Behavioral decision theory: An introduction.* Beverly Hills, CA: Sage Publications.

Wulczyn, F. (2009). Epidemiological perspectives on maltreatment prevention. *The Future of Children, 19*(2), 39–66.

Wulczyn, F., Barth, R. P., Yuan, Y.-Y. T., Jones Harden, B., & Landsverk, J. (2005). *Beyond common sense: Child welfare, child well-being, and the evidence for policy reform.* New Brunswick, NJ: AldineTransaction.

CHAPTER 4

ACTION for Child Protection. *Training expectations.* Trenton, NJ: New Jersey Department of Children and Families, 2007.

Albers, E. C., Reilly, T., & Rittner, B. (1993). Children in foster care: Possible factors affecting permanency planning. *Child & Adolescent Social Work Journal, 10*(4), 329–341. doi:10.1007/BF00758263.

Alsop, R., & Winterfeld, A. (1999). Protecting children. *American Human Association Quarterly, 15*(3/4), 15–18.

American Humane Association. (2002). Combating the workforce crisis in child protective services. *Protecting Children, 17*(3).

American Humane Association, National Association of Public Child Welfare Administrators, & Texas Department of Protective and Regulatory Services (Eds.). (1993). *First national roundtable on outcome measures in child welfare services: Summary of the proceedings.* Englewood, CO: American Humane Association.

Annie E. Casey Foundation. (2003). *The unsolved challenge of system reform: The condition of the frontline human services workforce.* Baltimore, MD: Annie E. Casey Foundation.

Associated Press. (2010, February 2). Child abuse drops sharply in the U.S. *The Associated Press.* Retrieved from http://www.msnbc.msn.com/id/35205114/ns/health-kids_and_parenting/.

Behn, R. D. (2001). *Rethinking democratic accountability.* Washington, DC: Brookings Institution Press.

Bess, R., Leos-Urbel, J., & Geen, R. (2001). *The cost of protecting vulnerable children II.* Occasional Paper No. 46. Washington, DC: The Urban Institute.

Booz Allen & Hamilton. (1987). *The Maryland social work services job analysis and personnel qualifications study.* Baltimore, MD: National Association of Social Workers.

Bremner, R. H. (1971). *Children and youth in America: A documentary history, Vol. 2: 1866–1932, Parts 7–8* (1st ed.). Cambridge, MA: Harvard University Press. Retrieved from http://www.worldcat.org/oclc/215369533.

Brittain, C., & Hunt, D. E. (2004). *Helping in child protective services.* New York: Oxford University Press.

Carbonara, E., Parisi, F., & Wangenheim, G. von. (2008). Lawmakers as norm entrepreneurs. *Review of Law & Economics, 4*(3), 779–799. doi:10.2202/1555–5879.1320.

Cash, S. (2001). Risk assessment in child welfare: The art and science. *Children and Youth Services Review, 23*(11), 811–830. doi:10.1016/S0190–7409(01)00162–1.

Center for the Study of Social Policy. (2007). *Period III monitoring report for Charlie and Nadine H. v. Corzine.* July 1, 2006–December 31, 2006. Washington, DC: CSSP.

Center for the Study of Social Policy. (2010). *Progress of the New Jersey department of children and families: Period VII monitoring report for Charlie and Nadine H. v. Christie.* July 1–December 31, 2009. Washington, DC: CSSP.

Child Welfare League of America. (1999). *Minimum education required by state child welfare agencies, percent, by degree type, 1998: State child welfare agency survey.* Washington, DC: Child Welfare League of America.

Cooper, P. J. (1988). *Hard judicial choices: Federal district court judges and state and local officials.* New York: Oxford University Press.

Cotton, E. (2003). *New Jersey child safety assessment.* Trenton, NJ: New Jersey Department of Children and Families.

Courtney, M. E., Needell, B., & Wulczyn, F. (2004). Unintended consequences of the push for accountability: The case of national child welfare performance standards. *Children and Youth Services Review, 26*(12), 1141–1154.

Crary, D. (2010, February 2). APNewsBreak: US study shows drop in child abuse. *The Associated Press.* Retrieved from www.nola.com.

Crosby, P. (1995). *Quality without tears: The art of hassle-free management,* 2nd ed. New York: McGraw-Hill.

Deming, E. W. (1986). *Out of crisis.* Cambridge, MA: MIT Press.

DeParle, J. (2004). *American dream: Three women, ten kids, and a nation's drive to end welfare.* New York: Viking.

DePanfilis, D., & Salus, M. K. (2003). *Child protective services: A guide for caseworkers.* Washington, DC: U.S. Department of Health and Human Services.

Dickinson, N., & Gil de Gibaja, M. (2004). University-child welfare partnerships: Familiar collaborations, new possibilities. *Protecting Children, 19*(3), 27–36.

Ellett, A., Ellis, J., Westbrook, T., & Dews, D. (2007). A qualitative study of 369 child welfare professionals' perspectives about factors contributing to employee retention and turnover. *Children and Youth Services Review, 29*(2), 264–281. doi:10.1016/j.childyouth.2006.07.005.

English, D. J., Brandford, C. C., & Coghlan, L. (2000). Data-based organizational change: The use of administrative data to improve child welfare programs and policy. *Child Welfare, 79*(5), 499–515.

English, D. J., Brummel, S. C., Coghlan, L. K., Novicky, R. S., & Marshall, D. B. (1998). *Decision-making in child protective services: A study of effectiveness, phase II: Social worker interviews.* Olympia, WA: Office of Children's Administrative Research.

Fisher, H., Pecora, P., Fluke, J., Hardin, M., & field, T. (1999). *Improving the quality of children's services: A working paper on outcome-based decision making and managed care.* Englewood, CO: American Humane Association.

Freund, A. (2005). Commitment and job satisfaction as predictors of turnover intentions among welfare workers. *Administration in Social Work, 29*(2), 5–21. doi:10.1300/J147v29n02_02.

Gainsborough, J. F. (2010). *Scandalous politics: Child welfare policy in the States.* Washington, DC: Georgetown University Press.

Gambrill, E. (1997). *Social work practice: A critical thinker's guide.* New York: Oxford University Press.

Gambrill, E. (2008). Providing more effective, ethical services: The philosophy and process of evidence-based (-informed) practice. In D. Lindsey & A. Shlonsky (Eds.), *Child welfare research. Advances for practice and policy* (pp. 51–66). Oxford, UK: Oxford University Press.

Geen, R., Boots, S. W., & Tumlin, K. C. (1999). *The cost of protecting vulnerable children: Understanding federal, state and local child welfare spending.* Washington, DC: The Urban Institute.

Geen, R., & Tumlin, K. C. (1999). *State efforts to remake child welfare: Responses to new challenges and increased scrutiny.* Occasional Paper No. 29. Washington, DC: The Urban Institute.

Gibbs, L. E., & Gambrill, E. (1999). *Critical thinking for social workers: Exercises for the helping professions.* Thousand Oaks, CA: Pine Forge Press.

Golden, O. A. (2009). *Reforming child welfare.* Washington, DC: Urban Institute Press. Retrieved from http://www.worldcat.org/oclc/311768820.

Graef, M. I., & Potter, M. E. (2002). Alternative solutions to the child protective services staffing crisis: Innovations from industrial/organizational psychology. *Protecting Children, 17*(3), 18–31.

Gustavsson, N., & MacEachron, A. (2002). Death and the child welfare worker. *Children and Youth Services Review, 24*(12), 903–915.

Hagen, J. L. (1993). *Implementing JOBS: The perspective of frontline workers (JOBS implementation study).* Albany, NY: State University of New York: Nelson A. Rockefeller Institute of Government.

Hagen, J. L., Lurie, I., & Wang, L. (1993). *Implementing JOBS: The perspective of frontline workers.* Albany, NY: State University of New York: Nelson A. Rockefeller Institute of Government.

Hirsch, B. T., & Macpherson, D. A. (2003). Union membership and coverage database from the Current Population Survey: Note. *Industrial and Labor Relations Review, 56*(2), 349–354.

Howing, P. T., Kohn, S., Gaudin, J. M., Jr., Kurtz, P. D., & Wodarski, J. S. (1992). Current research issues in child welfare. *Social Work Research and Abstracts, 28*(1), 5–12.

Jagannathan, R., & Camasso, M. (2006). Public assistance workers' confidence in welfare-to-work programs and the clients they serve. *Administration in Social Work, 30*(1), 7–32. doi:10.1300/J147v30n01_02.

Kim, A. K., Brooks, D., Kim, H., & Nissly, J. (2008). *Structured decision making and the child welfare service delivery project.* Berkeley: University of California Press.

Light, P. C. (2003). *The health of the human services workforce.* Washington, DC: Brookings Institution Press.

Lindsey, D. (1994). Mandated reporting and child abuse fatalities: Requirements for a system to protect children. *Social Work Research, 18*(1), 41–54.

Lindsey, D. (2004). *The welfare of children,* 2nd ed. New York: Oxford University Press.

Littell, J. H. (2008). How do we know what works?: The quality of published reviews of evidence-based practices. In D. Lindsey & A. Shlonsky (Eds.), *Child welfare research. Advances for practice and policy* (pp. 66–93). Oxford, UK: Oxford University Press.

Livio, S. K. (2004, July 9). Assessing families by the numbers: DYFS retrains its staff in structured decisions. *The Star-Ledger.*

Mahon, B. (2008). *Changing the culture of child welfare in New Jersey.* New Brunswick, NJ: Rutgers School of Social Work.

Malm, K., Bess, R., Leos-Urbel, J., Geen, R., & Markowitz, T. (2001). *Running to keep in place: The continuing evolution of our nation's child welfare system* (Occasional Paper Number 54). Washington, DC: The Urban Institute.

McDaniel, N. (2004). Examining the results of our work: Outcome measures in child welfare services. *Protecting Children, 18*(3), 2–3.

Milner, J., & Hornsby, W. (2004). Training of child welfare staff and providers: Findings from the child and family service review. *Protecting Children, 19*(3), 4–14.

Mor Barak, M. E., Nissly, J. A., & Levin, A. (2001). Antecedents to retention and turnover among child welfare, social work, and other human service employees: What can we learn from past research? A review and metanalysis. *Social Service Review, 75*(4), 625–661. doi:10.1086/323166.

Moynihan, D. P., & Landuyt, N. (2008). Explaining turnover intention in state government: Examining the roles of gender, life cycle, and loyalty. *Review of Public Personnel Administration, 28*(2), 120–143. doi:10.1177/0734371X08315771.

Moynihan, D. P., & Pandey, S. K. (2007). The TIES THAT BIND: Social networks, person-organization value fit, and turnover intention. *Journal of Public Administration Research and Theory, 18*(2), 205–227. doi:10.1093/jopart/mum013.

National Research Council. (2007). *Taking science to school.* Washington, DC: National Academies Press.

New Jersey Department of Children and Families. (2006). DCF partners with Rutgers on MSW program. Trenton, NJ. Retrieved from http://www.state.nj.us/dcf/news/press/approved/061026.html.

New Jersey Department of Children and Families. (2007). *About the division of youth and family services.* Retrieved from http://www.state.nj.us/dcf/divisions/dyfs/.

New Jersey Department of Children and Families. (2007). *Implementing the case practice model.* Trenton, NJ.

New Jersey Department of Human Services. (2004). *A New beginning: The future of child welfare in New Jersey.* Trenton, NJ.

Nissly, J., Mor Barak, M., & Levin, A. (2004). Stress, social support, and workers' intentions to leave their jobs in public child welfare. *Administration in Social Work, 29*(1), 79–100. doi:10.1300/J147v29n01_06.

Nolan, R. B. (2007). *Rutgers SSW creates institute to strengthen families.* New Brunswick, NJ: Rutgers University Press.

Noonan, K. G., Sabel, C. F., & Simon, W. H. (2009). Legal accountability in the service-based welfare state: Lessons from child welfare reform. *Law & Social Inquiry, 34*(3), 523–568.

Pear, R. (2004, April 26). U.S. finds fault in all 50 states' child welfare programs, and penalties may follow. *The New York Times.* Retrieved from http://query.nytimes.com/gst/fullpage.html?res=9806E2DE103AF935A15757C0A9629C8B63.

Peters, T. J., & Waterman, R. H. (1982). *In search of excellence: Lessons from America's best-run companies,* 1st ed. New York: Harper & Row.

Peters, T. J., & Waterman, R. H. (2004). *In search of excellence: Lessons from America's best-run companies,* 2nd ed. New York: Harper & Row.

Preston, M. (2004). Mandatory management training for newly hired child welfare supervisors. *Administration in Social Work, 28*(2), 81–97. doi:10.1300/J147v28n02_06.

Price, T. (2005). Child welfare reform: The issues. *The CQ Researcher, 15*(15), 345–368.

Roberts, A. R., & Greene, G. J. (Eds.). (2002). *Social workers' desk reference.* New York: Oxford University Press.

Roberts, A. R., & Yeager, K. R. (2004). (Eds.). *Evidence based practice manual.* New York: Oxford University Press.

Robinson, S. E. (2004). Punctuated equilibrium, bureaucratization and budgetary changes in schools. *The Policy Studies Journal, 32*, 25–39.

Rosenthal, J., & Waters, E. (2006). Predictors of child welfare worker retention and performance. *Journal of Social Service Research*, *32*(3), 67–85. doi:10.1300/J079v32n03_04.

Rossi, P. H., Schuerman, J., & Budde, S. (1999). Understanding decisions about child maltreatment. *Evaluation Review*, *23*(6), 579–598. doi:10.1177/0193841X9902300601.

Rutenberg, J., & Kaufman, L. (2006, January 25). New York acts to coordinate child welfare. *The New York Times*.

Ryan, J., Garnier, P., Zyphur, M., & Zhai, F. (2006). Investigating the effects of caseworker characteristics in child welfare. *Children and Youth Services Review*, *28*(9), 993–1006. doi:10.1016/j.childyouth.2005.10.013.

Sandler, R., & Schoenbrod, D. (2003). *Democracy by decree: What happens when courts run government*. New Haven: Yale University Press. Retrieved from http://www.worldcat.org/oclc/473297671.

Schmid, D. L. (1993). *Opening remarks: First annual roundtable on outcome measures in child welfare services*. Englewood, CO: American Humane Association.

Schorr, A. L. (2000). The bleak prospect for public child welfare. *Social Service Review*, *74*(1), 124–138. doi:10.1086/514460.

Sedlak, J., Mettenburg, J., Basena, M., Petta, I., McPherson, K., Greene, A., & Li, S. (2010). *Fourth national incidence study of child abuse and neglect (NIS-4): Report to Congress*. Washington, DC: USDHHS, ACF.

Shlonsky, A., & Wagner, D. (2005). The next step: Integrating actuarial risk assessment and clinical judgment into an evidence-based practice framework in CPS case management. *Children and Youth Services Review*, *27*, 409–427.

Silimperi, D. R., Veldhuyzen Van Zanten, T., & Miller Franco, L. (2004). Framework for institutionalizing quality assurance. In A. R. Roberts & K. Yeager (Eds.), *Evidence-based practice manual. Research and outcome measures in health and human services* (pp. 867–881). Oxford, UK, New York: Oxford University Press.

Smith, B. D., & Donovan, S. E. F. (2003). Child welfare practice in organizational and institutional context. *Social Service Review*, *77*(4), 541–563. doi:10.1086/378328.

Steib, S. D., & Blome, W. W. (2003). Fatal error: The missing ingredient in child welfare reform: Part 1. *Child Welfare*, *82*(6), 747–750.

Therolf, G. (2010, October 19). Deaths from abuse and neglect increasing among children under L.A. county oversight. *Los Angeles Times*.

U.S. Department of Health and Human Services, Children's Bureau, Administration for Children and Families. (2002). *Child maltreatment 2000*. Washington, DC: USDHHS. Retrieved from http://www.acf.hhs.gov/programs/cb/pubs/cm00/cm2000.pdf.

U.S. Department of Health and Human Services. (2003). *National study of child protective services systems and reform efforts: Review of state CPS policy*. Washington, DC: USDHHS.

U.S. Department of Health and Human Services, Children's Bureau, Administration for Children and Families. (2006). *Child maltreatment 2004*. Washington, DC: USDHHS. Retrieved from http://www.acf.hhs.gov/programs/cb/pubs/cm04/cm04.pdf.

U.S. Department of Health and Human Services, Children's Bureau, Administration for Children and Families. (2007–2010). *Child welfare monitoring: Child and family services reviews*. Washington, DC: USDHHS. Retrieved from http://www.acf.hhs.gov/programs/cb/cwmonitoring/index.htm.

U.S. Department of Health and Human Services. (2008). *Statewide automated child welfare information systems: SACWIS assessment review guide*. (OMB No: 0970–0159). Washington, DC: USDHHS.

U.S. Department of Health and Human Services, Children's Bureau. (2009). *Children's Bureau: Child and family services reviews fact sheet.* Washington, DC: USDHHS. Retrieved from http://www.acf.hhs.gov/programs/cb/cwmonitoring/index.htm.

U.S. Department of Health and Human Services, Children's Bureau, Administration for Children and Families. (2009). *Child maltreatment 2007.* Washington, DC: USDHHS.

U.S. Department of Health and Human Services, Children's Bureau, Administration for Children and Families. (2010). *Child maltreatment 2009.* Washington, DC: USDHHS.

U.S. Department of Health and Human Services, Children's Bureau, Administration for Children and Families. (2011). *Statistics and research.* Washington, DC: USDHHS. Retrieved from http://www.acf.hhs.gov/programs/cb/stats_research/index.htm.

United States Government Accountability Office. (1995). *Child welfare: Complex needs strain capacity to provide services* (No. GAO/HEHS-95-208). Washington, DC: USGAO.

United States Government Accountability Office. (1997). *Child protective services: Complex challenges require new Strategies* (No. GAO/HEHS-97-115). Washington, DC: USGAO.

United States Government Accountability Office. (2003a). *States face challenges in developing information systems and reporting reliable child welfare data.* Washington, DC: USGAO Retrieved from http://www.gao.gov/new.items/d04267t.pdf.

United States Government Accountability Office. (2003b). *Child welfare: Most states are developing statewide information systems, but the reliability of child welfare data could be improved* (No. GA-03-809). Washington, DC: USGAO.

United States Government Accountability Office. (2006). *Federal oversight of state IV-B activities could inform action needed to improve services to families and statutory compliance* (No. GAO-06-787T). Washington, DC: USGAO.

Utah Division of Human Services. (1999). *DCFS practice guidelines and rules.* Salt Lake City, UT. http://www.hspolicy.utah.gov/dcfc/.

Vroom, V. H. (1960). The effects of attitudes on perception of organizational goals. *Human Relations, 13,* 229–240.

Waldfogel, J. (1998). *The future of child protection.* Cambridge, MA: Harvard University Press.

Westbrook, T., Ellis, J., & Ellett, A. (2006). Improving retention among public child welfare workers. *Administration in Social Work, 30*(4), 37–62. doi:10.1300/J147v30n04_04.

Willingham, D. (2007). Critical thinking: Why is it so hard to teach? *American Educator, 31*(2), 8–19.

Yeager, K. R. (2004). Establishing and utilization of balanced scorecards. In A. R. Roberts & K. R. Yeager (Eds.), *Evidence based practice manual* (pp. 891–896). New York: Oxford University Press.

Zell, M. C. (2006). Chile welfare workers: Who they are and how they view the child welfare system. *Child Welfare, 85*(1), 83–103.

CHAPTER 5

Aber, J. L., Brooks-Gunn, J., & Maynard, R. (1995). The effects of welfare reform on teenage parents and their children. *The Future of Children, 5*(2), 53–71.

Allen, M. (1996). *The implications of the Welfare Act for child protection.* Washington, DC: The Children's Defense Fund.

American Association for the Protection of Children. (1987). *Highlights of official child abuse and neglect reporting—1986.* Denver, CO: American Humane Association.

Ards, S. D., Myers, S. L., Jr., Chung, C., Malkis, A., & Hagerty, B. (2003). Decomposing black-white differences in child maltreatment. *Child Maltreatment, 8*, 112–121.

Baker, R., & Ball, S. (1969). *Mass media and violence: A report to the national commission on the causes and prevention of violence.* Washington, DC: Government Printing Office.

Barth, R. P. (2005). Child welfare and race: Models of disproportionality. In D. Derezoes et al. (Eds.), *Race matters in child welfare. The overrepresentation of African American children in the system* (pp. 25–46). Washington, DC: Child Welfare League of America.

Bartholet, E. (1999). *Nobody's children: Abuse and neglect, foster drift, and the adoption alternative.* Boston, MA: Beacon Press.

Belsky, J. (1978). Three theoretical models of child abuse: A critical review. *Child Abuse and Neglect, 2*, 37–49.

Bennie, E., & Sclare, A. (1969). The battered child syndrome. *American Journal of Psychiatry, 125*, 975–979.

Berger, L. M. (2004). Income, family structure and child maltreatment risk. *Children and Youth Services Review, 26*(8), 725–748.

Berrick, J. D., Frame, L., Langs, J., & Varchol, L. (2006). Working together for children and families: Where TANF and child welfare meet. *Journal of Policy Practice, 5*(2/3), 27–42.

Billingsley, A., & Giovannoni, J. (1972). *Children of the storm: Black children and American child welfare.* New York: Harcourt, Brace and Jovanovich.

Birrell, R., & Birrell, J. (1969). The maltreatment syndrome in children: A hospital survey. *Medical Journal of Australia, 2*, 1023.

Blank, R., & Schmidt, L. (2001). Work, wages and welfare. In R. Blank & R. Haskins, (Eds.), *The new world of welfare* (pp. 70–102). Washington, DC: Brookings Institution Press.

Blank, R. M. (2002). Evaluating welfare reform in the United States. *Journal of Economic Literature, 40*(4), 1105–1166.

Blank, R. M. (2007). What we know, what we don't know, and what we need to know about welfare reform. Paper prepared for the conference "Ten Years After: Evaluating the Long-Term Effects of Welfare Reform on Children, Families, Work, and Welfare," organized by the University of Kentucky Center for Poverty Research. Lexington, KY.

Bronfenbrenner, U. (1977). Toward an experimental ecology of human development. *American Psychologist, 32*, 513–531.

Bronfenbrenner, U. (1979). *The ecology of human development.* Cambridge, MA: Harvard University Press.

Brown, J., & Daniels, R. (1968). Some observations on abusive parents. *Child Welfare, 47*, 89.

Brown, S. (1984). Social class, child maltreatment and delinquent behavior. *Criminology, 22*(2), 259–278.

Burrell, B., Thomson, B., & Sexton, D. (1994). Predicting child abuse potential across family types. *Child Abuse and Neglect, 18*, 1039–1049.

Camasso, M. J., & Jagannathan, R. (2012). Welfare reform and poverty: A latent trajectory model analysis. *Research on Economic Inequality, 20*, 393–422.

Camasso, M. J., & Wilkinson, K. P. (1990). Severe child maltreatment in ecological perspective: The case of the western energy boom. *Journal of Social Service Research, 13*, 1–18.

Cancian, M., Haveman, R., Kaplan, T., Meyer, D., & Wolfe, B. (1999). Work, earnings, and well-being after welfare reform. In S. Danziger (Ed.), *Economic conditions and welfare reform* (pp. 161–186). Kalamazoo, MI: W. E. Upjohn Institute for Employment Research.

Chaffin, M., Kelleher, K., & Hollenberg, J. (1996). Onset of physical abuse and neglect: Psychiatric, substance abuse, and social risk factors from prospective community data. *Child Abuse and Neglect, 20*, 191–203.

Chasnoff, I., Landress, H., & Barrett, M. (1990). The prevalence of illicit-drug or alcohol use during pregnancy and discrepancies in mandatory reporting in Pinellas County, Florida. *The New England Journal of Medicine, 332*(17), 1202–1206.

Chibnall, S., Dutch, N. M., Jones-Harden, B., Brown, A., Gourdine, R., Smith, J., Boone A., & Snyder, S. (2003). *Children of color in the child welfare system: Perspectives from the child welfare community.* Washington, DC: U.S. Department of Health and Human Services, Children's Bureau, Administration for Children and Families.

Child Welfare League of America. (1998). Child Welfare League of America decries results of new welfare law: Predicts foster care population will double. http://www.cwla.org/cwla/communic/resultsofnewwelfarelaw.htm.

Church, W. T. (2006). From start to finish: The duration of Hispanic children in out-of-home placements. *Children and Youth Services Review, 28,* 1007–1023.

Coley, R. L., Lohman, B. J., Votruba-Drzal, E., Pittman, L. D., & Lindsay Chase-Lansdale, P. (2007).Maternal functioning, time, and money: The world of work and welfare. *Children and Youth Services Review, 29*(6), 721–741.

Coulton, C., Korbin, J., Su, M., & Chow, J. (1995). Community level factors and child maltreatment rates. *Child Development, 66*(5), 1262–1276.

Coulton, C., & Pandey, S. (1992). Geographic concentration of poverty and risk to children in urban neighborhoods. *American Behavioral Scientist, 35,* 238–257.

Council of Economic Advisors (CEA). (1999). *Technical report: The effects of welfare policy and the economic expansion on welfare caseloads: An update.* Washington, DC: The White House.

Courtney, M. (1997). Welfare reform and child welfare services. In A. Kahn & S. Kamerman (Eds.), *Child welfare in the context of welfare reform.* New York: Cross National Research Studies Program, Columbia University of Social Work.

Courtney, M. E., Barth, R. P., Berrick, J. D., Brooks, D., Needel, B., & Park, L. (1996). Race and child welfare services: Past research and future directions. *Child Welfare, 75,* 99–137.

Courtney, M. E., Piliavin, I., Dworsky, A., & Zinn, A. (2001). *Involvement of TANF families with child welfare services.* Presented at the annual meeting of the Association for Public Policy Analysis and Management, Washington, DC.

Danielson, C., & Klerman, J. A. (2008). Did welfare reform cause the caseload decline? *Social Service Review, 82*(4), 703–730.

Derr, M., & Cooley, V. (2001). *Does welfare grant sanctioning increase child welfare involvement among TANF recipients?* Paper presented at the Council on Social Work Education Annual Meeting, March 8–11.

Drake, B., Johnson-Reid, M., Way, I., & Chung, S. (2003). Substantiation and recidivism. *Child Maltreatment, 8*(4), 248–260.

Drake, B., Lee, S. L., & Johnson-Reid, M. (2009). Race and child maltreatment reporting: Are blacks overrepresented? *Children and Youth Services Review, 31*(3), 309–316.

Drake, B., & Pandey, S. (1996). Understanding the relationship between neighborhood poverty and specific types of child maltreatment. *Child Abuse & Neglect, 20*(11), 1003–1018.

Elmer, E. (1967). *Children in jeopardy.* Pittsburgh, PA: University of Pittsburgh Press.

Elmer, E., & Gregg, G. S. (1967). Developmental characteristics of abused children. *Pediatrics, 40,* 596–602.

Fang, H., & Keane, M. P. (2004). Assessing the impact of welfare reform on single mothers. *Brookings Papers on Economic Activity, 2004*(1), 1–116.

Fein, D., & Lee, W. (2003). The impacts of welfare reform on child maltreatment in Delaware. *Children and Youth Services Review, 25*(1/2), 83–111.

Figlio, D. N., & Ziliak, J. P. (1999). Welfare reform, the business cycle, and the decline in AFDC caseloads. In S. H. Danziger (Ed.), *Economic Conditions and Welfare Reform* (pp. 17–48). Kalamazoo, MI: W. E. Upjohn Institute Employment Research.

Fluke, J. D., Yuan, Y. T., Hedderson, J., & Curtis, P. A. (2003). Disproportionate representation of race and ethnicity in child maltreatment: Investigation and victimization. *Children and Youth Services Review, 25*, 359–373.

Fontana, V. (1971). *The maltreated child.* Springfield, IL: Thomas.

Frame, L. (1999). Suitable homes revisited: An historical look at child protection and welfare. *Children and Youth Services Review, 21*(9/10), 719–754.

Freisthler, B., Bruce, E., & Needell, B. (2007). Understanding the geospatial relationship of neighborhood characteristics and rates of maltreatment for black, Hispanic and white children. *Social Work, 52*(1), 7–16.

Fryer, G., & Miyoshi, T. (1995). A cluster analysis of child maltreatment incidents in rural Colorado. *Child Abuse and Neglect, 19*(3), 363–369.

Gainsborough, J. F. (2010). *Scandalous politics: Child welfare policy in the States.* Washington, DC: Georgetown University Press.

Galdston, R. (1965). Observations of children who have been physically abused by their parents. *American Journal of Psychiatry, 122*, 440–443.

Garbarino, J. (1981). An ecological approach to child maltreatment. In L. H. Pelton (Ed.), *The social context of child abuse and neglect* (pp. 228–267). New York: Human Sciences Press.

Garbarino, J., & Gilliam, G. (1980). *Understanding abusive families.* Lexington, MA: D. C. Health.

Geen, R., Boots, S. W., & Tumlin, K. C. (1999). *The cost of protecting vulnerable children: Understanding federal, state and local child welfare spending.* Washington, DC: The Urban Institute.

Geen, R., Fender, L., Leos-Urbel, J., & Markowitz, T. (2001). *Welfare reform's effect on child welfare caseloads.* Washington, DC: The Urban Institute.

Gelles, R. J. (1992). Poverty and violence toward children. *American Behavioral Scientist, 35*(3), 258–274.

Gil, D. (1970). *Violence against children: Physical child abuse in the United States.* Cambridge, MA: Harvard University Press.

Gil, D. (1971). Violence against children. *Journal of Marriage and the Family, 33*, 637–648.

Gil, D. (1974). *A holistic perspective on child abuse and its prevention.* Paper presented at the Conference on Child Abuse and Neglect, National Institute of Child Health and Human Development, Washington, DC.

Green, A. H. (1976). A psychodynamic approach to the study and treatment of child abusing parents. *Journal of Child Psychiatry, 15*, 414.

Green, A. H., Gaines, R. W., & Sandgrun, A. (1974). Child abuse: Pathological syndrome of family interaction. *American Journal of Psychiatry, 131*, 882–886.

Green, M. Y. (2006). Minorities as majority: Disproportionality in child welfare and juvenile justice. *Residential Group Care Quarterly, 7*(2), 3–7.

Grogger, J., & Karoly, L. A. (2005). *Welfare reform: Effects of a decade of change.* Cambridge, MA: Harvard University Press.

Groth, A. N., & Birnbaum, H. J. (1978). Adult sexual orientation and attraction to underage persons. *Archives of Sexual Behavior, 7*, 175–181.

Harris, M. S., & Hackett, W. (2008). Decision points in child welfare: An action research model to address disproportionality. *Children and Youth Services Review, 30*, 199–215.

Harvey, C., Camasso, M. J., & Jagannathan, R. (2000). Evaluating welfare reform waivers under section 1115. *Journal of Economic Perspectives, 14*(4), 165–188.

Haskins, R. (2001). *The welfare reform law of 1996: What has been accomplished? What remains to be done?* Acton Institute Policy Forum No.2. 1–25.

Hill, R. B. (2006). *Synthesis of research on disproportionality in child welfare: An update.* Washington, DC: Casey-CSSP Alliance for Racial Equity in the Child Welfare System.

Hill, R. B. (2007). *An analysis of racial/ethnic disproportionality and disparity at the national, state and county levels.* Washington, DC: Casey-CSSP Alliance for Racial Equity in the Child Welfare System.

Holder, W., & Corey, C. (1995). *Child protective services risk management: A decision-making handbook.* Charlotte, NC and Denver, CO: ACTION for Child Protection.

Iverson, T. J., & Segal, M. (1990). *Child abuse and neglect: An information and reference guide.* New York: Garland Publishing, Inc.

Jagannathan, R. (2011). Welfare reform's impact on caseload decline in the United States: An application of latent trajectory model. *Social Science Journal, 48*, 703–721.

Johnson, B., & Morse, H. (1968). Injured children and their parents. *Children, 15*, 147.

Johnson, E. P., Clark, S., Donald, M., Pedersen, R., & Pichotta, C. (2007). Racial disparity in Minnesota's child protection system. *Child Welfare, 86*(4), 5–20.

Jonson-Reid, M., Drake, B., & Kohl, P. L. (2009). Is the overrepresentation of the poor in child welfare caseloads due to bias or need? *Children and Youth Services Review, 31*(3), 422–427.

Kempe, H. C. (1973). A practical approach to the protection of the abused child and rehabilitation of the abusing parent. *Pediatrics 51*, 804–812.

Kempe, H. C., Silverman, F. N., Steele, B. F., Droegemueller, W., & Silver, H. K. (1962). The battered child syndrome. *Journal of the American Medical Association, 181*, 17–24.

Knitzer, J., & Bernard, S. (1997). The new welfare law and vulnerable families: Implications for child welfare/child protection systems. *Children and welfare reform*, Issue Brief 3. New York: Columbia University Press.

Lauer, B., Ten Broeck, E., & Grossman, M. (1974). Battered child syndrome: Review of 130 patients with controls. *Pediatrics, 54*, 67–70.

Levin-Epstein, J. (2003). *Lifting the lid off the family cap: State revisit problematic policy for welfare mothers.* Childbearing and Reproductive Health Policy Brief no. 1. Washington, DC: Center for Law and Social Policy.

Lindsey, D. (1994). *The welfare of children.* New York: Oxford University Press.

Magruder, J., & Shaw, T. V. (2008). Children ever in care: An examination of cumulative disproportionality. *Child Welfare, 87*(2), 169–188.

Martin, H., Conway, E., Breezley, P., & Kempe, H. C. (1974). The development of abused children, Part I: A review of the literature. *Advances in Pediatrics, 21*, 43.

McCabe, K., Yeh, M., Hough, R., Landsverk, J., Hurlburt, M., Culver, S., & Reynolds, B. (1999). Racial/ethnic representation across five public sectors of care for youth. *Journal of Emotional and Behavioral Disorders, 7*, 72–82.

McKernan, S-M., & Ratcliffe, C. (2006). *The effect of specific welfare policies on poverty.* Washington, DC: The Urban Institute.

Melnick, B., & Hurley, J. R. (1969). Distinctive personality attributes of child-abusing mothers. *Journal of Consulting and Clinical Psychology, 33*, 746–749.

Mersky, J. P., Berger, L. M., Reynolds, A. J., & Gomoske, A. N. (2009). Risk factors for child and adolescent maltreatment: A longitudinal investigation of a cohort of inner-city youth. *Child Maltreatment, 14*(1), 73–88.

Mezey, S. G. (2000). *Pitiful plaintiffs: Child welfare litigation and the federal courts.* Pittsburgh, PA: University of Pittsburgh Press. Retrieved from http://www.worldcat.org/oclc/42812830.

Moffitt, R. A. (1999). The effect of pre-PRWORA waivers on AFDC caseloads and female earnings, income and labor force behavior. In S. H. Danziger (Ed.), *Economic conditions and welfare reform* (pp. 91–118). Kalamazoo, MI: W. E. Upjohn Institute for Employment Research.

Morris, M., & Gould, R. (1963). Role reversal: A necessary concept in dealing with the battered child syndrome. In *The neglected/battered child syndrome.* New York: Child Welfare League of America.

Morton, T. (1999). The increasing colorization of America's child welfare system: The over-representation of African American children. *Policy and Practice, 57*(4), 23–30.

Newberger, R., Reed, R., Daniel, J., Hyde, M., & Kotelchuck, M. (1975). *Pediatric social illness: Toward an etiologic classification.* Paper presented at the biennial meeting of The Society for Research in Child Development, Denver, CO.

NSPCC. (2008). *Child protection research briefing: Poverty and child maltreatment.* London, UK: National Society for the Prevention of Cruelty to Children.

Owens, D. J., & Strauss, M. A. (1975). The social structure of violence in childhood and approval of violence as an adult. *Aggressive Behavior, 1,* 193–211.

Paulson, M., & Blake, P. (1969). The physically abused child: A focus on prevention. *Child Welfare, 48,* 86.

Paxson, C., & Waldfogel, J. (1999). Parental resources and child abuse and neglect. *American Economic Review Papers and Proceedings, 89,* 239–244.

Paxson, C., & Waldfogel, J. (2002). Work, welfare, and child maltreatment. *Journal of Labor Economics, 20*(3), 435–474.

Paxson, C., & Waldfogel, J. (2003). Welfare reforms, family resources, and child maltreatment. *Journal of Policy Analysis and Management, 22*(1), 85–113.

Pelton, L. H. (1989). *For reasons of poverty: A critical analysis of the public child welfare system in the United States.* New York: Praeger Publishers.

Pelton, L. H. (1994). The role of material factors in child abuse and neglect. In G. Melton & F. Barry (Eds.), *Protecting children from abuse and neglect* (pp. 131–181). New York: Guilford Press.

Polansky, N. A., Chalmers, M. A., Buttenwieser, E., & Williams, D. P. (1981). *Damaged parents: An anatomy of neglect.* Chicago: University of Chicago Press.

Primus, W., Rawlings, L., Larin, K., & Porter, K. (1999). *The initial impacts of welfare reform on the incomes of single mother families.* Washington, DC: Center on Budget and Policy Priorities.

Rector, R E., & Youssef, S. E. (1999). *The determinants of welfare caseload decline.* Report No. 99–04. Washington, DC: Heritage Foundation, Center for Data Analysis.

Roberts, D. (2002). *Shattered bonds: The color of child welfare.* New York: Basic Civitas Books.

Roberts, D. (2007). *The racial geography of state child protection.* Working paper. Evanston, IL: Institute for Policy Research, Northwestern University.

Schneider, C., Hoffmeister, J. K., & Helfer, R. E. (1976). A predictive screening questionnaire for potential problems in mother-child interaction. In R. E. Helfer & C. H. Kempe (Eds.), *Child abuse and neglect: The family and the community* (pp. 393–407). Cambridge, MA: Ballinger.

Schneider-Rosen, K., & Cicchetti, D. (1984). The relationship between affect and cognition in maltreated infants: Quality of attachment and the development of visual self-recognition. *Child Development, 55,* 648–658.

Schoeni, R. F., & Blank, R. M. (2000). *What has welfare reform accomplished? Impacts on welfare participation, employment, income, poverty, and family structure.* National Bureau of Economic Research Working Paper No. 7627. Cambridge, MA: National Bureau of Economic Research.

Schuck, A. M. (2005). Explaining black-white disparity in maltreatment: Poverty, female-headed families, and urbanization. *Journal of Marriage and Family, 67*(3), 543–551.

Sedlak, A., & Broadhurst, D. D. (1996). *Third national incidence study of child abuse and neglect: Final Report.* Washington, DC: U.S. Department of Health and Human Services.

Sedlak, A., Mettenburg, J., Basena, M., Petta, I., McPherson, K., Greene, A., & Li, S. (2010). *Fourth national incidence study of child abuse and neglect (NIS–4): Report to Congress.* Washington, DC: U.S. Department of Health and Human Services, Administration for Children and Families.

Sedlak, A., & Schultz, D. (2005). Racial differences in child protective services investigation of abuse and neglected children. In D. Derezotes, J. Poertner, & M. Testa (Eds.), *Race matters in child welfare: The overrepresentation of African American children in the system* (pp. 97–118). Washington, DC: Child Welfare League of America.

Shook, K. (1999). Does the loss of welfare income increase the risk of involvement with the child welfare system? *Children and Youth Services Review, 21*(9/10), 781–814.

Shorkey, C. T. (1980). Sense of personal worth, self-esteem, and anomia of child-abusing mothers and controls. *Journal of Clinical Psychology, 36,* 817–820.

Slack, K. S., Holl, J. L., Lee, B. J., McDaniel, M., Altenbernd, L., & Stevens, A. B. (2003). Child protective intervention in the context of welfare reform: The effects of work and welfare on maltreatment reports. *Journal of Policy Analysis and Management, 2294,* 517–536.

Slack, K. S., Holl, J. L., McDaniel, M., Yoo. J., & Bolger, K. (2004). Understanding the risks of child neglect: An exploration of poverty and parenting characteristics. *Child Maltreatment, 9*(4), 395–408.

Steele, B., & Pollock, C. (1968). A psychiatric study of parents who abuse infants and small children. In R. Heller & C. H. Kempe (Eds.), *The battered child* (pp. 89–133). Chicago: University of Chicago Press.

Ten Broeck, E. (1977). *The extended family center, 1972–1975: Final report.* Washington, DC: USDHEW, OCD-CB-366.

Tumlin, K., & Geen, R. (2000). *The decision to investigate: Understanding state child welfare screening policies and practices.* Assessing the New Federalism Policy Brief A-38. Washington, DC: The Urban Institute.

Turbett, J., & O'Toole, R. (1980). *Physician's recognition of child abuse.* Paper presented at the Annual Meeting of the American Sociological Association.

U. S. Census Bureau. (2011). Children below poverty level by race and Hispanic origin: 1980 to 2008. *The 2011 Statistical Abstract.*

U. S. Department of Health and Human Services. (1981). *National Study of the incidence and severity of child abuse and neglect.* Washington, DC: DHHS Publication No. (OHDS) 81–30325.

U. S. Department of Health and Human Services. (1988). *Study findings: Study of national incidence and prevalence of child abuse and neglect.* Washington, DC: DHHS Publication No. CD-17794.

U. S. Department of Health and Human Services. (1994). *National study of protective, preventive and reunification services delivered to children and their families.* Washington, DC: U.S. Government Printing Office.

U.S. Department of Health and Human Services. (2000). *Dynamics of children's movement among the AFDC, Medicaid, and foster care programs prior to welfare reform: 1995–1996.* Washington, DC: Office of the Assistant Secretary for Planning and Evaluation.

Waldfogel, J. (1998). *The future of child protection: How to break the cycle of abuse and neglect.* Cambridge, MA: Harvard University Press.

Waldfogel, J. (2004). Welfare reform and the child welfare system. *Children and Youth Services Review, 26*(10), 919–939.

Waldfogel, J., Danziger, S. K., Danziger, S., & Seefeldt, K. (2002). Welfare reform and lone others' employment in the U.S. In J. Millar & K. Rowlingson (Eds.), *Lone mothers, employment, and social policy: Cross national comparisons* (pp. 37–60). Bristol, UK: Polity Press.

Wells, K., & Tracey, E. (1996). Reorienting intensive family preservation services in relation to public child welfare practices. *Child Welfare, 75*(6), 662–692.

Wolfe, D. A. (1985). Child-abusing parents: An empirical review and analysis. *Psychological Bulletin, 97,* 462–482.

Wolfe, D. A., & Mosk, M. D. (1983). Behavioral comparisons of children from abusive and distressed families. *Journal of Consulting and Clinical Psychology, 51,* 702–708.

Wulczyn, F., & Lery, B. (2007). *Racial disparity in foster care admissions.* Chicago, IL: Chapin Hall Center for Children. Available at www.chapinhall.org.

Wulczyn, F., Lery, B., & Haight, J. (2006). *Entry and exit disparities in the Tennessee foster care system.* Chicago, IL: Chapin Hall Center for Children. Available atwww.chapinhall.org.

Young, L. (1964). *Wednesday's children: A study of child neglect and abuse.* New York: McGraw-Hill.

Zalba, S. (1967). The abused child: A typology for classification and treatment. *Social Work, 12,* 70.

Zalba, S. (1971). Battered children. *Transaction, 8,* 58–61.

Zedlewski, S., Giannarelli, L., Morton, J., & Wheaton, L. (2002). Extreme poverty rising, existing government programs could do more. *Assessing New Federalism Series B,* No. B-45. Washington, DC: The Urban Institute.

Ziliak, J. P., Figlio, D. N., Davis, E. E., & Connolly, L. S. (2000). Accounting for the decline in AFDC caseloads: Welfare reform or the economy? *Journal of Human Resources, 35*(3), 570–586.

CHAPTER 6

Baumgartner, F. R., & Jones, B. D. (2009). *Agendas and instability in American politics,* 2nd ed. Chicago, IL: University of Chicago Press.

Council of Economic Advisors (CEA). (1997). *Technical report: Explaining the decline in welfare receipt, 1993–1996.* Washington, DC: The White House.

Council of Economic Advisors (CEA). (1999). *Technical report: The effects of welfare policy and the economic expansion on welfare caseloads: An update.* Washington, DC: The White House.

Fording, R. C. (2003). Laboratories of democracy or symbol politics? The racial origins of welfare reform. In S. F. Schram, J. Soss, & R. C. Fording (Eds.), *Race and the politics of welfare reform* (pp. 72–97). Ann Arbor: University of Michigan Press.

Gainsborough, J. F. (2010). *Scandalous politics: Child welfare policy in the States.* Washington, DC: Georgetown University Press.

Kaushal, N., & Kaestner, R. (2001). From welfare to work: Has welfare reform worked? *Journal of Policy Analysis and Management, 20*(4), 699–719.

Lieberman, R. C., & Shaw, G. M. (2000). Looking inward, looking outward: The politics of State welfare innovation under devolution. *Political Research Quarterly, 53,* 215–240.

Mezey, S. G. (2000). *Pitiful plaintiffs: Child welfare litigation and the federal Courts.* Pittsburgh, PA: University of Pittsburgh Press. Retrieved from http://www.worldcat.org/oclc/42812830.

Nelson, B. S. (1984). *Making an issue of child abuse: Political agenda setting for social problems.* Chicago, IL: University of Chicago Press.

Paxson, C., & Waldfogel, J. (2002). Work, welfare, and child maltreatment. *Journal of Labor Economics, 20*(3), 435–474.

Paxson, C., & Waldfogel, J. (2003). Welfare reforms, family resources, and child maltreatment. *Journal of Policy Analysis and Management, 22*(1), 85–113.

Reihl C, Harfeld, A. Weichel, E. & Carr, J. (2012). State Secrecy and Child Deaths in the U.S. 2nd ed. San Diego School of Law. Available at: http://caichildlaw.org/Misc/StateSecrecy2ndEd.pdf.

Schiller, B. R. (1999). State welfare reform impacts: Content and enforcements effects. *Contemporary Economic Policy, 17*(2), 210–222.

Soss, J., Schram, S. F., Vartanian, T. P., & O'Brien, E. (2001). Setting the terms of relief: Explaining State policy choices in the devolution revolution. *American Journal of Political Science, 45*(2), 378–395.

United States Government Accountability Office. (2011). *Child Maltreatment: Strengthening National Data on Child Fatalities Could Aid in Prevention* (No. GAO-11-599). Washington, DC: U.S.GAO.

Zgoba, K., Veysey, B., & Dalessandro, M. (2010). An analysis of the effectiveness of community notification and registration: Do the best intentions predict the best practices? *Justice Quarterly, 27*(5), 667–691. doi:10.1080/07418820903357673.

CHAPTER 7

Baumann, D., Law, J., Sheets, J., Reid, G., & Graham, J. (2005). Evaluating the effectiveness of actuarial risk assessment models. *Children and Youth Services Review, 27*(5), 465–490.

Bloom, H. S., Michalopoulos, C., & Hill, C. J. (2005). Using experiments to assess nonexperimental comparison-group methods for measuring program effects. In H. S. Bloom (Ed.), *Learning more from social experiments. Evolving analytic approaches* (pp. 173–236). New York: Russell Sage Foundation.

Brown, M. G. (2007). *Beyond the balanced scorecard: Improving business intelligence with analytics.* New York: Productivity Press.

Camasso, M. (2007). *Family caps, abortion, and women of color: Research connection and political rejection.* New York: Oxford University Press.

Camasso, M. J., & Jagannathan, R. (1992). *Coding the structure of child welfare decision making processes.* New Brunswick, NJ: Rutgers University School of Social Work.

Center for the Study of Social Policy. (2010). *Progress of the New Jersey department of children and families: Period VII monitoring report for Charlie and Nadine H. v. Christie.* July 1–December 31, 2009. Washington, DC: Center for the Study of Social Policy.

Cohen, B., Kinnevy, S., & Dichter, M. (2007). The quality of work life of child protective investigators: A comparison of two work environments. *Children and Youth Services Review, 29*(4), 474–489. doi:10.1016/j.childyouth.2006.09.004.

Collins-Camargo, C., McBeath, B., & Ensign, K. (2011). Privatization and performance-based contracting in child welfare: Recent trends and implications for social service administrators. *Administration in Social Work,* 35: 494–516.

Cook, T. D., & Payne, M. (2002). Objecting to the objections to use random assignment in educational research. In F. Mosteller & R. Boruch (Eds.), *Evidence matters. Randomized trials in education research* (pp. 150–178). Washington, DC: Brookings Institution Press.

Cook, T. D. (2010). An alien parachutes into economic research on low-income populations. *Focus, 27*(2), 27–32.

Covello, V. T., Peters, R. G., Wojtecki, J. G., & Hyde, R. C. (2001). Risk communication, the West Nile virus epidemic, and bioterrorism: Responding to the communication challenges posed by the intentional or unintentional release of a pathogen in an urban setting. *Journal of Urban Health: Bulletin of the New York Academy of Medicine, 78*(2), 382–391. doi:10.1093/jurban/78.2.382.

Covello, V., & Sandman, P. M. (2001). Risk communication: Evolution and revolution. In A. B. Wolbarst (Ed.), *Solutions for an environment in peril* (pp. 164–178). Baltimore, MD: The Johns Hopkins University Press.

Covello, V., Sandman, P., & Slovic, P. (1988). *Risk communication, risk statistics, and risk comparisons: A manual for plant managers.* Washington, DC: Chemical Manufacturers Association.

Crocker, D. C. (1990). *How to use regression analysis in quality control. The ASQC basic references in quality control: Vol. 9.* Milwaukee, WI: American Society for Quality Control.

Donabedian, A. (1980). *The definition of quality and approaches to its assessment. His explorations in quality assessment and monitoring: Vol. 1.* Ann Arbor, MI: Health Administration Press.

Duflo, E.. (2004). Scaling up and evaluation. In *Proceedings from the annual World Bank Conference on development economics.* Washington, DC: World Bank.

Gambrill, E. (2008). Decision making in child welfare: Constraints and potentials. In D. Lindsey & A. Shlonsky (Eds.), *Child welfare research. Advances for practice and policy* (pp. 175–193). Oxford, UK: Oxford University Press.

Gambrill, E., & Shlonsky, A. (2001). The need for comprehensive risk management systems in child welfare. *Children and Youth Services Review, 23*(1), 79–107. doi:10.1016/S0190-7409(00)00124-9.

Golden, O. A. (2009). *Reforming child welfare.* Washington, DC: Urban Institute Press. Retrieved from http://www.worldcat.org/oclc/311768820.

Inamdar, N., & Kaplan, R. S. (2002). Applying the balanced scorecard in healthcare provider organizations. *Journal of Healthcare Management, 47*(3), 179–195.

Johnson, W. (2006). The risk assessment wars: A commentary: Response to "Evaluating the effectiveness of actuarial risk assessment models." *Children and Youth Services Review, 28*(6), 704–714. doi:10.1016/j.childyouth.2005.07.007.

Johnson & Johnson. (2010). *Our credo values.* New Brunswick, NJ. Retrieved from http://www.jnj.com/connect/about-jnj/jnj-credo/?flash=true.

Kaplan, R. S. (2010). *Conceptual foundations of the balanced scorecard: Working paper.* Boston, MA: Harvard Business School Press.

Kaplan, R. S., & Norton, D. P. (1992). The balanced scorecard: Measures that drive performance. *Harvard Business Review, 70*(1), 71–79.

Kaplan, R. S., & Norton, D. P. (1996). *The balanced scorecard: Translating strategy into action*. Boston, MA: Harvard Business School Press.

Kaplan, R. S., & Norton, D. P. (2004). *Strategy maps: Converting intangible assets into tangible outcomes*. Boston, MA: Harvard Business School Press.

Lindsey, D., & Shlonsky, A. (Eds.). (2008). *Child welfare research: Advances for practice and policy*. Oxford, UK: Oxford University Press.

McCarthy, P. (2007). Foreward. In R. Haskins, F. Wulczyn, & M. B. Webb (Eds.), *Child protection. Using research to improve policy and practice* (pp. vii–viii). Washington, DC: Brookings Institution Press.

Mintzberg, H. (1979). *The structuring of organizations: A synthesis of the research*. Englewood Cliffs, NJ: Prentice-Hall.

Niven, P. R. (2004). *Balanced scorecard: Translating strategy into action*. New York: John Wiley & Sons.

Noonan, K. G., Sabel, C. F., & Simon, W. H. (2009). Legal accountability in the service-based welfare state: Lessons from child welfare reform. *Law & Social Inquiry, 34*(3), 523–568.

Rzepnicki, T. L., & Johnson, P. R. (2005). Examining decision errors in child protection: A new application of root cause analysis. *Children and Youth Services Review, 27*(4), 393–407.

Sandman, P. (2003). *Four kinds of risk communication*. Retrieved from http://www.psandman.com/col/4kind-1.htm.

Sandman, P. M., Sachsman, D., & Greenberg, M. (1987). *Environmental risk and the press: An exploratory assessment*. New Brunswick, NJ: Transaction Books.

Schorr, A. L. (2000). The bleak prospect for public child welfare. *Social Service Review, 74*(1), 124–138. doi:10.1086/514460.

The European Commission. (2004). *Nanotechnology: A preliminary risk analysis on the basis of a workshop organized in Brussels on 1–2 March 2004*. Brussels, Belgium.

Wiseman, M. (2007). Memoirs of a welfare warrior: Review of work over welfare: The inside story of the 1996 welfare reform law by Ron Haskins. *Journal of Policy Analysis and Management, 26*(4), 969–974.

Yeager, K. R. (2004). Establishment and utilization of balanced scorecards. In A. R. Roberts & K. Yeager (Eds.), *Evidence-based practice manual. Research and outcome measures in health and human services* (pp. 891–896). Oxford, New York: Oxford University Press.

INDEX

Page numbers followed by f indicate a figure. Page numbers followed by t indicate a table.